£6.00

Lobbying

AN INSIDER'S GUIDE TO THE PARLIAMENTARY PROCESS

Alf Dubs

PLUTO  PRESS

This edition first published 1989 by Pluto Press
345 Archway Road, London N6 5AA

First edition published 1988 by Pluto Press

Distributed in the USA by Unwin Hyman Inc.
8 Winchester Place, Winchester
MA 01890, USA

Typesetting: Ransom Electronic Publishing,
Woburn Sands, Bucks

Printed and bound in the United Kingdom by
Billing & Sons Ltd, Worcester

British Library Cataloguing in Publication Data

Dubs, Alf
  Lobbying.
  1. Lobbying—Great Britain
  I. Title
  328.41'078   JN611

ISBN 0-7453-0345-5

Contents

Acknowledgements   ix

1.   Introduction   1
2.   Getting to Know Your Politician   5
    Where to Obtain Information   6
    Restrictions on MPs with Government Posts   15
    The Opposition   17
    Other Jobs   17
    Membership of Committees   18
    Personalities and Politics   19
3.   How to Approach your MP   22
    Do You Know Who Your MP Is?   22
    How to Make Contact   23
4.   Raising an Issue in the House   29
    The Parliamentary Day   29
    Parliamentary Questions   36
    Government Business,
       Opposition Days, Adjournment Debates   50
    Early Day Motions, Petitions, Select Committees   59
5.   Legislation   73
    Second Reading   76
    Committee Stage   78
    Report Stage and Third Reading   83
    Private Bills   88
    Private Members' Bills   90
    Statutory Instruments   96
6.   How an MP Can Help in Other Ways   100
    Letters to the Minister   100
    Meetings with the Minister   103
    Mass Lobbies   105
    Select Committees   110
    Select Committee on European Legislation   114
    Party Groups   115
    All-Party (Country) Groups   117

	All-Party (Subject) Groups	118
	Receptions, Drinks or Dinners at Westminster	120
	Exhibitions in the Upper Waiting Hall	121
7.	MPs' Extra-parliamentary Activity	123
	Your Own MP or Another?	123
	Local Pressure Groups	124
	Why Invite an MP?	125
	Marches, Demos, Sit-ins	127
	Representations to Public Bodies and other Organisations	127
	Overseas Visits by MPs	128
8.	How to Use Election Campaigns	131
	National Pressure Groups	131
	Local Pressure Groups	132
9.	Influencing Political Parties	136
	Party Conferences	138
	Fringe Meetings	139
	Receptions	143
	Breakfast, Lunch, Dinner	143
	Stalls and Exhibitions	144
	Advertising in the Conference Guide/Handbook	145
	Other Conferences	145
10.	The House of Lords	147
	Similarities to the Commons	150
	Differences from the Commons	151
	Questions	151
	Legislation	153
	Other Debates	154
	Government Statements	154
	Select Committees	154
	The Select Committee on European Legislation	155
	Getting into Debates	156
	The House of Lords as the Highest Court of Appeal	156
	How to Contact Members	156
	Uses for Pressure Groups	158
11.	The European Parliament and Other International Bodies	160
	Where the Power Lies	161
	How to Contact an MEP	167
	What MEPs Can Do	169
	Other International Assemblies	178
12.	Councillors	181
	Structure	181

	Powers	182
	Finding Your Councillors	184
	How Councillors Raise Issues at Town Halls	185
	Subjects Councillors Can Raise	185
	How Councillors Can Help outside the Town Hall	186
	Issues Affecting Councillors	186
13.	Publicity: How MPs Can Help	188
	The Parliamentary Press Lobby	188
	Press Conferences	188
	Radio	189
	Local Newspapers	190
	Photo Opportunities	190
14.	Commercial Lobbying	192
	Criticisms of Commerical Lobbyists	193
	In-House Lobbyists	194
	Public Affairs Consultants	194
	Advantages of Going to a Consultancy	195
	Selecting and Briefing Public Affairs Consultants	196

Appendix I: Commons Glossary 198
Appendix II: Lords Glossary 211
Appendix III: European Glossary 214
Appendix IV: Political Lobbying Companies 217
    Specialist Public Affairs' Companies 217
    Public Relations Companies Offering 218
     Lobbying Services
    Monitoring Services 220
Appendix V: Useful Addresses and Phone Numbers 221
Bibliography 224
Index 226

Figures and Tables

Figures

2.1	Register of Member's Interests	7
2.2	Hansard (Commons)	9
2.3	Hansard (Lords)	10
2.4	Hansard (Standing Committee)	11
2.5	Weekly Information Bulletin	12
2.6	House Magazine	14
4.1	Whip (Labour Party)	32–3
4.2	Order of Business (Commons)	35
4.3	Hansard (extract)	41
4.4	Order of Questions (Commons)	43
4.5	Order Paper (Commons)	62
4.6	Petition (GLC)	67
4.7	Rules Concerning Petitions	68–9
5.1	Bill (Local Government Finance)	74
5.2	NCCL Briefing (Police and Criminal Evidence Bill)	77
5.3	Amendments (Housing and Planning Bill 1986)	79
5.4	Selection of Amendments (Representation of the People Bill)	84
6.1	Example of a Letter from a Pressure Group (Amnesty)	101
6.2	Mass Lobby Arrangements (World Development Movement)	108
6.3	Example of Typical Week's PLP Backbench Group Meetings	116

Table

10.1	Party Allegiances of Active Peers	148

Acknowledgements

Many people have helped and advised me on this book. I am extremely grateful to: Janet Anderson who works for the Parliamentary Labour Party, Roger Broad, Tony Belton, Jane Cooper of Amnesty International, Frances Crook, Director of the Howard League for Penal Reform, Bryan Davies, Secretary of the Parliamentary Labour Party, Eric Deakins, former MP for Walthamstow, Ann Dubs, Stuart Hercock, Emma MacLennan from Labour Party head office, Stan Newens MEP, Anita Pollack, Richard Percival, Gordon Prentice from Labour Party head office, Fred Silvester, former MP for Manchester, Withington, Rowan Bolton from the UK office of the European Parliament, David Natzler, Maurice Trowbridge, head of the UK office of the European Parliament and many others. They all gave a great deal of time to reading parts of the book and making useful comments and suggestions. Any errors are, however, my responsibility and not theirs.

To my friends in the following organisations who helped, supported, encouraged and lobbied me while I was Member of Parliament:

Battersea Labour Party
COHSE
JCWI
NCCL
Amnesty
CND
NACRO

1
Introduction

More and more organisations and individuals are seeking to make sure their views are known to politicians in the hope of influencing political decisions. This book is intended to help pressure groups and trade unions both at national and at local levels. I hope that ordinary members of the public who want to know more about how to influence our political system will find it useful. It may also interest students of politics. I realise that many commercial organisations are putting more emphasis on lobbying and I believe they too may find this book of help, even though my own experiences and attitudes come from the left.

Given an understanding of parliamentary procedures, much of the advice I give in this book is common sense. I make no apology for that. During my years as an MP I was frequently lobbied. All too often the obvious was overlooked by those who approached me. But I trust that even experienced members of pressure groups will still find a few things here that they did not previously know.

If you have never been involved in lobbying, how should you begin? Many pressure groups get a long way by concentrating on early day motions, parliamentary questions, both written and oral, getting MPs to write letters to a minister or have a meeting with him/her, briefing MPs for major debates like second readings of important bills and involving MPs in various events in the constituency. All it requires is a little knowledge of procedure and lots of common sense.

Not long after I was first elected I was due to take part in an all-night debate on the Consolidated Fund Bill. This consisted of a series of short debates on specific topics and my particular debate on the problems of London was expected to begin not earlier than 2am. I returned to the House of Commons about midnight to be greeted by the policewoman on duty with a crisp: 'Good evening, sir!' With all the pompous self-importance of a recently elected MP I replied: 'I am hoping to speak tonight.' 'Yes sir', she replied, 'Will it make any difference?' Five hours later, as dawn broke, I made my speech. I doubt if it did make any difference, though Hansard records what I said but not the tiredness of my voice. The press had gone home, the public gallery was empty and the handful of MPs present was more concerned to speak than to listen. I now know that skilled pressure groups and other interested organisations make it their business to know that an MP has referred to them or to a subject on which they have been lobbying.

With time I learned that even opposition backbench MPs can sometimes achieve minor victories. And if MPs can be effective then lobbyists can make an impact through them. That is the main theme of this book.

Democracy should not simply be a matter of voting for a government every four or five years and then letting the politicians get on with it. All of us, whether acting as individuals or as members of a pressure group, trade union or other organisation have the right to try to influence Parliament and the government at any point.

This is not a book about political science; it is not concerned with the philosophy of lobbying or its history. It is intended as a handbook for effective lobbying. I have tried to include plenty of examples to give you a better feel of what you may wish to ask MPs to do.

I should make it clear that for politicians there is a distinction between helping individual constituents with their problems, and trying to influence legislation and government policy. MPs spend a great deal of their time on the former. There is a difference, for example, between trying to help find a home for a homeless family in bed and breakfast accommodation and urging the government to change its housing policies so that fewer people become homeless. On the other hand it is important that MPs are able to draw generalised political conclusions from individual problems and this is something that is done much more by MPs in Britain than by legislators in other countries. There may of course be a more direct overlap between problems and issues. For example a group of residents in an area may object to a new road scheme which will go near their homes. For each of them it is a specific problem, but for the politician it is also a matter of local planning policy.

While the main emphasis of this book is on MPs, it also covers other lobbying targets. The House of Lords is becoming of greater interest to pressure groups as we have increasing evidence that peers are willing to vote against the government more frequently than the more docile Commons. Incidentally, throughout this book I have drawn a distinction between MPs in the Commons and peers in the Lords. It is also worth thinking of the European Parliament; MEPs do have influence even if relatively little power and they are less burdened by constituency casework. Local government should not be forgotten: it is true that the powers of local authorities have been reduced by the Tory Government but councillors are still worth lobbying on certain issues. Finally this book describes the work of lobbyists who work in commercial firms and what I call 'out of house' lobbyists who make their services available on a consultancy basis. I argue that their work follows similar principles to those used by 'social' pressure groups.

While on the subject of lobbying firms I should also refer to the lobbying of civil servants, both here and in Brussels at the European Community. It is important that pressure groups develop links with officials and there are no problems about doing this. The civil servants will normally be glad to be kept informed of what you are doing and will welcome copies of your briefings to MPs and reports. Indeed some pressure groups are a valuable source of information for officials.

Pressure groups, when sending out briefings, should also send copies to the House of Commons library. Its staff prepare numerous reports for MPs covering a variety of issues and it helps them to know your views – it is also a good way of feeding these indirectly to MPs. Incidentally, some pressure groups fail to amend their mailing lists after elections. It took many months after I lost my seat in June 1987 before briefings stopped being sent to me.

During my years in Parliament I was often asked to speak on lobbying to help members of pressure groups become more proficient. For example I spoke to Amnesty International, the Campaign for Nuclear Disarmament, Citizens Advice Bureaux and various trade unions; and all of them asked whether anything had been written about lobbying. From this it was a short step to writing a book based upon my parliamentary and other experiences.

I should stress that this is not intended simply to be another book about Parliament. There are plenty of them already. It is, however, necessary to understand something of how Parliament works in order to lobby effectively. So this book tries to explain the basic elements of procedure. Be warned: it's a complicated business. Soon after I was first elected one of the older hands suggested that it had taken him 18 months to understand most of what was going on. At the time I doubted this but in the event he was right.

For MPs, procedure can be a trap. To ignore it means being less effective; however, some MPs go to the other extreme and seem to spend virtually the whole of their parliamentary careers becoming expert at it.

If you want to influence politicians you must know something about them and how they operate. Unfortunately, there is a tendency for some MPs to cultivate the idea that there is some mystique about the House of Commons. They don't really want outsiders to understand it too well, perhaps because it would diminish their own sense of importance. Even if their speeches are not up to much, they are good at drawing a meeting to a close by muttering that they have to 'see the minister' or get back to the House for a division or over to *Newsnight* for an interview.

It is not easy for the outsider to follow what is going on in Parliament. Hansards, select committee reports and white papers are expensive. Newspaper coverage is often disappointing. As for what happens in standing committees or select committees, that barely gets any mention at all in the press.

This 'gap' between politicians and the people they represent is bad for democracy which surely requires an informed electorate. It is important that those who want to follow what is happening in Parliament should be able to do so and I hope the decision to televise the Commons will help by blowing away some of the cobwebs.

The more you understand what MPs can do the more you can get them to work for you. That means asking them to do specific things and not letting them brush you off by saying that they will look into it, with the consequence that you never hear from them again. They will find it harder to charm you into accepting no action if you make precise requests. It cannot be said often enough that the more you understand the system the more you can achieve.

The government, Parliament and the civil service – in fact the whole apparatus of the state – all too often appear to conspire to keep the public in ignorance; that way we can be manipulated. Knowledge, for ordinary people, is a necessary weapon to protect ourselves against the state. I hope this book will empower people to feel they can fight back.

Getting to Know Your Politician

To lobby effectively you must know your politician.

Politicians are ordinary people. They work hard and are vainer than most, appear to have lots of self confidence but can be very vulnerable especially if they have a small majority and an election is near. Their private lives are not their own and their smallest foibles, sins, weaknesses and misdemeanours hit the headlines. Most of them want to be liked. Above all almost all of them love being MPs, no matter how much they try to hide the fact.

When you meet your MP, if you have not already done so, there is no need to be awed or deferential; nor does it help to be particularly aggressive. Do bear in mind that MPs are often short of time so it helps to be clear about what you want to say. In the end remember they are there to serve you and your taxes pay their salaries.

MPs are not the only politicians who are important to lobbyists. There are thousands of councillors throughout the country, 650 members of Parliament and 81 members of the European Parliament. The vast majority of these are men, with only 12 women MEPs and 41 women MPs. This being said, there are quite a few women councillors. Since the 1987 general election there are four black MPs (all Labour) in the House of Commons but no MEPs, though some minorities are represented at councillor level. Politicians tend to come from a wide range of backgrounds but the middle class predominates. Surveys show certain jobs and professions are well represented in Parliament: there is a high proportion of lawyers, lecturers and teachers, local government employees and businessmen. In the Labour Party there are quite a few trade union officials and a fair number of MPs from the North and Scotland with working-class origins. Local councils might have more estate agents and small business people and some manual workers.

Some MPs give up their jobs on election, and some take on even more outside work in the form of consultancies and company directorships. If they do outside work, this may be in the mornings, and perhaps it is not surprising that there are a number of practising barristers and solicitors in the House of Commons. Councillors are usually either part time or do all their political work in the evenings and weekends. This chapter concentrates on MPs, how to find out about them and how to use this information.

Where to Obtain Information

Local Papers
Most politicians send out regular press releases and try to ensure that their activities are covered by their local papers. Read all of these regularly to keep up to date. It will help to keep cuttings which will build up a picture of what the politician is involved in over a period of time, and will be a useful resource. It may be that a particular press report could trigger a response from your group.

Useful Reference Books
There are a number of useful reference books, some of them rather expensive. If your group takes lobbying seriously you will need to have one or two of them easily available for quick reference. The others are often in public libraries. Fuller information about reference books is given in the Bibliography on p. 224.

- *The Times Guide to the House of Commons* lists all MPs with a photograph of each, gives their majorities and a very brief biography.
- *Parliamentary Profiles* by Andrew Roth gives detailed and often personal gossip as well as a political biography of every MP. Well worth a look as it is the most comprehensive and easy to read reference book, and has some wonderfully biting comments.
- *Vachers Parliamentary Companion* is a basic list of MPs, peers, departments, committees, etc.
- *Dod's Parliamentary Companion* is a glossy annual publication with photographs and brief political biographies.
- *Who's Who* gives details of all MPs and peers, as well as of thousands of other people.
- *Register of Members' Interests* (HMSO, £7.20) This lists interests as declared by MPs under nine possible headings: directorships; employment or office; trades or professions; clients; financial sponsorships, gifts, etc.; overseas visits; payments etc. from abroad; land and property; declarable shareholdings. (*See* Figure 2.1.) Unfortunately this register is neither comprehensive nor compulsory, as MPs can avoid declaring their financial interests.

Election Addresses and Leaflets
During election time all candidates produce a range of written materials

Figure 2.1 Register of Member's Interests

1987 Edition

Register of Member's Interests on 12th January 1987

Presented pursuant to the Resolutions of
22nd May 1974 and 12th June 1975

Ordered by The House of Commons *to be printed*
27th January 1987

LONDON
HER MAJESTY'S STATIONERY OFFICE
£7.20 net

155

7

which make promises and outline their policies. Election addresses and local and national manifestos are very useful as they will give details on policies, and local materials will give personal and political details about the politician. Get hold of copies by asking at the local party offices, and keep them for future reference. Many local parties will produce propaganda newsletters and leaflets designed to keep the electorate up to date with the politician's activities and these should be added to your files for reference, or could be used for a reply if appropriate.

Hansard

This is the record of everything that happens in the Commons chamber plus written questions and the answers (Figure 2.2). There is a similar Hansard covering the Lords and also one for every sitting of a standing committee (Figures 2.3 and 2.4). There are also similar reports covering evidence given to select committees.

There are indexes to each edition so you can look up your MP, or an issue, to see who has said what or asked a question. They are expensive to buy, but should be available for reference in a local library. It is a useful and fascinating exercise to have a look at these, and maybe to keep an eye on them regularly. They are published daily and weekly during sittings. The daily Commons Hansard costs £3.70 and the weekly edition £10.20; the comparable Lords Hansards cost £3.25 and £6.50. Annual subscriptions for the daily Commons Hansard are £630 and £357 for the weekly. Some national organisations have asked a friendly MP to send them their own copies of Hansard regularly (usually the weekly edition which the MP does not really need), but MPs and peers will normally only do this for national lobbying groups, and their supply is very limited.

Commons Weekly Information Bulletin

This publication is printed weekly, and comes out on Saturdays in advance of the next week's proceedings. It lists the previous week's business, and the coming week's business in both houses, progress of legislation, details of white and green papers, membership of standing and select committees, select committee reports and details of European Community documents (*see* Figure 2.5). Get a copy and see how useful you find it is. The cost is £1.95 per copy and the annual subscription is currently £71.30. Order it by letter or phone from the Stationery Office at HMSO Publication Centre, PO Box 276, London SW8 5DT. Telephone orders 01-622 3316; general enquiries 01-211 5656. Or you can buy it from HMSO bookshops.

Figure 2.2 Hansard (Commons)

Thursday
10 December 1987

Volume 124
No. 62

HOUSE OF COMMONS
OFFICIAL REPORT

PARLIAMENTARY
DEBATES

(HANSARD)

Thursday 10 December 1987

LONDON
HER MAJESTY'S STATIONERY OFFICE
£3·70 net

Figure 2.3 Hansard (Lords)

Vol. 492
No. 69

Tuesday
2 February 1988

PARLIAMENTARY DEBATES
(HANSARD)

HOUSE OF LORDS
OFFICIAL REPORT

CONTENTS

MONDAY, 1 FEBRUARY 1988

(Continuation of Proceedings)

Local Government Bill—Committee (Third Day) *(continued)* [Col. 933]

Written Answers [Col. 974]

TUESDAY, 2 FEBRUARY 1988

Questions—Westminster Pier: Proposed Development [Col. 985]
—Social Workers: Training [Col. 987]
—Cadaveric Organs: Donation [Col. 989]
—NHS Hospitals: Staff Costs [Col. 991]

Multilateral Investment Guarantee Agency Bill—First Reading [Col. 993]

Local Government Bill—Committee (Fourth Day) [Col. 993]

United Kingdom Central Council for Nursing, Midwifery and Health Visiting (Electoral Scheme) (Variation) Order 1988—Motion for Approval

Written Answers

LONDON
HER MAJESTY'S STATIONERY OFFICE
£3·25 net

Figure 2.4 Hansard (Standing Committee)

PARLIAMENTARY DEBATES

HOUSE OF COMMONS
OFFICIAL REPORT

Standing Committee E

POLICE AND CRIMINAL
EVIDENCE BILL

Ninth Sitting

Thursday 8 December 1983

(Afternoon)

CONTENTS

CLAUSE 3, as amended, agreed to.
CLAUSE 4 under consideration when the Committee adjourned till Tuesday
13 December at half-past Ten o'clock.

LONDON
HER MAJESTY'S STATIONERY OFFICE
£1 · 35 net

Figure 2.5 Weekly Information Bulletin

Saturday 5 March 1988

Session 1987–88 No 22

House of Commons

Weekly Information Bulletin

THIS BULLETIN INCLUDES INFORMATION ON THE WORK OF THE HOUSE IN THE PERIOD
26 FEBRUARY – 4 MARCH 1988 AND ON FORTHCOMING BUSINESS FOR 7 – 11 MARCH 1988

	Page
Business of the House of Commons 26 February – 4 March 1988	1
Forthcoming Business of the House of Commons 7 – 11 March 1988	2
Forthcoming Business of the House of Lords 7 – 11 March 1988	4
Legislation – General Notes	5
Complete List of Public Bills before Parliament this Session	6
Progress on Bills during the period 26 February – 3 March 1988	11
Private Bills: Commons proceedings as at 3 March 1988	12
Order Confirmation and Provisional Order Bills: Commons proceedings as at 3 March 1988	14
Standing Committees Membership, Public Meetings	15
Select Committees: Membership, Meetings, Publications	18
Northern Ireland Legislation: proceedings thereon in the 1987–88 Session	22
White Papers and Green Papers received since the last Bulletin	23
European Communities Documents received since the last Bulletin	24
Further Information	25
State of the Parties in the House of Commons as at 3 March 1988	25
Selective Index to the Weekly Information Bulletin	Back Page

The House Magazine

This is published weekly and lists the progress of legislation as well as early day motions and private members' bills; it has feature editions on various topical issues. It costs £75 a year from 12-13 Clerkenwell Green, London, EC1R 0DP (01-250 1504). It is full of interesting information, and I do recommend local groups to keep an eye on it if they can get hold of a copy (*see* Figure 2.6). It is the most useful of the regular publications, particularly as it is the only one that lists what early day motions have been tabled (although it does not say who has signed them).

Parliamentary Information Services

House of Commons:
>   Public Information Office
>   House of Commons
>   London, SW1A 0AA
>   01-219 4272

House of Lords:
>   The Clerk
>   Journal and Information Office
>   House of Lords
>   London, SW1A 0PW
>   01-219 3107
>   (in recesses, 01-219 3000, ask for House of Lords information)

They are extremely efficient and helpful though very busy. They keep lists of the composition of standing and select committees, membership of other groupings, and government and opposition responsibilities. They will also provide lists of signatories to motions and updates on the progress of legislation.

Council Information Sources

Every council has a public information service which will probably have photographs of the councillors, addresses and phone numbers, and lists of which committees they serve on. Some will provide additional information on their backgrounds, and there is a log kept of their financial interests which is available to anyone who asks to see it. By law, councillors have to declare their interests in this book, and to state if they have any interest in a topic being discussed in committee and to withdraw from the debate if necessary. These rules are quite strict, unlike the parliamentary guidelines which are only voluntary. All that has been said about election addresses and leaflets and local papers

Figure 2.6 House Magazine

Publisher
KEITH YOUNG

Consultant Editor
PATRICK CORMACK MP FSA

Associate Editor
AUSTIN MITCHELL MP

Publishing Director
RON McKAY

EDITORIAL

Associate Publisher
RUSSELL DEXTER

Head of Information
ANN MacDONALD

Editorial Assistant
CHRISTABEL KERR-DINEEN

Council View
CHRISTIAN WOLMAR

ADVERTISING

Associate Publisher
JENNIFER DOHERTY

Sales Executive
BEN JAMAL

THE HOUSE *magazine*

12-13 Clerkenwell Green, London EC1R 0DP. Tel: 01-250 1504

CONTENTS

FEATURES

SIDELINES 2
Cobbett's Corner, Council of Europe

COMMITTEE CORRIDORS 4
Watchman

HOUSE DIARY 6
David Harris

US REPORT 7
Bruce Carey

PROFILE 8
Lord Hesketh

AGRICULTURE
John MacGregor 11
David Clark 12
National Farmers Union 13

I.P.T. 14
Countryside Commission 15
Food from Britain 16

MEMBERS ONLY 17
Michael Colvin

BUSINESS

COMMONS CHAMBER 18

COMMONS COMMITTEES 20

LORDS CHAMBER 21

PROGRESS OF LEGISLATION 22

LAST WEEK IN PARLIAMENT 26

NOTICEBOARD 27

HOUSE DIRECTORY 28

CLASSIFIEDS 32

On May 11th, Lord Callaghan unveiled Sir Jacob Epstein's bust of Ernest Bevin in the Lower Waiting Hall. The bust, one of Epstein's most powerful portraits, has been lent to the House by the Trustees of the Tate Gallery, but both Lord Callaghan and the Speaker made eloquent pleas that its loan, negotiated by the House of Commons Works of Art Committee, should be a permanent one. The ceremony, attended by many of those who served with Ernest Bevin, was a notable parliamentary occasion, made memorable by Lord Callaghan's speech which we hope to print in full in next week's edition.

Opinion

'I have no intention of taking an early bath', said Mr Speaker in his recent Weekend World TV interview. Thus he squashed rumours that he would soon be retiring. The bathtub imagery was doubtless appropriate for the grubby world of politics.

No Speaker can live without controversy. The adversarial nature of the Commons makes this inevitable. The Speaker has to balance the competing claims of Government and Opposition and of backbenchers and their nominal superiors on the front benches. Even the most skilled parliamentary juggler must expect some plates to crash.

The Speaker deserves explicit support and the benefit of our doubts. It is not helpful when his authority is challenged in the Chamber.

One recent issue has symbolised the difficulties for the Speaker. It concerns the granting of a Standing Order No 20 debate on Social Security. The debate was sought immediately upon the Commons return from the Easter Recess. The demand was instant, and the terms of SO 20 meant the debate also would be speedy.

Charles Kennedy and I, visiting a North Sea oil rig, were frustrated and inconvenienced observers of the process. Even so, the Speaker was absolutely right. No one with a shred of social sensitivity can doubt that the issue was causing distress to our constituents. No one knows how the topic would have obtruded upon the business of the House had an SO 20 debate not been provided. The action of the Speaker secured an early opportunity for debate and a safety valve for a situation where passions ran high.

The Speaker has a first obligation to the House of Commons generally, and to the Government and Opposition Front Benches in that context. He has a formidable and onerous task; but it is being carried out with a sense of fairness and with a reverence for Parliament. Such sweet smelling success certainly has no need of 'an early bath'.

JOHN BIFFEN MP

applies equally to councillors.

European Parliament Information Services

The European Parliament has an office in each of the 12 countries and publishes many pamphlets about its work in the official languages. These can be obtained free of charge from the London office: European Parliament Information Office, 2 Queen Anne's Gate, London, SW1H 9AA (01-222 0411). The list of members is also free, and lists their committees and addresses and phone numbers. It is worthwhile contacting this office and asking for general information about the European Parliament and related organisations, as the pamphlets are easy to read and do explain the complicated set-up clearly.

It is less easy to keep a track on MEPs because the press does not cover their activities so often, so it may be better to contact them direct and ask to be kept informed, particularly if they produce a regular newsletter or briefing. (See Chapter 11.)

Restrictions on MPs with Government Posts

If target MPs hold a government position or opposition frontbench responsibility it may restrict what they are able to do for you and it will affect their attitude and reaction to approaches from constituents. This is equally true whatever political party is in power. There are conventions which rule what government MPs and opposition frontbenchers may do. Ministers will never sign early day motions and nor will Parliamentary Private Secretaries (PPSs). Strictly speaking opposition front benchers should not sign EDMs either. In practice members of the shadow cabinet probably will not but other frontbenchers may sign – provided the motion is not against party policy. An example worth quoting occurred when Amnesty International groups all over the country asked their MPs to sign an EDM on human rights violations. While some Labour Party frontbenchers signed, others refused saying they were not allowed to because of their jobs. Try it anyway; you will normally get them to add their names. Of course there are sometimes EDMs sponsored by the shadow cabinet member responsible and that is a signal that it has official approval.

Currently 84 MPs hold a government post, including whips, plus 41 PPSs. (In addition there are 21 peers with a post, including whips.) The 84 ministers plus the 41 PPSs are sometimes called the 'payroll' vote, even though the PPSs are unpaid. This means that they are called out to vote whenever there is a government 'line' and this can be especially important on occasions where there is no formal whip.

Among this number are the cabinet, other ministers, and PPSs. Although ministers, whips and PPSs have constraints on what they may do, including asking questions, they are given more leeway on constituency matters to make up for it, and it appears that more weight is given to private representations on behalf of constituents to other ministers simply because they cannot make a public fuss. These constraints mean that they have to make use of informal approaches.

The Cabinet
By statute, the cabinet can have up to 22 members; any over 22 cannot, by statute, get paid. The precise posts in the cabinet may vary, and some posts get added depending on how much political importance is attached to that issue by the prime minister. For instance, James Callaghan had a minister for overseas development in his cabinet, and Margaret Thatcher has not. At present there are 22 cabinet members, including 3 from the Lords. The cabinet has evolved as the centre of political power, and has centralised executive power.

Ministers
There are 28 ministers (of which five are peers) not in the cabinet who have specific areas of policy responsibility under the direction of the secretary of state, and 41 junior ministers, including whips. The junior ministers are often given the title of 'parliamentary under-secretary of state'. For example, Home Office ministerial responsibilities in February 1988 were:

Secretary of State: Rt Hon Douglas Hurd CBE MP
Overall responsibility for the work of the department. Deals personally with emergencies; Royal matters; security

Minister of State: Timothy Renton MP
Deals with immigration, nationality and passports; broadcasting; data protection; refugee resettlement; shops; Home Office interest in deregulation; and obscenity

Minister of State: John Patten MP
Deals with criminal policy and criminal justice, other than life sentence cases and mental health policy and casework; crime prevention; juvenile offenders; probation and after-care; criminal justice casework; magistrates' courts; gambling; voluntary services; sex discrimination; community relations and inner cities; extradition and House of Commons business on charities law; fire; and civil defence

Parliamentary Under-Secretary of State: The Earl of Ferrers
Deals with police; fire service; Channel Islands and Isle of Man; civil
defence; charities law and is spokesman (sic) in the House of Lords on
Home Office matters. The Earl of Arran assists the Earl of Ferrers as
Home Office spokesman (sic) in the House of Lords.

Parliamentary Under-Secretary of State: Douglas Hogg MP
Deals with prisons; drugs; liquor licensing; electoral matters; summer
time; animal welfare; coroners; local legislation/bye-laws; mentally
disordered offenders policy and casework; life sentence cases; and House
of Commons business on police; Channel Islands and Isle of Man.

A minister will write to another minister on behalf of constituents, can
undertake public or speaking activities unless it conflicts with
government policy, and can take up an issue within his/her own
department if necessary. Ministers act as constituency MPs but will
normally closely follow official policies and are bound by collective
responsibility. In lobbying terms, having a minister of one kind or
another as a constituency MP has both advantages and disadvantages. It
virtually guarantees local publicity if you set it up properly and may
result in national publicity; if s/he is sympathetic to the issue it could
result in a direct line to the ear of ministerial colleagues. But it can
prevent the possibility of canvassing widespread support among
backbenchers and action on the floor of the House.

The Opposition

The official opposition has a shadow cabinet which functions similarly
to the cabinet on policy formulation, except that it cannot enact it!
Members of this are under similar restrictions as to the actions they may
not undertake.

Other Jobs

A parliamentary private secretary is a sort of unpaid aide to a minister.
The only member of the opposition who has a PPS is the leader. Being a
PPS is really the first rung on the ladder to preferment – with luck. They
may not normally table oral parliamentary questions or sign early day
motions.

The Speaker and three deputy Speakers have, in effect, relinquished
party membership and all political activity in the House where they
are traditionally politically neutral. However they still represent

their constituencies like any other MPs and will act on constituency problems. While they were not challenged in elections in the past, nowadays they have to fight general elections. Despite this they are unlikely to respond to calls for open political action but will do things informally and behind the scenes. In some ways the public constraints on the Speaker and on the deputy Speakers are similar to those affecting ministers.

Membership of Committees

There are innumerable committees of one kind or another in Parliament and these are explained in Chapters 4 and 5. Suffice it to say here that with a bit of digging the lobbyist can find out whether a local MP is an officer of an all-party committee on penal reform, or international human rights, or on transport, or whatever. These backbench or party committees can often be influential in policy terms, they may visit foreign countries or have other outside contacts. They will conduct investigations and may produce reports, and may also have some influence on party thinking.

International Committees

The Inter-Parliamentary Union (IPU) and the Commonwealth Parliamentary Association (CPA) have widespread international contacts and some limited influence. They each have sub-committees of MPs and peers to handle contacts with individual countries. Officers of the sub-committees will usually meet diplomatic representatives of that country socially once in a while, and will arrange and participate in visits to and from the country. Both the IPU and the CPA restrict what issues can be raised by parliamentarians during their events, so that discussion of human rights violations and individual cases is banned, unless it concerns a parliamentarian. The House of Commons information office has lists of all the officers of both and will send out copies on demand.

NATO

Some MPs are delegates to NATO and sit on its committees, and some of them have used this forum to raise human rights and nuclear disarmament issues quite effectively.

Foreign travel

Most MPs go on visits abroad during their careers and many do a fair amount of foreign travelling in one capacity or another. Unfortunately no central list is kept of who goes where and who is paying for it, although some MPs do declare this in the *Register of Members' Interests* if they have been paid for by a government or company. The problem with even this information is that it comes out months later. The only way to find out where they are going, who is paying and what the purpose of the visit is, is to ask them regularly. The all-party whip (a paper circulated to all MPs weekly) lists IPU and CPA trips coming up, and it may be possible to get hold of this occasionally, but regular information is very hard to obtain. This is possibly intentional.

Personalities and Politics

Subtle lobbying will involve not just barging into the MP's advice session and demanding immediate action, but doing a little detective work first. Their political stance within the party, their past experience and the issues they have taken up, are all things that can be discovered. Delving into their personalities and their politics will pay dividends as it may guide tactics. Diligence and guile should contribute to a productive association.

Religions

Some MPs practise a religion. It is well known that John Selwyn Gummer MP is a member of the Church of England Synod and that Greville Janner MP is actively associated with Jewish causes. Denominational year books list MPs who are practising members of each religion and these books can be consulted in libraries. Other parliamentary reference books may also show this information.

If a member of the lobbying group, or a sympathetic contact, is also a member of that religion it may be useful to take them along on a delegation, or get them to coordinate approaches to the MP. CND has shown how this technique can be used very effectively at a national and local level. It makes it difficult for a Catholic MP to give short shrift to a delegation which includes a priest, or a Jewish MP to dismiss a request for action from a rabbi.

Party Contacts

It might be a good idea to get a member of the same party to liaise with the MP. Use a respected party member, a councillor, or a friend, if possible. While you are about it, it is worthwhile finding out where the politician stands inside his/her own party. All political parties have sub-groups and divisions.

Trade Union Sponsorship

Many Labour MPs are either sponsored by trade unions or act as consultants for a union. If the local MP has this type of formal relationship with a particular union, it will be useful for a lobbying group to make contact with local branches. The union could be asked to discuss the issue at one of its meetings (offer a speaker and a draft resolution) and this could be relayed to the MP. Perhaps a local union officer or member would take part in a delegation to the MP. Remember that sponsorship involves the union paying money towards the election expenses of the MP and sometimes extra funds throughout the year, so this relationship can be a powerful lever on the MP. However the sponsored MP does *not* get any money for himself/herself.

Politicians' Backgrounds

The background of a politician could have a bearing on any approach, depending on the issue. A lot of MPs are lawyers and some still practise. This could affect the way they respond to lobbying on law reform or related matters. An MP may have been a social worker, a teacher, or in business, and this could be relevant when lobbying on educational issues or even on environmental problems or the like. It is always useful to know, just in case.

Financial Interests

Financial holdings and interests are important. MPs do not have to declare whether they are on the board of directors of a company, or if they act as a parliamentary adviser, but in practice most will. Have a look at the *Register of Members' Interests*. For example, a lobbying group concerned with apartheid should know if the local MP has shares in a company which has invested heavily in South Africa. This is an obvious example, but financial ties may affect attitudes in all sorts of subtle ways, so it is best to know as much as possible. It can also be a useful publicity tool if a conflict of interest is perceived between the MP's financial holdings and the concerns of constituents.

Political Interests

Most politicians will develop political interests or expertise on one or two issues. It is impossible to become an expert on everything, and usually politicians will decide to specialise in subjects, either related to past work experience, their constituencies, or because they sit on particular committees. They may raise certain issues repeatedly in the House, because they have a genuine concern, or possibly as the result of concerted lobbying. Jack Ashley, Alf Morris and Tom Clarke are well known for their work on behalf of the disabled. Clare Short is known for her interest in Ireland, and her campaign against the exploitation of women's bodies in some popular newspapers. Tam Dalyell has been the scourge of the Government on the sinking of the *Belgrano* and all attempts to suppress information from the media on grounds of 'security'. The list could be endless. A picture of these concerns can be built up from the local press, from Hansard and probably best of all from Roth's *Parliamentary Profiles*.

3

How to Approach your MP

Do You Know Who Your MP Is?

This is not such a silly question – most people cannot name the MP representing their constituency. Indeed, quite a few people may not know in which constituency they live or work. Finding out is easy and there are several ways of getting the information.

It is important that you should contact your own MP (defined by your home address) even if you don't like him/her or his/her politics. There are two reasons for this. The MP for another constituency will normally pass your letter etc. to your own MP. Workloads for politicians, especially for those representing inner city areas, are very heavy and there simply isn't time to deal with non-constituency matters. Of course there are exceptions, such as if you are commenting on a particular speech made by the MP, or if s/he has frontbench responsibilities, serves on a particular committee or is leading a specific campaign on some issue. Even so there is no guarantee that your letter won't be passed on to your own MP. You could try writing from your work address to the MP of that constituency; also pressure groups and other organisations covering several constituencies can contact all the MPs in their areas.

The second reason for contacting your own MP even if s/he is unsympathetic to your issue is that it is important not to let hostile MPs off the hook. It is natural that we should feel more comfortable in contacting politicians who share our views but that lets the other MPs say that none of their constituents cares about the matter so it can't be important. And there is nothing like pressure from within the constituency for influencing an MP.

Ways of finding out who your MP is:

- Phone the *local town hall* and ask who the MP is for your address; you can also find out which party s/he belongs to and the name of the constituency.
- Ask in the *local public library* – indeed the MP may have a notice there giving the dates and times of advice sessions.

- Check the *local press* to see if there's anything about the local MP. If you live in a town with one constituency, such as Cambridge, then you should find the answer easily. But in Oxford, for example, where there are two MPs and in larger towns and cities where there are many more you will need to identify your MP through the constituency name, assuming it is given in the paper.
- *Citizens Advice Bureaux, law centres, Age Concern* and other voluntary agencies will all be able to tell you.
- You could ask the *local political party office*, if there is one and if it is staffed; it's probably better to ask the party to which the MP belongs but if you make a mistake it hardly matters. At worst they'll tell you they don't know!

How to Make Contact

1. *By letter*. The easiest way is to write to the House of Commons. For example: John Smith MP, House of Commons, London, SW1A 0AA. If the surname is fairly common it obviously helps to put in the first name and the name of the constituency as well. For several years there were, for example, two Labour MPs called Ron Brown and they kept getting letters intended for the other. Do not enclose a stamped addressed envelope as MPs get free postage within the UK for parliamentary matters. It is worth putting contact phone numbers, day and evening, in case the MP wants more information though s/he will usually be too busy to do that often. MPs get free phone calls from the House of Commons to anywhere in the UK.

If MPs are away from Westminster, especially during the recesses, they can ask the Commons post office to send post to home or constituency addresses. This is a very efficient system so there is no need for you to try and find the MP's home address. Indeed when I was away my assistant dealt with virtually all the post. On the other hand letters sent to my home address did not get looked at till I returned. So unless you have clear information to the contrary it is best to write to your MP at the Commons. If your MP is a minister then you still write to him/her at the Commons if you are asking him/her to do something as your constituency MP.

If you are approaching MPs because they are ministers it would seem logical to write to them at their departments. *Don't do that*, unless you are from an organisation which is well known and important enough to get ministerial replies. Otherwise you will only get an answer from a civil servant. In Chapter 6 I cover this in more detail and suggest you should contact the appropriate minister through your MP.

What do you do if your organisation wants to write to a large number of MPs, perhaps to all 650? Logic would suggest that to avoid postage you take the letters in person to the central lobby. You cannot do that. The central lobby attendants will take two letters only. So if you want to deliver a bulk mailing you must either post them away from Westminster or buy and attach stamps at the post office in the central lobby. At this point you probably think the answer is to put your mailing in a large parcel for a friendly MP and ask him/her to distribute them. The rules are against this too; MPs can only put six letters at a time on the board in the members' lobby and this rule seems to be intended to prevent your organisation sending bulk mailings without postage. Don't blame me – I tried to get the system changed. Incidentally all this is different in the Lords; see Chapter 10.

2. *By phone.* Phone the MP at the House of Commons (01-219 3000). Be warned: MPs are hard to find in their offices. Each has a direct line but these are not publicly available, though some MPs will give them to you or even have them on their headed House of Commons paper. If the MP is not available or busy the call should automatically be put through to the secretary/assistant; if s/he is busy or not there the call goes through to a very efficient message system. Your message will be taken but please keep it short as the system is not geared to cope with more than a sentence or so. This message should then reach the MP concerned quickly if s/he is in the building. A light on the phone in the office alerts him/her that there's a message, attendants go through the building to the chamber, the committee rooms, the tea room, the bars etc. looking for the MP and another copy is placed on the 'board' in the members' lobby. If the member is not at Westminster the message will be put in the post and s/he should get it the next day. The message system also works during parliamentary recesses though then the MP is only alerted by a warning light on his/her office phone or by the message in the post.

If you are telephoning from outside London you could try reversing the charges, though that will work only if the MP or secretary/assistant are there and probably if they know who you are. Do not try it for messages.

Some MPs get to the Commons as early as 9am but others, especially those with outside occupations, may not get there till noon or perhaps not before question time at 2.30pm. MPs on standing committees will be busy on certain mornings and evenings. Equally it may also be worth trying to phone your MP on Monday to Thursday evenings up to nearly 10pm or later if you know a late sitting is taking place. Remember there are often divisions at 10pm so the MPs won't be at their desks then. A useful tip, if you cannot get your MP directly, is to leave a message for him/her just before 10pm so he/she gets it on going through the members' lobby to vote. (See Chapter 4 for further details of times when Parliament sits and Chapter 5 for times of standing committee sessions.)

If you can find the MP's home or constituency phone numbers it is worth trying there at weekends or during recesses. Most non-London MPs leave the Commons on Thursday evenings for their constituencies, depending on whether there's a vote late on Thursday or a compelling reason for being present on a Friday. London members tend to be easier to find at the Commons on Fridays, though they may also be at constituency engagements.

This may amuse you: a tired Scottish MP had finished an all-night standing committee at about 5.00am. He went to the post office in the members' lobby and began going through his mail. A particularly irate constituent ended his letter by saying: 'I demand you phone me immediately on receipt of this letter.' The MP did just that.

3. *At the House of Commons.* If you want to see your MP at the House of Commons you do not need an appointment while the House is sitting. Enter through the St Stephen's entrance opposite Westminster Abbey (you can't get in any other way unless you have a pass or are with an MP). After a security check proceed through St Stephen's Hall to the central lobby. At the desk on the left there is an attendant who will give you something called a 'green card' which, rather unusually for the Commons, is an accurate description. When you have completed it the attendants will try to find the MP in the same way as with telephone messages. It can take a long time; indeed the MP may not be at Westminster at all and you will have spent many hours watching life in the central lobby. For the first half hour you may feel there are worse places to wait but afterwards the novelty wears off.

I once spent an evening in my Battersea constituency and was given a green card on returning to vote at 10pm. The constituents had spent most of the evening waiting and left just before I got back. The irony is that I had spent a couple of hours at a meeting about 100 yards from their home! If the MP cannot be found, the green card is put in the post, as with messages, and I expect most MPs send a note to the constituent suggesting they make contact again. MPs are, of course, not obliged to come to the central lobby when they get a green card. They may be reluctant anyway if the address is not from their constituency. Equally they may be in standing committee or in the chamber. Clearly the MP could hardly be expected to come out while about to ask a parliamentary question or even just when prime minister's questions are about to start.

On another occasion I received a green card on which the constituents had written that they wanted to lobby me about a certain aspect of immigration policy. This was passed to me in the chamber during question time when I had a question down on that very subject. All I could do was send a note out explaining I was already acting on the matter and could not leave the chamber.

On the other hand MPs may sometimes leave a standing committee and meet constituents outside in the committee corridor (this is on the first floor). Clearly a minister or opposition frontbencher might find it hard to leave the committee even for a few minutes as might the member moving a particular amendment. Other MPs might not be intending to speak so they could leave the committee room provided they can return at short notice (within seconds) for any votes that are called.

While it is your right to ask to see your MP without appointment whenever the Commons is in session my strong advice is, unless it is very urgent, do not do it without an appointment.

There is another reason why it is best to have an appointment. It sometimes takes a long time to get in through the St Stephen's entrance, especially as you have to clear the security check and have your cases etc. searched. There may be a mass lobby with long queues waiting for admission. (See Chapter 6 about organising mass lobbies.) Without an appointment you might have to wait a long time in the early afternoon. However with a letter of appointment from the MP you can avoid the queue and just show your letter to the police officer at the St Stephen's entrance and then go straight in.

When the Commons is not in session you must have an appointment; this applies in the recess as well as on sitting days (Mondays to Thursdays before 2.30pm and on Fridays after 3.00pm). MPs are unlikely to make appointments after about 4.30pm during the recess because the Commons closes down; the MPs themselves can get in and out at any time but would have to go out of the building to escort you in.

A few points to note about meeting an MP at the Commons:

- It is always helpful to tell the MP how long you would like to talk, and find out how long s/he has for you. An obvious point, but hardly anybody remembers it.
- If there are several of you, warn the MP in advance.
- If there are more than two of you or if you want privacy and quiet you might suggest that the MP book an interview room. These are sometimes called the 'W' rooms and are off Westminster Hall. If such a room has been booked the police at the security check will usually direct you there without the need to go to the central lobby. In any

case it is best to tell the police where your meeting is otherwise you might first be directed to the central lobby.

- If you want to take photographs, or tape record or film the interview (ask the MP first if it is all right) then you will need a W room.
- If the W rooms are all booked up there are other committee rooms, many of them larger, but with two exceptions you can't film in the others. These exceptions are also off Westminster Hall and are the Grand Committee Room and the Jubilee Room. This is especially important if you want the MP to hold a press conference (for more about this see Chapters 6 and 13).

4. *At MPs' local advice sessions/surgeries.* Most MPs have local advice sessions. Check with the town hall, library, Citizens Advice Bureau, law centre, local political party office, or phone the MP at the House of Commons or look in the local paper to see if the advice sessions are advertised. Some MPs require appointments; others have open access. Be careful: you and the MP might feel uncomfortable if you sit discussing housing policy, human rights or abortion, say, while there is a waiting room full of people, including mothers with young children, who need help with social security, housing repairs or other problems. It is probably best, where there is no appointment system, to arrange to be last so your discussion with the MP can be more relaxed.

5. *At other local venues.* The MP may suggest meeting at his/her local party offices or at some other local venue. You might even suggest your house, or a pub or café. Another possibility might be, if appropriate, the offices of your local organisation. (The benefits of inviting the MP to visit your local organisation are discussed more fully in Chapter 7.)

6. *Wining and Dining.* You could invite the MP for a meal or a drink. This might make sense if you know the MP quite well. If not, be careful. While some MPs may not be averse to accepting a free meal they may be the very ones not worth lobbying. Others might be suspicious. Clearly if they accept an invitation to visit an organisation then it's reasonable to offer a (snack) lunch. Also if you are from a large wealthy organisation a meal might be in order, though some MPs might refuse on principle. In any case a busy MP is often unlikely to have time to be taken for an expensive meal. Perhaps attitudes vary between the parties? *My advice is: if in doubt, don't offer lavish entertainment to an MP.*

On the other hand the MP may invite you for a meal/snack/drink at the Commons. It'll probably be in the cafeteria or, in the summer, on the terrace. There are more expensive restaurants in the Palace of Westminster, but don't expect to be taken there. Being an MP can be quite an expensive business; when I was there I had a succession of people for tea and meals and the costs mounted up. You could offer to contribute; some MPs will refuse to accept this, others might be persuaded. This applies equally to drinks in the bar or on the terrace. Strictly speaking only MPs are allowed to buy drinks. Incidentally it is not permitted to have refreshments in the interview or committee rooms. If you are interested in receptions with food and/or drink then you'll have to use the private dining rooms. The MP has to make the booking. (See Chapter 6 for details.)

4

Raising an Issue in the House

This chapter deals mainly with some of the ways an MP can raise issues on the floor of the House. (Legislation is covered in Chapter 5.) In order to cover this adequately, it is necessary to give some explanation of parliamentary procedure.

One of the first problems facing a newly elected MP is how to deal with the request: 'Please raise this in the House.' There are so many ways of doing this that it takes experience and judgement to decide on the best approach. It is the task of the effective lobbyist to understand the procedures well enough to be able to know what the options are and thus to be able to suggest how the MP might go about it. Let us first consider how the Commons operates and what happens when the House is sitting.

The Parliamentary Day

A first time visitor to the public gallery is bound to be confused by the House in action. Not only is the procedure complicated but much of what happens is not predictable, the mood changes, tempers flare, MPs are shouted down, the Speaker calls for order, there is tension and hostility; then laughter, and suddenly calm descends again. At one moment the chamber is packed; five minutes later there is hardly anyone present.

From the public gallery you may wonder why on occasion there are so few members in the chamber. After all there are 650 MPs but the chamber only has seats for under 450 so why are there ever empty benches? Remember on Mondays to Thursdays the Commons sits for eight hours at least and quite often much longer. To be effective MPs must specialise and therefore not everything in the Commons will be of overwhelming interest. MPs like everyone else have a boredom threshold, and they do not find all of their colleagues' speeches compelling.

The burden of constituency casework is increasing. For me it was the largest single task each day. I estimated I received 20,000 items a year in the post and sent out about 10,000 letters. Not all the incoming post needed a reply as some items were journals and briefing documents.

Equally some of the letters I wrote were as a result of constituency advice sessions; nevertheless, writing 10,000 letters a year is time-consuming. Almost certainly, dealing with constituency problems is a much greater burden for inner city MPs than for others.

Here are a few examples of what MPs might be doing if not in evidence in the chamber:

dealing with incoming post
dictating or signing letters
phoning constituents
in standing committee
in select committee
in meetings, visits in the
  constituency
party meetings
backbench group meetings
meetings of all-party groups
being lobbied
meeting constituents at the House
working in their departments,
  if ministers

opposition shadow cabinet or
  other frontbench meetings
TV, radio, press interviews,
  press releases
meeting ministers
political campaigning
eating and drinking
research, reading documents
writing speeches, PQs etc
political gossiping
working at an outside job
foreign visits
UK visits ...

On Mondays to Thursdays, after prayers, the sitting normally begins with questions at 2.30pm. This lasts an hour and may be followed by a private notice question and one or more statements by government ministers. Then comes the main debate of the day, which can be the second reading of a bill, or a debate on a topic chosen by the government such as public expenditure or a debate initiated by the opposition called an 'opposition day' or a white paper or any other issue which the government wants to debate or is under pressure to have discussed. At 10 o'clock there may be one or more votes and these can be followed by debates on one or more 'orders' or statutory instruments, each lasting up to one and a half hours. Finally the last half hour is an adjournment debate.

Whips are a vital aspect of the operation of the Commons (and are also important in the Lords and in local authorities). They are MPs with the responsibility for keeping discipline within their parties, ensuring attendance and that members turn up to vote. If an MP has reason to be absent from a vote s/he must get permission from the whips. Clearly this was very important during the 1974–9 Parliament when the Labour Government for much of the time did not have an overall majority. Since 1979 the Tories have easily dominated votes in the Commons and this became especially marked after the 1983 election.

Every Thursday evening the whips issue a sheet (*see* Figure 4.1) showing the debates for the following week, and whether there will be 'official' party votes and how important they are. The degree of importance is determined by whether the vote will be on a two line or three line whip; one line whips mean a vote is unlikely. However, votes can also be called by the minor parties and by backbenchers, so the government has to keep enough MPs present for such contingencies.

Throughout the Palace of Westminster you will see what look like TV screens but which in fact are annunciators or monitors. At 1pm on Mondays to Thursdays they show whether there are any ministerial statements or private notice questions at 3.30 after normal question time. Then when the House is actually sitting they show what the subject of the debate is, who is speaking, the time the speech began and the actual time. Whenever another MP starts speaking, or there is a new debate or other change, the annunciator gives a 'ping'. If a division is called there are very loud bells and police officers shouting 'division' so they can be heard above the division bells! In case that isn't enough, the annunciator also shows if there is a division, and the result. It does not show names of individual MPs during question time but merely the approximate number of the question reached. Nor does it show the names of the individual MPs on their feet during ministerial statements or points of order.

During debates the annunciator looks like this:

In some parts of the building you may also see similar House of Lords annunciators.

Let us consider the Commons order of business, as shown on page 35, Fig. 4.2. Please note the distinction between items marked 'n', indicating that they require notice and will therefore be shown on the order paper, and items which do not require notice but are taken at the appropriate time if they arise. Note also the different

Figure 4.1 Whip (Labour Party)

PARLIAMENTARY LABOUR PARTY
ON MONDAY, 4th February, 1985, the House will meet at 2.30 p.m.
          TRANSPORT Questions. Tabling for ENERGY.

 OPPOSITION DAY (7th allotted day)
    There will be a debate on an Opposition Motion on the COAL MINING DISPUTE.
    (Rt.Hon. Stan Orme & Alex Eadie)

  DIVISIONS WILL TAKE PLACE AND YOUR ATTENDANCE BY 9 P.M. IS ESSENTIAL.

    Motion relating to the Immigration Appeals (Procedure) Rules.
    (Alf Dubs)
            YOUR CONTINUED ATTENDANCE IS REQUESTED.

ON TUESDAY, 5th February, the House will meet at 2.30 p.m.
          EMPLOYMENT Questions. Tabling for EDUCATION & SCIENCE.
 Ten Minute Rule Bill: Freedom of Probate – Ken Weetch.

    FILMS BILL: REMAINING STAGES.
    (Bryan Gould)
  DIVISIONS WILL TAKE PLACE AND YOUR CONTINUED ATTENDANCE FROM 5 P.M. AND

  UNTIL THIS BUSINESS IS CONCLUDED IS NECESSARY.

    SHIPBUILDING BILL: REMAINING STAGES.
    (Geoffrey Robinson)
    YOUR CONTINUED ATTENDANCE IS REQUESTED.

    MILK (CESSATION OF PRODUCTION) BILL: REMAINING STAGES.
    (Brynmor John & John Home Robertson)
  DIVISIONS MAY TAKE PLACE AND YOUR CONTINUED ATTENDANCE IS NECESSARY.

    TOWN AND COUNTRY PLANNING (COMPENSATION) BILL: PROCEEDINGS.
    (David Clark)
    YOUR CONTINUED ATTENDANCE IS REQUESTED.

ON WEDNESDAY, 6th February, the House will meet at 2.30 p.m.
          ENVIRONMENT Questions. Tabling for F.C.O.
 Ten Minute Rule Bill: People's Right to Fuel – Dennis Canavan.
    Motion on the Rate Limitation (Prescribed Maximum) (Precepts) Order.
    (John Cunningham)
    A DIVISION WILL TAKE PLACE AND YOUR ATTENDANCE BY 6.30 P.M. IS ESSENTIAL.

    HONG KONG BILL: REMAINING STAGES.
    (George Robertson)
    YOUR CONTINUED ATTENDANCE IS REQUESTED.

ON THURSDAY, 7th February, the House will meet at 2.30 p.m.
        NORTHERN IRELAND Questions. Tabling for TREASURY.

Motions relating to the Water Authorities (Return on Assets) Orders
(Jeff Rooker)   1984 and 1985.

DIVISIONS WILL TAKE PLACE AND YOUR ATTENDANCE BY 6 P.M. IS ESSENTIAL.

Ways and Means Resolution relating to the GLC Grant to London Regional
(Gwyneth Dunwoody)   Transport.
A DIVISION WILL TAKE PLACE AND YOUR CONTINUED ATTENDANCE IS ESSENTIAL.

Motion on the London Regional Transport (Levy) Order.
(Gwyneth Dunwoody)
A DIVISION WILL TAKE PLACE AND YOUR CONTINUED ATTENDANCE IS ESSENTIAL.

    THIS VOTE WILL BE LATE - PLEASE MAKE YOUR ARRANGEMENTS ACCORDINGLY.

ON FRIDAY, 8th February, the House will meet at 9.30 a.m.
        PRIVATE MEMBERS' BILLS

WILDLIFE AND COUNTRYSIDE (AMENDMENT) BILL: SECOND READING. - David Clark.
(David Clark)
EDUCATION (SCHOOL BUDGETS) BILL: SECOND READING. - David Madel.
(Andrew Bennett)

        YOUR ATTENDANCE IS REQUESTED.

ON MONDAY, 11th February, the House will meet at 2.30 p.m.
        WALES Questions. Tabling for TRANSPORT.

PRIVATE MEMBERS' MOTIONS until 7 p.m.

SOCIAL SECURITY BILL: REMAINING STAGES.

Colleagues are asked to be ready to respond to a THREE LINE WHIP.

                MICHAEL COCKS

arrangements on Fridays when there is no question time. Items that are not taken at all on Fridays or at that time on Fridays are marked #. Petitions are taken directly after prayers on a Friday instead of just before the adjournment debate as on other days.

There is no such thing, however, as a typical parliamentary day. All sorts of different combinations of matters may be debated. Sometimes proceedings finish at 11.30pm while on other days the debate continues till the early hours or longer. On some days MPs will know precisely when they will vote or when they can go home, while on other days nothing can be predicted. Some of the reasons for the vagaries of voting and finishing times are explained below.

The parliamentary day is unpredictable. The government can change the business at short notice; more important is the fact that the length of time any item will take cannot always be estimated or anticipated. Sometimes there has to be a vote at, say, 10 o'clock, or the length of a particular debate is determined by standing orders. Other business is open ended and on occasion the debate collapses, giving more time for something else, especially for the MP who spots what is happening and is quick off the mark. Usually, however, debates take longer than expected as MPs can generally find many things to say; and tiredness, an empty House, no possible news value in the topic, as well as a partner waiting at home, do not appear to be sufficient incentive to brevity.

There is usually much competition by MPs to speak, and at the end of many debates there will be MPs who failed to get called by the Speaker. It can thus be very frustrating when constituents comment, 'I haven't heard much from you on '*Yesterday in Parliament*', been away have you?' When deciding which members to call at questions or for a debate the Speaker is influenced by whether an MP is a privy councillor or has a constituency, specialist or a regional interest.

The opposition frequently demand that a government minister make a statement. Understandably the minister often declines. On occasion there can be sudden moments of high drama. For example there were numerous compelling incidents at the height of the Westland saga following the resignation of Michael Heseltine, the Defence Secretary. Leon Brittan, the Trade and Industry Secretary, made a statement after questions at 3.30 pm one day. There was much anger and dissatisfaction among members that all the facts had not emerged. Eventually at about 10.15 that night Leon Brittan made another statement which contradicted some of the things he had said earlier. On both occasions the House was packed!

A word about Fridays. Unless there is important Commons business, MPs head for their constituencies late on Thursday evenings or on Friday

Figure 4.2 Order of Business (Commons)

HOUSE OF COMMONS

Order of Business

The Business of the House is transacted in the order set out below. Items marked *n* require notice and any business arising under these heads will be found on the Order Paper. The remaining items do not require notice, and may therefore not be placed on the Order Paper, but will be taken in their appropriate place if they arise. Notification of the Royal Assent to Acts may be given at any time, and any proceedings may be interrupted for this purpose.

1 AFTER PRAYERS

    Reports of Queen's Answers to Addresses.
    Formal Communications by Mr Speaker.
    Motions for New Writs.
  n Private Business.
  * Presentation of Public Petitions.
  n Motions for Unopposed Returns.

2 QUESTIONS

  †*n* Questions for oral answer.
    Private Notice Questions.

3 AFTER QUESTIONS

    Ministerial statements (and statements by Mr Speaker).
    Introduction of new Members.
  † Proposals to move the Adjournment under Standing Order No. 20.
    Motions for leave of absence.
    Ceremonial speeches.
    Giving notice of motions and (*n*) holding of ballot.
    Personal explanations.
    Consideration of Lords amendments (if not of substance) or messages.

4 AT THE COMMENCEMENT OF PUBLIC BUSINESS

  n Presentation of Public Bills.
  n Business Motions moved by the Government.
  †*n* Motions under Standing Order No. 19 for leave to bring in Bills or nomination of Select Committees.

5 PUBLIC BUSINESS ('ORDERS OF THE DAY')

  n Orders of the Day and Notices of Motions to be proceeded with in the order in which they appear.

      †[Private Business set down under Standing Order No. 16 starts at 7 p.m., any business then under discussion being postponed until such proceedings are over. Motions for the Adjournment under Standing Order No. 20 stand over until the commencement of public business on the following day (on Thursday, until Monday) or, if Mr Speaker so directs, until 7 p.m. on the same day, any business then under discussion being postponed.]

  n Business motions under Standing Order No. 14(2).
  n Business exempted under Standing Order No. 14 (including proceedings on Statutory Instruments etc.)
  † Presentation of Public Petitions.
    Adjournment motion under Standing Order No. 9.

The Order Paper also contains :

    List of Committees to sit this day.
  n Questions for written answer.

      * Fridays only.
      † Not on Fridays.

13th November 1986

    [This issue replaces that issued on 12th November 1986]

mornings. Friday business is therefore often regarded as somehow being less important. Most Fridays are set aside for private members' bills or motions though a few are devoted to government business, though never for second readings of major government bills. (Debates on certain private members' bills such as those dealing with abortion or official secrets keep MPs in London.)

There is no question time, except for the possibility of a private notice question. Occasionally business is interrupted at 11am for a ministerial statement. Business starts at 9.30am and generally finishes at 3pm, the last half hour being the usual adjournment debate. As on other days the government has the power to propose an extension of the debating time and although the decision is Parliament's, the government invariably gets its way. In practice it is extremely rare for Friday's business to go beyond the normal time.

Incidentally, the government can also call the House for a sitting on a Saturday, or during the recess. The last Saturday sitting was the day after the Falklands/Malvinas were invaded and though no vote was taken the government subsequently claimed that the House had on that fateful Saturday endorsed the policy of sending the Task Force to recapture the islands.

It is clear that the nature of parliamentary business with all its surprises does provide opportunities for the MP who has been well briefed by the lobbyist and is ready to seize any chance of arguing a particular case. Skilled MPs keep themselves well informed on their special subjects and an effective lobbying organisation ensures that they are helped in this.

Parliamentary Questions

The parliamentary question is often the best way of drawing the attention of a minister or the House as a whole to a specific topic. A PQ is quick and simple to table (put down) and effective lobbyists make a great deal of use of PQs. To do so to full advantage they need to understand how the system works. The questions are printed on the order paper after being tabled and again on the day they are due to be answered; the questions and answers also appear in Hansard.

MPs ask about 50,000 parliamentary questions a year and an assiduous MP has been known to ask as many as 1,000! Most of these are put down for written answer and there is no limit to how many an MP may table. About 3,000 a year are answered orally. Written questions are used essentially to get factual information but additionally they signal that there is concern about the topic. They are therefore an obvious means of exerting pressure on a minister, especially if a number are asked about the same subject. Tam Dalyell MP probably asked hundreds over a period of months in his efforts to investigate and press the government on the circumstances surrounding the sinking of the *Belgrano* during the Falklands War.

The minister has to approve each draft reply prepared by the civil servants, knowing that interested lobbyists, journalists, MPs and others will scrutinise the answers for any sign of change of policy, or any information which can be used subsequently against the government in debate, press releases or letters to the minister.

There are strict rules about the wording of questions. The PQ on the order paper (agenda) must be factual, and seek information rather than give it. Nor should it lead to an argument or cover a subject that is blocked. Examples of blocked subjects include many aspects of the security services, details of defence policy and information about sales of arms to specific overseas governments. Ministers may also simply refuse to answer questions about certain matters but such a 'block' may only be temporary. It is thus not permitted to ask the Prime Minister a PQ about when a matter relating to the security services was first brought to her attention; she can, however, be asked to refer a specific issue to the Security Commission. It is not permitted to ask the Attorney General why persons named or unnamed have not been prosecuted; it is possible to ask him to consider such a prosecution.

Irony is not allowed. For example, when some time ago the press was full of stories about the government being accident prone I was allowed a question to the Secretary of State for Trade and Industry about the amount of bananas imported but was told that a similar question to the Prime Minister would not be permitted. MPs take their PQs to an office in the House of Commons called the table office, whose officials are very helpful and will often be able to suggest an acceptable form of words.

When questions are tabled they are always addressed to the senior minister in the department. However, the answer may come from one of the other ministers. Ministers may refuse to answer a question on the grounds that the information is not available or could only be provided at excessive cost. There is a broad rule that if it costs the civil service more than £250 the PQ will not be answered. If that is the case, there is little that can be done about it.

Mrs Clwyd: To ask the Secretary of State for Wales if he will list all women who have been appointed to public bodies for which he has responsibility since 1979.

Mr Wyn Roberts: This information can be supplied only at disproportionate cost. (Hansard, 10 November 1987, col 132).

The following example is also quite amusing.

Mr Dubs asked the Secretary of State for the Home Department how many prisoners held on remand in police or court cells have escaped since the beginning of 1983; with which offences they had been charged; and how many were not recaptured on the day of escape.

Mr Hurd: This information cannot all be obtained without dispropor- tionate cost, but I will see what can be collected and write to the hon. member. (Hansard, 17 March 1984, col 328).

An answer like that makes one wonder how many prisoners had, in fact, escaped for such information to be too costly to obtain.

Apart from questions to the prime minister, MPs must put them down to the minister whose department has responsibility for the topic covered. If by some chance the table office accepts a PQ for the wrong minister, the department will send the MP a letter telling him/her that the PQ has been transferred to another minister. This may not matter much in the case of questions for written answer beyond causing a little delay. The point may however be crucial in the case of oral answers because a transfer to another minister will, for the reasons given below, remove an oral PQ from its place in the 'shuffle'.

Ministers are obviously not responsible for the policies of foreign governments, or for the detailed decisions made by local authorities, health authorities or nationalised industries (if there are any left). Nevertheless a skilled MP can usually find ways of obliging the minister to give some sort of answer, though such a tactic works better with oral questions. For example, Mr Ieuan Wyn Jones asked the Secretary of State for Transport when he last met the chairman of British Rail; and what issues were discussed.

Mr Channon: Last week. We discussed a variety of railway matters.
Mr Jones: When the Secretary of State next meets the chairman of British Rail will he discuss with him the state of the North Wales railway line between Holyhead and Crewe. (Hansard, 9 November 1987, col 11).

The supplementary went on to ask about electrification, a point also taken up by another MP.

Questions for Written Answer

Written questions are usually intended to elicit facts. They may provide statistics not normally published, or in advance of publication; they may reveal when a report or white paper will be issued or when a minister expects to do something.

> **Mr Haynes**: To ask the Chancellor of the Duchy of Lancaster by how much the trade balance in textiles changed between the second quarter of 1979 and the second quarter of 1987; and what was the comparable figure in the average, best and worst performing Organisation for Economic Co-operation and Development country.

The answer was a table containing over 160 figures.

However, written questions are also a way of drawing attention to an issue, and making it clear to ministers and civil servants that there is concern. For example, there was a barrage of questions from many MPs during the campaign against the abolition of the Greater London Council.

Sometimes ministers themselves want an opportunity to make some information available. They get one of their own backbenchers to put down a PQ for written answer and this is normally called a 'planted question'. This device is sometimes used, much to the annoyance of the opposition, as a means of making a statement which cannot immediately be questioned or challenged, especially if it happens on say the day before a recess. (The device of a planted question may also be used in the case of oral questions.) For example:

> **Mr Wolfson**: To ask the Secretary of State for Social Services when he intends to publish the report of the committee of inquiry into the future development of the public health function and community medicine; and if he will make a statement.
>
> **Mr Moore**: I have today published the report ...

On occasion a minister, in answering, will say that s/he has placed relevant papers in the Commons library. The only way for you to get hold of these is to ask a friendly MP to photocopy them for you.

While ordinary written questions are normally answered within a week, an MP can ask for priority; this will get a reply within 12 sitting days but it may simply result in a briefer answer or in the minister saying s/he will write to the MP.

Questions for Oral Answer

Oral questions are the most newsworthy and politically effective way of pressing the government on an issue. Apart from the fact that the exchange takes place on the floor of the House in the early afternoon, the main advantage is the chance to ask a supplementary question. While the strict rules relating to written questions also apply to the tabling of oral questions, with a supplementary virtually anything is possible, provided it conforms to the usual parliamentary constraints about bad language, unparliamentary expressions, describing another MP as a liar, or excessive length.

Skilled lobbyists can thus make very effective use of oral PQs. It may be necessary to brief the MP on the background so that the supplementary can have maximum political impact. Normally the lobbyist, and the MP, should know roughly what reply the minister will give so that the supplementary can be planned in advance. However the minister does sometimes give an unexpected reply and a well-briefed MP who thinks quickly can avoid being disconcerted by this.

Where the PQ covers an area in which the government's policy is clear, the purpose of the PQ may simply be to keep the minister under open and obvious pressure. As civil servants and ministers will try to anticipate the possible supplementaries, a battle of wits sometimes ensues (*see* Figure 4.3).

Supplementaries have to relate to the subject matter of the original question; the skill is to catch the minister unawares or cause embarrassment by putting him/her on the spot. Usually ministers, well prepared by their officials, survive question time without giving anything significant away. Sometimes, however, the result may not be quite what the minister intended. The following is from Hansard, 14 December 1983, col 988:

Mr Dubs asked the Secretary of State for Trade and Industry whether his policy of encouraging exports is limited by any non-commercial criteria.

Mr Tebbit: Yes, Sir.

Mr Dubs: Is the minister aware that there is a firm in the Midlands which manufactures and exports gang chains, leg shackles, and other such items, which are sold to countries where there are known violations of human rights and where they can be used only for the purposes of coercion, degradation and torture? Will the minister look into this matter and see whether he can take the necessary powers to stop the export of such items?

Figure 4.3 Hansard (extract)

Gentleman mentioned a figure that his own Government when in office regarded as wholly unrealistic. We are getting ahead and studying the position in the hope of coming forward fairly early with an answer.

Mr. Sims: Will my hon. and learned Friend take into account the representations made by a wide range of bodies that support the idea of family courts? The representations included those from some who combined to form the family courts campaign. These bodies went to a lot of trouble to respond to the consultation document, since when nothing seems to have happened. When will we get some action?

The Solicitor-General: My hon. Friend points out that a number of bodies have made representations. They made a very diverse range of representations. The concept of the family court covers all those good ideas. It is for the Lord Chancellor, in company with colleagues, to decide which ideas to choose.

Prosecutors (Guidelines)

65. **Mr. Allen:** To ask the Atorney-General if he has any plans to change the guidelines to prosecutors arising from his experience in the Spycatcher case.

The Attorney-General (Sir Patrick Mayhew): No, Sir.

Mr. Allen: In view of the allegations in the book "Spycatcher" that the security services sought to undermine the democratically elected Government of this country, and as the book is still being pursued through the courts by the Attorney-General, will he now change his mind and allow the book to be published without further hindrance? Will he further investigate by public inquiry the security services, that are meant to defend our democracy and not to undermine it?

The Attorney-General: No. The principle underlying the Government's litigation here and elsewhere is very well understood in Britain. It is that those who have served in the security services owe a lifelong duty of confidentiality to the Crown. That must be maintained and that is why the Government are bringing this litigation.

Mr. Stanbrook: Is not one of the lessons to be learned from the "Spycatcher" cases the need to revise the conditions of service of members of MI5 in order to emphasise to them that the duty of confidentiality is a lifelong duty and to discourage them from any thought that they might be serving the public interest by breaching that duty?

The Attorney-General: I note what my hon. Friend says about the importance of conditions of service, and I shall see that that point is brought to the attention of my right hon. Friend the Home Secretary. However, it is well understood that this duty of confidentiality.is lifelong and that this is absolutely inherent in the obligations of those who serve the Crown in that service.

Mr. Alex Carlile: Does the right hon. and learned Gentleman not agree that decisions such as those made in the "Spycatcher" case in Australia have damaged the very principle of confidentiality that he seeks to establish? Does he agree that his decisions and those of his predecessor in the "Spycatcher" case have made the British common law system the laughing stock of the common law world?

The Attorney-General: I am suspicious of those who claim to know what has made and what may not make

something the laughing stock of something else. However, it is perfectly clear that the British Government have made abundantly plain throughout the world the importance that they attach to the obligation that I described. As the matter is still under appeal in Australia, I will not, I am afraid, yield to the temptation to comment on the remainder of the hon. and learned Gentleman's question.

Mr. Aitken: We all agree with the Government's tactics — *[Interruption.]* I am sorry; that was a slip of the tongue. We all agree with the Government's principle, but my hon. and learned Friend makes it sound as though the tactics are perfect. If my right hon. and learned Friend is interested in avoiding a repetition of the expensive grand opera of legal folly that has characterised the "Spycatcher" case so far, will he not agree that the time has come to issue new guidelines, not just to humble prosecutors, as was suggested in the question, but to future Treasury Solicitors, Law Officers, Cabinet Secretaries and perhaps even higher personages? Perhaps the guidelines should be published in a book, then banned and turned into a bestseller, but we certainly need a change.

The Attorney-General: The line between tactics and strategy is notoriously difficult to define. Perhaps my hon. Friend will recall what I told the House three weeks ago. With regard to section 2, which remains in force, work has been in hand for some time on devising provisions which would be an effective, enforceable and reasonable alternative. That task is not without difficulty. My hon. Friend knows that in 1979 the Government introduced their Protection of Official Information Bill. That was found to be unacceptable, but work is in hand.

Mr. Fraser: If there has been a serious impropriety in the Government service or even a serious breach of constitutional principles, at what point is a civil servant entitled to stop biting his lip and blow the whistle without fear of prosecution?

The Attorney-General: It is well understood that there are procedures within the Civil Service for drawing attention to perceived improprieties. Each case turns upon its own circumstances, as the hon. Gentleman will be the first to recognise. That must be the only general answer capable of being given to a general question.

Director of Public Prosecutions

66. **Mr. Janner:** To ask the Attorney-General when he last met the Director of Public Prosecutions; and what subjects were discussed.

The Attorney-General: I last met the Director on Monday 23 November. We discussed matters relating to the Crown Prosecution Service.

Mr. Janner: Did not the right hon. and learned Gentleman discuss that evil and offensive emanation known as "Holocaust News"? Does he know of the alleged decision not to prosecute those who have perpetrated it? Will he repeat the undertaking given to the hon. Member for Rutland and Melton (Mr. Latham) and myself by his hon. and learned Friend the Solicitor-General—namely that if we produce counsel's opinion to say that the case of "Holocaust News" is covered by the Public Order Act, he and his colleagues will reconsider their previous view, stated in a written answer last week that this publication

315

Mr Tebbit: I note what the hon. gentleman says, but I understand that the truth of the matter is not entirely established. Of course, we have to understand that while there are no international understandings on the export of such items, if this country did not export them someone else would. [Interruption.] Oh yes, indeed. If that happened, the right hon. member for Bethnal Green and Stepney (Mr Shore) would grumble further about our trade position.

Even the normally staid Hansard could not refrain from indicating that Tebbit's answer had caused a storm. Afterwards I understand that protests poured in from all over the world at the revelation that Britain was in the business of exporting torture equipment. The minister's reference to Peter Shore was because of the latter's front bench responsibilities. Within a few weeks Norman Tebbit had to climb down and ban the export of such items. But such successes for a backbench questioner are few and far between.

There is a rota (*see* Figure 4.4) which determines on which days each department is first to answer, and most ministers answer every four weeks. MPs put down the questions between 10am and 4pm, ten sitting days before the appropriate day. In practice ten sitting days usually means exactly a fortnight beforehand; the occasional bank holiday or recess means that PQs have to be tabled longer in advance. Note that PQs for answer in October after the summer recess have to be tabled at the end of July. It is difficult to anticipate in July what subject will be topical three months later. An additional complication is that oral PQs cannot be tabled for answer after a recess until the date when the House resumes has been announced. This means that several days' worth of PQs may be tabled in one afternoon following the announcement of the recess dates. If that happens, MPs will usually have till 6pm that day to table their questions.

Far more MPs put down PQs for oral answer each day than the particular minister can answer. Those that are not reached get a written answer unless the MP withdraws the question beforehand. Otherwise the MP may not immediately table an identical question – although with skill s/he can word the question slightly differently to, say, ask for the latest information on a particular matter, a sort of moving target.

The order in which the questions are printed and reached is determined by a random process called a 'shuffle' which ensures fairness. Individual MPs are limited to eight oral questions on the order paper at any one time and may not put down more than two for any one day. It's easy to exceed the total of eight as at most question times at

Figure 4.4 Order of Questions (Commons)

ORDER OF QUESTIONS

Monday 20th June — Thursday 28th July 1988

Mon. 20 June	Tues. 21 June	Wed. 22 June	Thurs. 23 June
Transport, Wales, Energy, Attorney General[1], Foreign & Commonwealth (Overseas Development Questions)[3]	Educ. & Science, Defence, Employment, Social Services	Environment, Scotland, Foreign & Commonwealth, Trade & Industry	Home Office, Northern Ireland, Ag. Fish & Food, Treasury
At 3.15 p.m. Prime Minister			At 3.15 p.m. Prime Minister

Mon. 27 June	Tues. 28 June	Wed. 29 June	Thurs. 30 June
Wales, Energy, Transport, Member answering for Church Commissioners[5], Member answering for House of Commons Commission[2], Lord President of the Council[3,4]	Defence, Employment, Social Services, Educ. & Science	Scotland[6], Foreign & Commonwealth, Trade & Industry, Environment	Northern Ireland, Ag. Fish & Food, Treasury, Home Office
	At 3.15 p.m. Prime Minister		At 3.15 p.m. Prime Minister

Mon. 4 July	Tues. 5 July	Wed. 6 July	Thurs. 7 July
Energy, Transport, Wales, Arts[1], Civil Service[3]	Employment, Social Services, Educ. & Science, Defence	Foreign & Commonwealth (other than Overseas Development Questions), Trade & Industry, Environment, Scotland	Ag. Fish & Food, Treasury, Home Office, Northern Ireland
At 3.15 p.m. Prime Minister			At 3.15 p.m. Prime Minister

Mon. 11 July	Tues. 12 July	Wed. 13 July	Thurs. 14 July
Transport, Wales, Energy, Attorney General[1], Foreign & Commonwealth (Overseas Development Questions)[3]	Social Services, Educ. & Science, Defence, Employment	Trade & Industry, Environment, Scotland, Foreign & Commonwealth	Treasury, Home Office, Northern Ireland, Ag. Fish & Food
At 3.15 p.m. Prime Minister			At 3.15 p.m. Prime Minister

Mon. 18 July	Tues. 19 July	Wed. 20 July	Thurs. 21 July
Wales, Energy, Transport, Chancellor of the Duchy of Lancaster[5] and Member answering for Church Commissioners[5], Member answering for Public Accounts Commission[2], Lord President of the Council[3,4]	Educ. & Science, Defence, Employment, Social Services	Environment, Scotland, Foreign & Commonwealth, Trade & Industry	Home Office, Northern Ireland, Ag. Fish & Food, Treasury
At 3.15 p.m. Prime Minister			At 3.15 p.m. Prime Minister

Mon. 25 July	Tues. 26 July	Wed. 27 July	Thurs. 28 July
Energy, Transport, Wales, Arts[1], Civil Service[3]	Defence, Employment, Social Services, Educ. & Science	Scotland[6], Foreign & Commonwealth, Trade & Industry, Environment	Northern Ireland, Ag. Fish & Food, Treasury, Home Office
At 3.15 p.m. Prime Minister			At 3.15 p.m. Prime Minister

[1] Starting not later than 3.10 p.m.
[2] Starting not later than 3.15 p.m.
[3] Starting not later than 3.20 p.m.
[4] Also answers as Leader of the House and Chairman of the Select Committee on House of Commons (Services).
[5] Starting not later than 3.10 p.m. Questions to the Chancellor of the Duchy of Lancaster have precedence.
[6] Also answers on behalf of Lord Advocate.

NOTE:
For the Departments shown in bold type, Questions for oral answer should be submitted between 10 a.m. and 4 p.m. exactly ten *sitting* days before the date of answer, in order to be included in the random shuffle to determine the order of questions.

least two ministers or the prime minister and one other minister are top of the list to answer.

Prime minister's questions are different.

Mr Rooker: To ask the Prime Minister if she will list her official engagements for Thursday 3 December.

Indeed most of the oral questions to the PM are identical. In her answer the Prime Minister stated her engagements and Jeff Rooker then went on to ask a supplementary about poll tax. Other supplementaries concerned a possible Post Office strike, nurses' pay and the health service, and the National Union of Miners before the next question was reached.

Why is everyone so interested in what she is doing on a particular day? Traditionally, prime ministers would not answer questions on subjects that were the responsibility of a departmental minister. In order to pin the PM down, with the intention of asking a supplementary, MPs devised questions that only the prime minister could answer. Hence the preoccupation with the day's engagements.

Of course there are other questions which the prime minister has always answered, relating to foreign heads of government, the TUC or visiting a town in a member's constituency. The trouble with these questions is that they may limit the scope of the supplementary. Asking a question about meeting the TUC, for example, may prevent the member from following issues concerning, say, a statement by the Irish prime minister the previous day, a sudden industrial dispute, a report about the effect of cuts at a particular hospital or US policy in Central America which may have become the big subjects of the day.

Despite this, the order paper, full of identical and seemingly meaningless questions to the PM about her engagements that day, continues to be a target for reformers who would like to make the procedure seem more sensible and comprehensible to outsiders.

Incidentally it is quite possible to ask the prime minister a question for written answer, in which case the procedures are similar to those for other written questions. Present practice suggests that even when the question relates to a strictly departmental matter, the PM may answer the question herself though the reply will obviously be drafted in the relevant department. However, except in matters of great national importance, it makes more sense that such questions should be aimed at the departmental minister.

While on average something like 10 to 15 questions are covered by departmental ministers in their question times, only about the first five are reached in PM's questions. Competition is intense and MPs invariably complain that they are never lucky. In practice the best part of a year may go by without an MP getting his PM's question in the first four or five or being called for a supplementary on another MP's question.

Question time is important. It gets MPs coverage in their local papers (if they have sent out their press releases) and may sometimes lead to radio interviews and other publicity. Above all, oral questions keep the pressure on ministers. Those who are bad at question time don't improve their promotion prospects. Similarly for a newly elected opposition MP, questions may be the best way of making an impact.

It is clear that questions are very important for the lobbyist. Information otherwise unobtainable (except perhaps by an MP's letter to the minister) can be revealed, issues highlighted and pressure brought to bear. In fact, in spite of all their publicity value, questions to the prime minister, except perhaps written ones, are less effective as a weapon simply because there is such a small chance that a particular MP may be called. Equally if the point is detailed the prime minister will hardly be able to give much of an answer except perhaps to draw it to the attention of the appropriate minister. PM's questions therefore become point-scoring on major issues of the day with the leader of the opposition taking a prominent part.

Private Notice Questions

Private notice questions are a special form of question to deal with emergency matters and are tabled on the day they are to be answered. An MP may ask for a PNQ by giving notice to the Speaker before 12 noon, or 10am on a Friday. It is up to the Speaker's discretion whether he allows it or not. If the decision is 'no' then that is the end of the matter as he cannot be challenged. If the PNQ is allowed then it is taken at 3.30pm after questions. The procedure is the same as for ordinary questions except that the MP asking the question has to read it out as it will not be on the order paper. However more time is generally allowed. The Speaker appears to grant a PNQ when there is a fairly urgent matter of national importance or when it is the only way that an MP can raise something that has come up suddenly in his/her constituency, say a major accident. In practice it seems that PNQs on non-constituency matters are more likely to be granted to opposition frontbenchers than to any backbenchers.

The following are examples of subjects raised through PNQs:

Britoil
West Bank and Gaza

British Caledonian
Tamil refugees
Stock Exchange crash
Exports of military equipment to the PLO
Air traffic (air misses)

Except in rare instances PNQs will not be of great interest to the lobbyist because of the short notice involved. Unless a colleague has indicated to another MP that s/he has asked for a PNQ, the first that MPs hear of one being granted is when it is displayed on the House of Commons annunciator at 1pm (10.30am on a Friday). The MP asking for the PNQ can find out a little earlier by contacting the Speaker's secretary at about 12.30pm.

If an MP phones you to this effect then you may provide some ideas for supplementary questions. Better still, if you have good contacts with an MP then you can ask him/her to try for a PNQ. This means acting very quickly, as any delay detracts from the urgency of the matter and will discourage the Speaker from granting the question. Usually the MP must try to ask his/her PNQ the same day as the incident or event referred to or on the very next day. Clearly anything that has happened over the weekend could be the subject of a PNQ on a Monday morning and similarly for the other days. Note than on Fridays PNQs are taken at 11am. Another point to bear in mind is that the Speaker is unlikely to grant a PNQ if the same issue could be raised by an MP as a supplementary to a PQ already down for answer that day.

Business Questions (or Business Statement)
Every Thursday afternoon, normally at 3.30pm after the PM has completed her question time, the House moves to what are called 'business questions'. The leader of the opposition first asks the leader of the House to announce next week's business. The leader lists matters which will arise in the following week starting with the coming Monday and usually going on up to and including the following Monday. Then follows a period during which the leader of the House is asked further questions theoretically about the following week's business but in practice about virtually anything. The length of this question period is not fixed. Normally the Speaker allows about half an hour, though on a particularly busy day this may be shorter.

This gives MPs an opportunity of raising particular issues and of course those who failed to get called during prime minister's questions can have a second bite. This means that most MPs have a chance of being called. The difficulty is that the leader of the House cannot deal authoritatively with issues which are directly the responsibility of departmental ministers. On the other hand he is a leading member of the cabinet and MPs try to get him to commit the government. It doesn't usually work. Yet being leader of the House is clearly a hazardous occupation: all those who have held this post under Margaret Thatcher – Norman St John Stevas, Francis Pym and John Biffen – ended up being fired and returning to the backbenches!

Incidentally the planned business is not sacrosanct and may be changed at short notice. This means that the leader of the House can at any time make a 'business statement' and this too is subject to questioning. Sometimes this is a consequence of opposition pressure for a debate on a specific issue. Ordinarily such changes are only effected by agreement with the opposition. It is obviously best to use business questions to ask for debates on issues, sometimes ones which are the subject of an early day motion.

Mr Brian Wilson: Will the leader of the House consult early-day motion 319? (about sport) Will he consider the possibility of setting up a select committee on sport? ... Would he make available an opportunity for a major debate ...?

But MPs are inventive and try to pin down the leader of the House. The answer may be something on the lines of: 'I shall draw the attention of my right honourable friend to what the honourable member has said.' In ordinary English this means: 'I'm not falling into the trap of answering that one.' Kenneth Baker's (or some other minister's) civil servants will refer him to the page in Hansard, but in any case nothing's going to happen. Even so, the MP has got his point on the record and can use the Hansard extract as the basis of a press release in his/her constituency.

The point for the lobbyist is straightforward. If you want an issue raised on the floor of the House and the MP has failed to get called at question time then suggest that business questions may be appropriate.

Incidentally the leader also uses the opportunity to announce dates of recesses though this is sometimes left till late in July, much to the annoyance of MPs, especially those with children who are anxious about family holidays. If Parliament sits into August it is tough on Scots members because school holidays there start and finish earlier than in England.

Ministerial Statements

Several times a week ministers make statements to the House. These are usually at 3.30pm after question time or at 11am on a Friday. On a Monday to Thursday MPs are alerted at 1pm on the Commons annunciator which puts up a cryptic message like: 'Ministerial Statement: Social Security.' On a Friday a PNQ or statement is shown on the annunciator at about 10.30am but then the anouncement is flashed on at intervals to interrupt the usual details while a debate is in progress.

Opposition frontbenchers may be tipped off a little in advance and are usually given a preview of the statement some time around 3pm. Some statements can be anticipated, such as those given by the Prime Minister following a summit meeting or an EEC Council of Ministers meeting. Other ministers also report on the outcome of EEC meetings. For the rest, MPs can often make a rough guess at what is likely to be announced. Occasionally, though, even frontbenchers are puzzled. I remember colleagues asking what was happening when a statement saying 'Westland' was flashed on the screen. This proved to be the precursor to high drama in the Commons as the saga unfolded, ending in the resignation of two cabinet ministers and, as we have learned more recently, almost that of the Prime Minister herself!

The importance for the lobbyist is that each statement is followed by a period of questions. The length varies but may be as long as half an hour. If there are several statements the Speaker will try to cut them down to a shorter period. Clearly a well-briefed MP can make an effective intervention. Equally it is possible for an MP to phone a pressure group after the announcement goes up at 1pm. I have done this in the past, but it clearly works best if there is a close relationship between the MP and the pressure group and if the latter is geared up to dealing with a request for background information.

You will have noticed in the order of business that statements follow questions and that a PNQ therefore takes precedence over any statement. There was one occasion when the Speaker accepted a request from me for a PNQ about Tamil refugees. The Prime Minister was making a statement that day and she would have had to wait for some 10 to 15 minutes while my PNQ was being dealt with. In the event the annunciator at 1pm indicated that there would be two statements that afternoon, the first by the Prime Minister (she takes precedence over all other ministers) and the second by the home secretary about Tamil refugees. And so Mrs Thatcher was spared the indignity of waiting.

Ministerial statements can cover a wide range of topics as the following examples indicate:

Extra social security payments following
  discovery of error in retail price index
Rate support grant
British Steel Corporation (privatisation)
Upholstered furniture (fire resistance)
Airbus A330/A340 projects
Haemophiliacs (financial assistance)
Health authorities (financial allocations)
European Space Agency
Terrorist attack (Enniskillen)
BBC (injunction)

Action Check List

1. If you are just seeking factual information, ask your MP to put down a written question. Unless the MP is known to you s/he may ask for background information – a reasonable point because the press sometimes discusses PQs with the MP.

2. You can simply write to the MP requesting that s/he ask a question on a particular topic.

3. If you are from a lobby that often wants questions asked it may help the MP if you ask him/her for a supply of question forms so you can send them along already filled in. Then the MP has merely to sign them and hand them in or post them to the table office.

4. Do not ask for priority written answers unless this is strictly necessary.

5. If the same question has already been asked the MP will normally be told by the table office and s/he can let you have the earlier answer.

6. Where ministers refuse to answer certain classes of questions the matter can be raised again in the following session.

7. For oral questions, study the order of questions (ask the MP) so that your question reaches the MP at the latest on the morning it should be tabled but preferably the day before in case the MP is away. Remember that MPs who follow particular subjects may already have a PQ to put down.

8. When oral questions have been tabled for a particular day check if you want to brief friendly MPs for supplementaries. It is best to do this at least a couple of days ahead. Each opposition frontbench team usually meets about a day ahead to plan its strategy for question time.

9. Questions cannot be answered during recesses but can be tabled for answer when the House resumes. Oral questions for, say, the end of

October can usually be tabled towards the end of July. If the recess has not been announced at least 10 sitting days before it begins MPs can put down several lots of oral questions when the announcement is actually made. If the recess is announced at 3.30pm then MPs usually have till 6pm that day to table.

Government Business, Opposition Days, Adjournment Debates

Government Business

The government controls most of the time in the Commons. A large proportion of government time is devoted to legislation and this is considered in Chapter 5. There are still quite a number of days devoted to debates other than legislation. Some of these can be predicted and even their timing can, within limits, be anticipated. The most important of these is the Queen's Speech debate which takes place at the beginning of each session in early November, except in an election year when it takes place two weeks after polling day. Then there are the four days devoted to the budget debates, usually in March. Normally there will be a two-day defence debate and a foreign affairs debate. There are also single days devoted to debates on the Army, Navy and the Air Force. There are also debates on the annual rate support grant settlements, and on public spending. In addition the government will arrange debates on a wide variety of topics, sometimes at the request of the opposition. These have, in recent years, covered such things as select committee reports, the Commission on Racial Equality, technology, the Anglo-Irish agreement, Cyprus, the Channel Tunnel, the regions, the multifibre agreement (on textiles) and many others. Sometimes the first that is known of such a debate is the announcement at business questions on a Thursday afternoon.

Nevertheless the opportunity is there and the lobbyist can suggest issues that MPs could cover in their speeches. Indeed MPs often get representations from pressure groups before major debates of this kind. In some of these debates it is not too difficult for MPs to get called; in others the chances are small, but the effort is worth making.

Opposition Days

We have seen that the government controls most of the time in the Commons. However opposition parties are given a number of days each session and these are called 'opposition days'. The Labour Party gets 17 days a session and the smaller parties get three between them.

Most of these will deal with major topical issues, though the opposition will obviously not choose a subject on which the government will in any case have a debate. As aften as not the Labour Party will divide the day into two half-day debates; almost always there will be a vote on a three line whip, probably at 7pm and at 10pm. Normally the government will put down an amendment to the Labour motion; the question proposed is 'that the original words stand part of the question', enabling the opposition to vote 'Aye'. The following are examples of topics for opposition days:

Firearms
Education
Transport
The real economy
Government of Scotland
National Health Service
Unemployment
Future government of Scotland (Alliance)

Opposition day topics are often decided a couple of days beforehand so nobody has much notice of what will be debated. Nevertheless there are two reasons why they are of interest to the lobbyist. The first is that a pressure group may wish to brief MPs who will want to speak, especially the opposition frontbenchers. Such briefings will be similar to those for other debates (see below). The second reason is that pressure groups may try to suggest topics for opposition days.

The choice of subject for such a debate is made by Labour's shadow cabinet. There is usually a queue of subjects waiting for an opportunity to be debated. Suggestions come from members of the shadow cabinet, who often press for a debate within their area of responsibility, and from other Labour MPs. It is normally best for a pressure group to make a proposal through an MP, preferably one of the frontbenchers responsible for the area. Don't be too hopeful of success as competition for opposition day subjects is very fierce. The opposition is seeking to make political capital out of this highly valuable time and the choice of subjects will normally reflect immediate political priorities.

Backbench Debates

Backbenchers or private members have certain opportunities to initiate debates. In this chapter I cover all the non-legislative opportunities; legislation is covered in Chapter 5.

There are five main ways in which ordinary MPs can initiate debates:

Daily adjournment debates
Adjournment debates on last day before a recess
Consolidated fund debates
Christmas/Easter/Spring/Summer adjournments
Private members' motions

Daily Adjournment Debates

Not all adjournment debates are in private members' time. Sometimes the government will give the opportunity for a debate, and indicate the topic, even though the formal wording will be on the motion: 'That this House do now adjourn.' I am here concerned only with debates initiated by the ordinary member. The last half hour of debate every day is devoted to an adjournment debate. This is an opportunity for an MP to raise virtually any subject provided it meets two conditions: that a minister is responsible for the subject; and that the MP is not asking for legislation.

In practice there is great scope as it is possible to pin responsibility on a minister for a wide range of issues. MPs often use the opportunity to raise matters specific to their constituencies or regions, or to raise national or even international issues. It would not however be appropriate to seek an adjournment debate to cover an issue as major as the government's economic policies or defence policies. However, no hard and fast rules exist and the following examples indicate subjects that have been debated:

Future policy for sport and recreation
The Scottish penal system
Transport for the disabled in Greater London
European Regional Development Fund grants to
   the Northern Region.
The North Sea Cod quota
Smoke detectors
Stockport (road schemes)
IRA bomb damage
Truro and St Austell
St Saviour's School, Ealing
Gipsies (South Leeds)
Local authority search enquiries
Mr Jim Cormack
Firbeck Hospital

Each adjournment lasts, as I have indicated, half an hour. The member normally speaks for up to 15 minutes and the appropriate minister (it's unlikely to be anyone as senior as a secretary of state) has the same time to reply. The MP initiating the debate can share his/her time with other members. Sometimes it is a good tactic for the MP to tell the minister (through the latter's private office) of the main points s/he wishes to raise, as this increases the chances of getting them answered.

MPs apply for adjournment debates by getting a letter into the Speaker's office not later than 10pm each Wednesday evening. The successful MPs are informed by a letter from the Speaker's office which is put on the board in the members' lobby about mid-morning the next day and the complete list of the following week's adjournment debates is available around noon; this covers debates from the next Tuesday to the following Monday. There is a ballot for each day except Thursday which is simply allocated by the Speaker. In practice the ballot is arranged so that government backbenchers get debates on two days of the week and opposition MPs on the other two days. (Applications during recesses for the first week back are made earlier but the basic procedures are the same.)

These debates seldom get much national press coverage, though the topic is occasionally interesting enough to attract some attention. Remember that the lucky MPs get their debates at 10pm, or a little later if there has been a division. Less lucky members have their debates at something like 3am by which time the House is empty and almost everyone has left. If the adjournment follows a division for which there was a three line whip the MP has not had to hang about unnecessarily. But if the adjournment follows a debate in which the MP had no interest and was not whipped to stay then s/he may be less enthusiastic about it. Obviously at the time the MP applies for a debate s/he has no idea when business will finish on any particular day. It is easier to predict that the adjournment will start around 2.30 on a Friday; that's fine for London members but others may, if there is no vote, feel frustrated at having to stay in London just for an adjournment when they ought to be in their constituencies.

Anyone watching an adjournment debate from the public gallery may be a little surprised. The House may be packed for the previous debate and then it suddenly empties. The MP with the adjournment will find him/herself talking to a junior minister and the deputy Speaker. All around are empty benches. The first time this happened to me I felt I was making a soliloquy rather than a speech and was grateful that there were perhaps 20 people in the public gallery.

Another problem for the MP is that s/he must be sure to be in the chamber when the adjournment is called, otherwise the House really does adjourn. If there is a preceding division, the MP only needs to stay in the chamber after voting. But without a division, the MP cannot afford to be far from the chamber. Business can collapse suddenly and there is no time even to sprint the 40 yards from the tea room.

I remember a Tory MP who issued press releases about a forthcoming adjournment debate. On the day the main debate ended, without a vote, members left the chamber to be confronted by a red-faced MP rushing in the opposite direction clutching a pile of papers, only to discover he was too late and the House had adjourned. The Speaker was kind and the MP had his adjournment debate a couple of Thursdays later.

What are the benefits of an adjournment? Clearly the MP puts the issue on the record and can get publicity for it. But more important for the lobbyist is the minister's 15 minute reply. A speech of this length may be quite revealing and with luck the minister may want to make some concession. For example I once did an adjournment debate after discussion with COHSE (the Confederation of Health Service Employees) about government proposals to sell houses and flats used by NHS employees such as nurses. In his speech the minister said he would stop these sales and review the policy.

Clearly there is a big demand among MPs for adjournment debates. Most applications will be unsuccessful and it's a matter of applying every week. During the last two parliaments it usually took me about six weeks to get a debate.

For the lobbyist the minister's reply is well worth detailed examination; even if the main point at issue has not been conceded, the reply may give facts and arguments useful for further lobbying and campaigning. If it is about a constituency matter it should provide material for a press release to the local papers and perhaps an interview on the radio.

Second Adjournments
It may sometimes happen that the main government business of the day does not run its full time and comes to an end before 10pm on a Monday to Thursday or before 2.30pm on a Friday. This means that the adjournment debate scheduled for that day can take longer – up to the normal finishing time of 10.30pm – which gives the MP an opportunity of getting colleagues to join in and add weight. However, it may be that the MP doesn't want more time because it is very much a constituency issue and can be covered adequately in 15 minutes. This gives scope for a second adjournment – provided advance notice has been given to the Speaker and of course to the minister, so that there can be a reply. The MP must inform the appropriate minister not later than 8pm on

a Monday to Thursday and by 10am on a Friday. This is yet another example of the opportunities that exist for the well-briefed MP who is quick off the mark. So ensure your MP is briefed with the material for an adjournment speech, ready for such an eventuality. I have known of evenings when there has also been a third adjournment but that is exceptional.

Adjournment Debates on Last Day Before a Recess (Holiday Adjournments)
The day before the recess begins, usually a Friday, is devoted entirely to adjournment debates. These start at 9.30am and are similar to the daily adjournments except that the Speaker permits the first four to last up to 45 minutes. A few days before the recess begins the Speaker will announce the arrangements for these adjournments. The process of applying is the same as before and the successful MPs have a week's warning (as do the ministers who answer).

The odds on getting such a debate are greater for two reasons. First, there are far more of them and secondly many members will not want to stay in London for the extra day. A further point is that if the last day is, say, Maundy Thursday, there may not be any quality newspapers on Good Friday and so the chances of press coverage are even worse than usual. Note that the last adjournment of the day is the ordinary end of day debate and the MP will have been selected earlier along with the successful MPs for the debates on the previous days that week. An MP may not speak twice in adjournment debates on such a day – unless, for technical procedural reasons, one of them is the last debate of all.

For the lobbyist the opportunity is well worth while, despite these drawbacks. Remember that London MPs are the most likely to agree to your request at this time as they can quickly get back to their constituencies after the debate. The subjects for holiday adjournments are similar to those for the daily adjournments, as the following examples show:

The work of the London Residuary Body
The Cornish tin industry
The safety of nuclear power stations
Aid for sub-Saharan Africa
British chess and the world chess championship
The future of National Health Service residential accommodation
Conditions on the A38 through Bromsgrove
Local authority tendering procedures
Vietnamese refugees

National Health Service (London)
Northern Ireland Schools
Poverty in Bradford
Oceanography
Coal Board housing
Cystic Fibrosis sufferers

Consolidated Fund Debates

The Commons debates the Consolidated Fund Bill three times a session: before Christmas, before Easter and before the Summer recess. This is, in effect, a series of short debates lasting through the night till 8.30am and followed by the usual half hour adjournment debate. MPs enter for the Consolidated Fund by ballot with their suggested subject. Most of the debates last one and a half hours but the Speaker may designate one or two of the more important subjects to last up to three hours. The importance of the subject is frequently measured by the number of MPs who have written in specifying their request to debate it.

The ballot determines the order of debates which usually start about 7pm. Invariably far more MPs apply than there will be time for. A typical entry might have 35 topics of which perhaps 11 will have been debated by 8.30am. The MP who has succeeded in the ballot for each debate speaks first. Note that these are proper debates and MPs on both sides can participate. Moreover a minister will respond and there will probably also be a contribution from the opposition front bench.

The early debates may well all go their full time but things become less predictable later in the night. Some MPs withdraw their subjects either because they think they will not be reached at all or because they do not want to wait up half the night. This means other MPs have to be alert to the possibility that their particular debate will start earlier. Equally MPs will check the list of subjects for debate to see if any have been withdrawn. It is possible for an MP to go home and arrange to be alerted by phone as his/her debate gets nearer. The following examples show the range of topics put forward:

Education policy
The problems facing sport
Trade unions and industrial relations
The Scottish beef industry
Nuclear power
Government funding of the research councils
Government policy towards Central America

The proposed by-pass around the village of Rillington, North
   Yorkshire
Regional policies and the future of H.M. Dockyard, Devonport
Nursery education and facilities for
   children under five in the United Kingdom
The establishment of the Sussex police force
The review of the supervision of charities
The BBC Glasgow police raid
The urban programme and its effect on West Leeds
Psychiatric care in Scotland – the case of Woodilee Hospital
The future of Whittle Colliery, Northumberland

Christmas/Easter/Spring/Summer Adjournments

Technically these short three-hour debates are about whether the
House should adjourn for the following recess and they usually take
place during the last week the House sits before the recess. In practice
MPs make short speeches about virtually anything on the pretext that
they do not want the House to adjourn until their subject has had its full
and proper airing. The leader of the House responds to the debate. The
difficulty is that the leader cannot speak on behalf of specific
departments and so is unable to reply in detail. Of course if the topic is a
House of Commons matter then it is reasonable to expect a fuller
response. Nevertheless the debate is an opportunity of getting
something on the record and this occasionally attracts publicity. There
is quite a lot of competition to speak, so a number of MPs will be
successful. The following are examples of topics that have been raised:

The legislative burden and the length of recesses
Spycatcher
Postal voting
A constituent's immigration problem
Remands in police cells

Private Members' Motions

On about 10 occasions every session time is allotted to private members'
motions. Some of these take the whole of a Friday, while a few are
given about three hours on certain Monday afternoons. For each of these
days three MPs will be selected by ballot about three weeks in advance
of the day. In practice the first topic will usually take the whole time.
The MP winning the ballot starts the debate and a government minister,
and opposition frontbencher, will both contribute. The days of such
debates are announced early each session; MPs sign to enter the ballot on

certain afternoons with the 'lucky' numbers being drawn in the chamber after question time and after statements. (Ordinary cloakroom tickets are used.)

Although most of these debates are not in 'prime time' (3.30–10pm on Mondays to Thursdays), they are more sought after than any of the other private members' debates. Obviously MPs may be advised on appropriate topics by their party leaderships so do not be too hopeful that you can persuade an MP to promote your particular interest. In any case the odds are very long: some MPs have never won the ballot despite years of trying.

Action Check List

1. For government and opposition day debates decide whether you have the resources to send briefings to all MPs or just to a target list.
2. Pay particular attention to the opposition frontbenchers who will be speaking in the debate and let them know when the briefing is coming, remember they are certain to be called to speak and are expected to make a longer speech so they need the information in good time.
3. Briefings should be short and the front page should make it clear what the subject is and for which day's debate.
4. Put day and evening contact names and telephone numbers for more information.
5. Make sure the briefings get to MPs before the debate begins. Obvious, you say – but it is surprising how often this does not happen!
6. Ask an MP to try to arrange gallery tickets; do this well beforehand.
7. For backbench debates, decide whom to approach. It is advisable to find out if the MP is willing to raise the issue before sending a full briefing. Ask the MP if he would like a meeting to discuss further points when he has had a chance to go through your material.
8. After the event thank the MP for the contribution, especially if it was in the early hours.

Early Day Motions, Petitions, Select Committees

Early Day Motions

Early day motions (EDMs) are the staple diet of the lobbyist. EDMs are not debated. They are motions which are printed on the full (blue) order paper and normally call on the House or the government or perhaps even an individual MP to do something. The scope is very wide and with a little skill virtually everything is possible, subject to the usual parliamentary rules and conventions. It takes only one MP to put down an EDM which then is printed with his/her name the next day the House is sitting. In practice it is usual to get six sponsoring MPs to start off an EDM.

Every time another MP signs the EDM it is reprinted the following day with his/her name and that of any others who signed that day together with the six sponsors. There is also a figure showing how many MPs in total have signed it and it is this figure which measures support. This means that if no further MPs sign, the EDM ceases to stay alive. In practice EDMs can continue throughout the session. Clearly the sponsoring MP(s) will collect signatures from their colleagues either by asking directly for signatures or by writing to them.

The attraction for the lobbyist is that it is a good means of approaching MPs and asking them to sign a particular EDM. They are all numbered so you can ask the MP if s/he will support, say, EDM 223 (in the 1987/88 session) opposing a value-added tax on books. This is how the EDM appeared on the order paper:

223 *VALUE-ADDED TAX ON BOOKS*
Mr Robert Adley
Mr Michael Foot
Mr A.J. Beith
Mr David Knox
Mr Merlyn Rees
Mr Michael McNair-Wilson

* 56

Mr Peter Pike   Mr Jimmy Wray   Mr Jimmy Hood

That this House requests Mr Chancellor of the Exchequer not to impose value-added tax on books and learned journals.

You will see that by that date (6 November 1987) a total of 56 members had signed, including three the previous (sitting) day. Notice also the significance of the six sponsoring MPs. As their names are reprinted each time this gives an important clue or signal as to the political support for the EDM. In this example there was all-party backing with three Tories, two Labour and one Liberal, although the three new signatories were all Labour. In fact under a Tory Government the majority of EDMs tend to be sponsored by Labour MPs.

Other MPs are influenced by who the sponsors are. Clearly it is virtually impossible to persuade Tory MPs to sign an EDM sponsored only by opposition members, and vice versa. Even within a party the six top signatures signal the basis of political support; for example, a Tribune Group EDM can be distinguished from one initiated by the Campaign Group, though in almost all instances EDMs attract names from all wings of the party.

Here is another example (6 November 1987) but in this instance the sponsors are all Labour:

257 *OVERSEAS AID TARGET*
  Mr Richard Caborn
  Joan Lestor
  Mr Robert N. Waring
  Mr Tony Lloyd
  Mr Andrew Smith
  Mr Brian Wilson

*22

Mr Dennis Skinner   Mr Peter Pike   Mr Chris Mullin
Mrs Gwyneth Dunwoody

    That this House regrets the Government's refusal to publish a white paper on overseas development as recommended by the Foreign Affairs Select Committee; believes that a new white paper is essential to clarify the objectives of the official aid programme which has been increasingly subject to the commercial pressures of the Department of Trade and Industry; believes that United Kingdom aid spending should be targetted on the poorest countries and the most disadvantaged groups; welcomes the small increase of about one per cent in real terms in 1988's net aid budget but recognises that much larger annual increases are necessary to restore the 15 per cent cuts borne by the aid budget since 1978/79; and urges the Government to publish a timetable of aid spending increases in order to reach the United Nations aid target of 0.7 per cent of gross national product.

Note the House of Commons style and that the EDM has to be in one sentence. In fact the very helpful officials in the table office sort out the wording for an MP so outsiders do not need to worry too much about the finer points of detail.

Some Labour MPs will not sign an all-party EDM but will show their support for the principle by making a small amendment. These amendments work the same way as the original motions with sponsoring MPs. The whole lot is reprinted whenever another MP signs either the original or the amendment, and there can be several such amendments to one EDM.

Note that government ministers do not sign EDMs and PPSs probably will not. With opposition parties the conventions are less rigid. Normally members of the shadow cabinet do not sign but the frontbench team may itself sponsor an EDM. Other opposition frontbenchers are free to sign though some prefer not to; clearly they will be concerned lest they put their names to something which is not official opposition policy. If it is not their specific subject, Labour frontbenchers check with the frontbencher responsible before sponsoring an EDM as the first signatory. While this often is only a formality it may sometimes take a little time for an MP to find his/her colleague, especially on a Friday when many members may be away.

The blue pages of the order paper every Monday (*see* Figure 4.5) give a complete list of the EDMs put down that session together with the name of the first sponsoring MP and the total number of signatures so far. If you want to know who has signed any particular EDM phone or write to the House of Commons public information office on 01-219 4272, or to ask a friendly MP to look it up in the House of Commons library.

For the lobbyist, EDMs present two opportunities:

• To get an EDM put down. Check that there is not one down already on the same subject (through an MP, or phone the Commons public information office). If you are acting on an individual basis, try your own MP first, unless you have reason to think s/he will be unsympathetic. Alternatively you could approach an MP whom you know takes the same view as you do. If the political point is obvious you should simply write to the MP and suggest s/he puts down an EDM on a particular topic. If you think the MP may not know the facts or the arguments put them in a letter or go and see the MP. Remember: as soon as an EDM is put down the press may approach the MP whose name is first, so make sure your briefing is adequate.

If you are a pressure group or trade union you will probably know MPs who would help. One of the key points to be decided is whether the EDM should have all-party or one-party sponsorship. This is a political judgement. You are most unlikely to influence the Government if the EDM is only signed by Labour MPs. Equally you may want to make a strong political point, say about the health service, or South Africa, and do not want to make the compromises which all-party support might require.

Figure 4.5 Order Paper (Commons)

ORDER PAPER

PRIVATE BUSINESS AFTER PRAYERS

CONSIDERATION OF LORDS AMENDMENTS
BILL WITH AMENDMENTS

Bexley London Borough Council Bill.

[*Copies of the Amendments may be obtained from the Vote Office or inspected
in the Private Bill Office.*]

NOTICE OF MOTION AT THE TIME OF PRIVATE BUSINESS

City of Westminster Bill [Ways and Means]

Mr Norman Lamont

That, for the purposes of any Act resulting from the City of Westminster Bill, it
is expedient to authorise payments into the Consolidated Fund.

QUESTIONS FOR ORAL ANSWER

Questions to Mr Attorney General will begin not later than 3.10 p.m.

**Questions to the Secretary of State for Foreign and Commonwealth Affairs will begin not later
than 3.20 p.m.**

★1 **Mr Matthew Taylor** (Truro): To ask the Secretary of State for Transport, if he has
any plans to give financial assistance to the building of an air terminal at the St.
Mawgan Royal Air Force air base.

★2 **Mr David Marshall** (Glasgow, Shettleston): To ask the Secretary of State for
Transport, what representations he has received about the eventual introduction in
the United Kingdom of cabotage in the road haulage and road passenger transport
industries; and if he will make a statement.

★3 **Mr Roger King** (Birmingham, Northfield): To ask the Secretary of State for
Transport, if he will give the date of the completion of the M40 extension.

★4 **Mr Michael Colvin** (Romsey and Waterside): To ask the Secretary of State for
Transport, when he next plans to meet the Chairman of the Civil Aviation
Authority to discuss the problems of air traffic control in British airspace.

★5 **Mr Tom Cox** (Tooting): To ask the Secretary of State for Transport, what
discussions he is having with London Regional Transport as to the policies to be
followed in relation to the deregulation of London bus services.

★6 **Mr John Bowis** (Battersea): To ask the Secretary of State for Transport, if he will
reconsider the guidelines for transport supplementary grant to enable more
schemes costing less than £1 million to be supported.

★7 **Mr Jerry Hayes** (Harlow): To ask the Secretary of State for Transport, what further
efforts are being made by the Government to reduce road casualties.

3U

Remember that in any session most EDMs attract fewer than 100 signatures; you are doing well if you reach three figures. If one gets 150 then it is reported to the cabinet. Hitting 200 is a real achievement and probably cannot be done without all-party backing. At that point it is possible to put real pressure on the government for a debate, especially at business questions. And to get 300 signatures is phenomenal. In the 1987–8 session there was one EDM which by March had obtained 254 signatures with an additional 86 for an amendment which strengthened the original motion concerning War Service Credits for overseas civil service pensioners.

It sometimes makes more impact for the sponsoring MPs to collect signatures for several days before tabling an EDM so that there are, say, 100 signatures already attached on the first day. It is a lot of work and may often not be worth the bother.

• *If an EDM is already down* then it makes a good focus for lobbying. Write to your MP (or to all MPs if you are a major pressure group) asking them to support a particular EDM, give the number, title, and the full wording, or failing that, the main point made by the motion. If you have the resources you could send a photocopy of the EDM – the MP then only needs to sign it and send or take it to the table office.

Here is an example of a pressure group, the British Association of Social Workers, seeking support for an EDM in a letter they sent to MPs:

Early Day Motion 118
Draughtproofing for Low Income Households
At least 5,000 community programme jobs will be lost if the Government's social fund proposals are implemented, and hundreds of thousands of elderly people will be deprived of home insulation. Yet insulation is the most effective way of cutting heating bills and helping to keep elderly people warm in winter. This and other effects of the social fund are little known or understood. Please sign EDM 118. If successful we hope to stimulate a debate on some of the social fund implications.

There is no order paper when the House is not sitting so EDMs cannot be tabled or signed during recesses. Any that get sent in when the House is in recess are printed the first day back except when this is the day of the Queen's Speech. The EDM procedure has a further benefit. After an election, a pressure group may want to know the views of newly elected MPs who have not previously made their positions clear. Putting down an EDM can help to pin-point potential support on such issues as human rights.

Note that the lists of EDMs also contain motions which are normally sponsored by Neil Kinnock as leader of the opposition and other leading members of the Labour Party and refer to statutory instruments. They can easily be recognised because of the reference to an SI after the title: 220 SOCIAL SECURITY (S.I.,1987,No 1692).

The point of this is explained in more detail in Chapter 5 but the purpose is to get a brief debate on a statutory instrument, i.e. subordinate legislation, led by the secretary of state.

In any session there are likely to be over 1,000 EDMs. The following is a selection of those put down early in the 1987–8 session. You will see that while the title is helpful in a general sense it does not always indicate the point of view taken in the EDM.

Legislative protection for the human embryo abortion
Government's lack of a mandate in Scotland and Wales
Democracy and human rights in South Korea
War service credits for overseas civil service pensioners
British Telecom profits
Child sexual abuse
World Court ruling on Nicaragua
Royal Shakespeare Company
Use of live animals for research
Iran–Iraq war
Privatisation of City and Hackney District Health Authority
Supply of Blowpipe missiles to rebels in Afghanistan
Televising of proceedings in the House
Opren compensation
Confinement of Anna Chertkova
Animals in warfare experiments
Swedish justice and the case of Captain Simon Hayward
Pensions for the elderly
London–Stranraer–Larne–Belfast rail service alterations
Execution of Sharpeville Six
Basildon Hospital accident and emergency unit
Proposed closure of Renishaw Park Colliery
Mountain rescue
Radio Leicester
North Sea cod quotas
Discrimination against Welsh football
Future of the *Financial Times*

Retention of the Southend radiotherapy unit
Visit of Adolfo Calero
Southend cancer unit
Health services in Leeds
Intermediate nuclear forces agreement and summit
Conduct of BLK Extrusions Ltd in Handsworth
EEC steel production capacity cuts
East Midland Bus Company
Overcrowding of detention centres on Merseyside
Reunification of Cyprus
Security services
Drinking and driving
Sale of Cumbernauld town centre

Action Check List

1. Check whether EDM is already down.
2. Decide whether you want all-party sponsorship.
3. Approach your own or another MP to put EDM down.
4. Discuss possible all-party or one-party sponsors with your MP.
5. Give your MP the suggested wording and title.
6. Decide on the best time to start. Putting down on a Thursday for a Friday may minimise the impact if few MPs are in London.
7. Avoid starting near a recess or at the end of a session.
8. Is it worth the effort to try and be number 1 in a session (there is lots of competition for this), or perhaps number 1,000 ?
9. Decide whether you will back up the MP by writing to other MPs for support.
10. Organise local approaches to MPs by letter or in person to request they sign the EDM.
11. Get the sponsoring MP to ensure a steady trickle of new signatures to ensure EDM gets continually reprinted on order paper to keep it before MPs.
12. Arrange publicity for MPs who have signed, or those that have not. Use your organisation's newsletter, local papers, etc.
13. Thank the sponsoring MP for his/her efforts.

Petitions

You might think that organising a petition for Parliament ought to be straightforward. While it is not difficult, there are a number of traps for the unwary; it is worthwhile doing your homework before starting, otherwise you may find your petition is not in order and cannot be presented. If you follow the 'rules' you should be all right. See

Figure 4.7 for the full instructions as issued by the House of Commons. If, however, you find you have a petition which does not conform to the rules, do not despair: you can still, as I explain below, do something useful with it to avoid making those who collected the signatures feel their efforts have been in vain.

The first thing to get right is the style. The petition *must* be worded as follows:

To the Honourable the Commons of the United Kingdom of Great Britain and Northern Ireland in Parliament assembled.
   The Humble Petition of [here insert a description of the Petitioner or Petitioners such as 'the constituents of Battersea'],
   Sheweth
      That [state the point of the petition]
   Wherefore your Petitioner(s) pray(s) that your honourable House [here state the particular object of the Petitioner or the nature of the remedy sought].
   And your Petitioner(s), as in duty bound, will ever pray, &c. [to be followed only by signatures, names and addresses].

This wording must be followed exactly. I can only think of two reasons for this ridiculous procedure. The first is that the Commons have simply forgotten to bring the system up to date, as the petition follows the medieval form of address to an absolute monarch. The alternative is that it is intended, by its ponderous complexity, to reduce the total number of petitions presented. I strongly advise you to check the wording before collecting signatures. Get an MP to do this or approach the appropriate official: the clerk of public petitions in the journal office of the House of Commons.

It may be helpful to consider the full wording of a petition and the example shown in Figure 4.6 was the one signed by thousands of Londoners opposing the abolition of the GLC.

There is more. The first page of the petition must be handwritten, though subsequent pages may be typed or printed (*see* Figure 4.7). More than once, I have had to handwrite a front page and then get at least one person – usually a parliamentary Labour Party official or an MP's assistant – to sign this page.

Only MPs can present petitions to Parliament and this has to be done while the Commons is sitting. There are two ways in which they can do this. The informal method is simply for the MP to put the petition in the green bag behind the Speaker's chair. If the petition is presented informally then the only references to it will be in the full order paper

Figure 4.6 Petition (GLC)

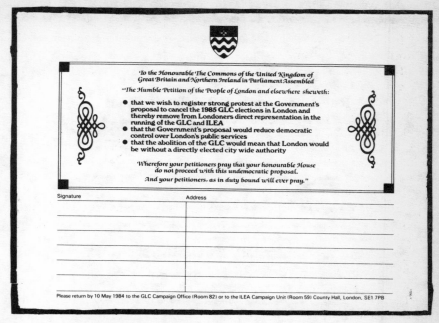

To the Honourable The Commons of the United Kingdom of Great Britain and Northern Ireland in Parliament Assembled

"The Humble Petition of the People of London and elsewhere sheweth:

● that we wish to register strong protest at the Government's proposal to cancel the 1985 GLC elections in London and thereby remove from Londoners direct representation in the running of the GLC and ILEA
● that the Government's proposal would reduce democratic control over London's public services
● that the abolition of the GLC would mean that London would be without a directly elected city wide authority

Wherefore your petitioners pray that your honourable House do not proceed with this undemocratic proposal.

And your petitioners, as in duty bound will ever pray."

Signature   Address

Please return by 10 May 1984 to the GLC Campaign Office (Room 82) or to the ILEA Campaign Unit (Room 59) County Hall, London, SE1 7PB

under 'votes and proceedings'.

The formal method is for the MP to present the petition in the House of Commons. There are specific occasions for doing this. On Mondays to Thursdays this is immediately after the main business and before the final half hour adjournment debate. Clearly this can be very late and often at an unpredictable time. So not surprisingly MPs prefer to use the Friday option when petitions are presented at 9.35am immediately after prayers and before the first debate.

MPs may not make a speech when presenting a petition but may simply read what it says, where it comes from and how many signatures it has. Often MPs slip in a brief sentence showing their support. This is how it appears in Hansard:

PETITION

British Citizenship

Mr Alfred Dubs (Battersea): I beg leave to present a petition, Mr Speaker, on behalf of the Action Group on Immigration and Nationality and more than 4,000 petitioners – a petition which has

Figure 4.7 Rules Concerning Petitions

HOUSE OF COMMONS

Rules concerning Public Petitions

Note—A Member wishing to present a Petition to the House in their place should consult the Clerk of Public Petitions in the Journal Office who, after examining the Petition, will advise the Member whether or not it is a Petition which can be received and is in Order. It will then be necessary for the Member to sign the paper in the Table Office before 12 noon on the day on which he or she desires to present the Petition.([¹])

Members wishing to present Petitions on Friday should enter their names on the paper in the Table Office before the rising of the House on Thursday.

Standing Orders Nos. 119 to 123 set out the procedures of the House relative to Public Petitions.

1. A Petition may only be presented to the House by a Member of Parliament. Every Member presenting a Petition to the House must affix his or her name at the head of the first sheet.([²])

2. Every Petition offered to be presented to the House must begin with the words " To the Honourable the Commons of the United Kingdom of Great Britain and Northern Ireland in Parliament assembled ; " or with an equivalent expression.

3. Every Petition must end with a prayer setting out the general object of the Petitioner or the nature of the relief asked for, which it must be within the competence of Parliament to grant.

4. Every Petition must be written by hand not printed, lithographed or typewritten.([³])

5. Every Petition must be signed by at least one person on the sheet on which the Petition is written.([⁴]) The first signature should be written at the foot of the Petition.

6. Every signature must be written upon the sheets upon which the Petition itself is written, and not pasted or otherwise transferred to it.([⁵])

7. If there are signatures on more than one sheet, the prayer only of the Petition must be repeated at the head of one side of each sheet ; but on every sheet after the first, the prayer may be reproduced in print or by other mechanical process. Signatures may be written on either side of any sheet, including that on which the Petition itself is written.([⁶]) The " prayer " is that part of the Petition which expresses the particular object of the Petitioners (i.e. the paragraph beginning " Wherefore "), as distinguished from the allegations, circumstances or evidence set out in the first part.

8. Every person signing a Petition must write his or her address after their signatures.

9. Every Petition must be written in the English language, or be accompanied by a translation certified by the Member who shall present it.([⁷])

10. Every Petition must be signed by the parties whose names are appended thereto by their names or marks, and by no one else except in case of incapacity by sickness.([⁸])

11. The Petition of a corporation aggregate should be under its common seal, if it has one.([⁹])

---

¹ H.C. Deb. (1946), vol. 427, cc. 1325-6.
² C.J. (1833) 190, (1883) 32.
³ C.J. (1651-59) 427, 462, (1792-3) 738-9, (1817) 156.
⁴ C.J. (1817) 155.
⁵ C.J. (1849) 283.
⁶ C.J. (1942-43) 128.
⁷ C.J. (1821-22) 172, 189.
⁸ C.J. (1667-87) 369, (1688-93) 285, (1772-74) 800, (1826-27) 118, (1836) 576.
⁹ C.J. (1797-98) 538-9.

[P.T.O.]

12. No letters, affidavits, or other documents, may be attached to any Petition.([10])

13. No erasures or interlineations may be made in any Petition.([11])

14. Every Petition must be respectful, decorous and temperate in its language.

15. No reference may be made to any Debate in Parliament nor to any intended Motion unless notice of such Motion stands upon the Notice Paper.([12])

16. No application may be made for any grant of public money, except with the recommendation of the Crown ; but Petitions praying for the grant of money by Bill are excluded from this rule.([12])

17. After presentation, all Petitions drawn up in accordance with the relevant Rules of the House are ordered to lie upon the Table and to be printed as a supplement to Votes and Proceedings and are transmitted by the Clerk of the House to a Minister of the Crown ; and observations made in reply by the Minister, or by any other Minister, are laid upon the Table by the Clerk of the House and ordered to be printed as a supplement to Votes and Proceedings.([13])

18. Members cannot present a Petition from themselves. While it is quite competent to any member to Petition the House, such a Petition ought to be presented by another Member. But this Rule is not to be understood to extend to cases in which Members present a Petition signed by them in their representative capacity as Chairman of a County Council or of any public incorporated body.

July, 1983.

APPENDIX

STYLE IN WHICH A PETITION TO THE HOUSE OF COMMONS SHOULD BE DRAWN UP

To the Honourable the Commons of the United Kingdom of Great Britain and Northern Ireland in Parliament assembled.

The Humble Petition of (*here insert the names of descriptions of the Petitioner or Petitioners*), Sheweth

That (*here set forth the case or circumstances to be brought to the notice of the House*).

Wherefore your Petitioner(s) pray(s) that your honourable House (*here set forth the prayer, shewing the particular object of the Petitioner or the nature of the relief asked for*).

And your Petitioner(s), as in duty bound, will ever pray, &c.

NOTE.—*The words " And your Petitioner(s), as in duty bound, will ever pray, &c. " constitutes the formal ending of the Petition. After the words " &c. " signatures and addresses only should follow, and no other matter should be added.*

SUMMARY OF RULES

Petitions must be written by hand and not printed, photocopied, lithographed, or typewritten. If signatures are affixed to more than one sheet, the prayer of the Petition (i.e., the paragraph beginning " Wherefore ") must be repeated at the head of each sheet ; but on every sheet after the first, the prayer may be reproduced in print or by other mechanical process.

The Clerk of Public Petitions is available in the Journal Office of the House of Commons to advise informally before signatures are collected as to whether a draft petition is likely to be acceptable for presentation to the House.

------

[10] C.J. (1826) 82, (1826-27) 41, (1856) 102.
[11] C.J. (1826-27) 262, (1830-31) 748.
[12] C.J. (1822-23) 150, (1826-27) 41.
[13] S.O. No. 109.
[14] S.O. No. 122.

502955 12/84

my wholehearted support – which seeks to show that the British Nationality Act 1981 and the Immigration Act 1971 are unjust. The petitioners go on to request:

1. To restore the principle of automatic citizenship by birth in the United Kingdom and confer British citizenship on British overseas citizens with no other citizenship,
2. To restore the rights of Commonwealth citizens settled in the United Kingdom before 1973.
3. To establish a nationality appeals system and a citizen's right to a passport,
4. To reform the immigration law to conform to international standards on human rights, respect family life and respect racial and sexual equality.

To lie upon the Table.

Formal petitions are also referred to in 'votes and proceedings' in the same way as informal ones. The petition is printed there and, some time later, there will be a reply printed again in 'votes and proceedings', from the appropriate minister. Here is an example of a reply to a petition arranged by Amnesty International about torture:

SUPPLEMENT TO THE VOTES AND PROCEEDINGS
Observations by the Secretary of State for Foreign and Commonwealth Affairs on the Petition (21 December) from residents of the United Kingdom.

Her Majesty's Government abhor torture and are determined to do everything possible to prevent it. We have made plain our concern at the United Nations and in other international fora, and will continue to do so, also mentioning specific cases, whenever we consider that this is likely to be productive.

British representatives played an active part in preparing the United Nations Convention against Torture and Other Forms of Cruel, Inhuman or Degrading Treatment or Punishment. This convention was adopted by the United Nations General Assembly on 10 December; the United Kingdom co-sponsored the resolution which proposed that it should be adopted.

The question of extending the right to compensation to victims of cruel, inhuman or degrading treatment, as well as victims of torture, was considered during negotiations, but it was agreed that such a provision should not be included.

Consideration at the United Nations of the proposal for the establishment of an international committee authorised to arrange visits to places of detention was deferred by general agreement, until after the adoption of the convention. The Council of Europe draft convention on the protection of detainees from torture, which contains similar provisions, is currently under consideration by an expert committee of the Council of Europe.

18 December 1984

Does it matter whether a petition is presented formally or informally? In my view, not greatly, though it is better for publicity purposes to be able to quote from Hansard. It may be more effective to involve as many MPs as possible in presenting a petition. Local signature collecting, with the MP playing a part, can give useful local press or other media coverage. It may be possible for MPs from all over the country to present their petitions to Parliament at roughly the same time, perhaps in the same week.

Is an MP likely to refuse to present a petition? Possibly. My own practice was to present those I agreed with formally in the chamber. If I felt unhappy about a petition I merely put it in the green bag. It is a basic constitutional right for constituents to have their petitions presented and to receive an answer. Certainly that is the argument I would advise you to use if your own MP shows signs of reluctance.

If your Petition does not conform to the Rules
All is not lost. Ask your MP, or in the case of a national petition, a sympathetic MP, to send it to the appropriate minister for his/her response. Your MP will get an answer by letter, instead of on the order paper, which can still be used for publicity purposes. Frankly I am not always convinced that the complicated procedures for petitions are always worth the trouble though there are clear benefits in gettting MPs involved at an early stage.

Action Check List
1. Check the wording of your petition.
2. Decide whether you want it to be presented as one national petition or as a series of local efforts. (Local efforts take more organising but may repay the effort through far more local publicity.)
3. Alert your MP that a petition is coming.
4. If it is part of a wider effort, suggest to your MP when it might be most usefully presented.
5. Check with your MP that it will be formally presented.
6. Decide on supporting publicity. You could, for example, be

photographed handing the petition to the MP either in the constituency or at the St Stephen's entrance to the Commons or on Westminster Bridge with Big Ben in the background. In any case issue a press release saying what you are doing.

Emergency Debates and Points of Order

If an urgent matter has arisen and the MP has failed to get the issue raised through a PNQ there are a couple of options open. On a Monday to Thursday, at the beginning of public business, an MP can seek to move the adjournment of the House, under S.O. (Standing Order) 20, for the purpose of discussing a specific and important matter that should have urgent consideration. The member may only speak briefly on the reason for the urgency and not on the substance of the matter. Such debates are very seldom granted by the Speaker but MPs often use the device as a means of getting the issue on the record. If a debate is granted it is usually for the following day and lasts three hours.

If all else fails, an MP can try and raise a matter as a point of order, usually after questions or after statements. The Speaker frowns on this device as it is seldom a genuine point of order. Again, however, it is used by MPs to get the matter on the record. In extreme cases MPs get themselves expelled for a few days by refusing to sit down or persistently interrupting the proceedings. This sometimes enables them to get publicity for an urgent problem.

5
Legislation

How often have you said: 'There should be a law against it'? Parliament spends much time making laws, many of which affect our daily lives. In recent years legislation has dealt with such varied topics as the police and public order, education, the poll tax, housing, trade unions, the abolition of the GLC and the metropolitan authorities, Sunday shopping, drink and driving, protecting the countryside, British nationality, immigration, homelessness and the rights of local authorities and councillors.

Legislation provides the best opportunity for lobbying organisations to influence what happens; many of the most successful pressure groups devote much time, thought and energy to lobbying through all stages. That is why anyone who is serious about lobbying has to have some understanding of how Parliament legislates. The better the lobbyist grasps the essentials the more influence s/he can exert. It isn't simple.

Although there is more to Parliament than legislation, the latter covers a fairly large proportion of Commons time. Do not be deterred; it is not necessary to become a walking *Erskine May* (the 1,200 page book on parliamentary procedure). With a bit of trouble you might even know a little more than some recently elected MPs, though it might not be tactful to make this obvious.

Most legislation is initiated by the government; other types of legislation are discussed later. Each proposed new law is called a 'bill' (*see* Figure 5.1) until it has gone through both Houses of Parliament and received the Royal Assent. Then it is called an Act of Parliament. Legislation has to be passed by both Houses. Bills, except finance bills, can start in either House, though the more important and controversial legislation will normally start in the Commons. Bills that start in the Lords have 'HL' after the title.

The government's main legislative proposals are normally mentioned in the Queen's Speech, which is studied carefully by pressure groups for information about the government's intentions. It marks the start of the parliamentary session and is usually in early November. Exceptionally the session may begin earlier and can last longer, say when there is a

Figure 5.1 Bill (Local Government Finance)

Local Government Finance Bill

EXPLANATORY AND FINANCIAL MEMORANDUM

This Bill provides for a new system of financing local government foreshadowed in the Green Paper "Paying for Local Government" (Cmnd 9714).

PART I—COMMUNITY CHARGES

Part I establishes a system of personal, standard and collective community charges to replace domestic rates for financial years from 1 April 1990. There is provision for the appointment of community charges registration officers who will compile and maintain community charges registers; for the payment, collection and recovery of community charges; for the inspection of registers and the provision of information; for the imposition of civil penalties; for rights of appeal against the decisions of charging authorities and registration officers; and for exemptions, reliefs and rebates.

PART II—CHARGES AND MULTIPLIERS

Part II establishes the powers and duties of charging authorities in relation to the setting of amounts for personal community charges for all financial years from 1 April 1990, and requires charging authorities to determine standard community charge multipliers for dwelling houses in their areas.

PART III—NON-DOMESTIC RATING

Part III provides for the rating of non-domestic hereditaments for financial years from 1 April 1990. Provision is made as to liability to be rated and the establishment and maintenance of local and central non-domestic rating lists. Provision is made for the valuation of hereditaments; the treatment of contributions in aid of rates by the Crown; collection and recovery; and the appointment and remuneration of valuation officers. Provision is also made for the establishment of a non-domestic rating pool for England and one for Wales.

PART IV—RESIDUAL RATING

Part IV makes provision for residual rating in England during the period 1990 to 1994. Provision is made for valuation and residual rating lists and for their maintenance; for liability to residual rates; for residual rating multipliers and residual rating standard amounts; and for collection and recovery.

[Bill 66]   50/1

June election. Then the Queen's Speech will follow almost immediately and the session lasts about 19 months till October of the following year. The following is an extract from the Queen's Speech on 25 June 1987:

Legislation wil be introduced to provide for a national curriculum for schools, delegation of school budgets and greater autonomy for schools. It will also reform the structure of education in Inner London, give greater independence to polytechnics and certain other colleges and support the establishment of city technology colleges.

Measures will be brought before you to effect a major reform of housing legislation in England and Wales ...

A bill will be introduced to abolish domestic rates in England and Wales and to make new arrangements for the finance of local government.

Measures will be introduced to promote further competition in the provision of local authorities' services.

Legislation will be introduced to enable the water and sewerage functions of the water authorities in England and Wales to be privatised ...

A bill will be introduced to reinforce the system of firm but fair immigration control.

Legislation will be introduced to give greater flexibility in licensing hours.

Legislation will be introduced to improve the rights of individual members with respect to their trade unions and to provide further protection against trade union enforcement of closed shops.

A bill will be introduced to reform the law of copyright and intellectual property.

A longer session makes things easier for the government for one important reason: all legislation (with the exception of private bills, which are discussed later) has to go through Parliament within one session. A long and complicated bill, if it is hotly contested, is difficult to get through in a normal session. That is why governments often have to resort to the use of the 'guillotine' to cut short debate either in committee or on the floor of the House. Understandably governments always say they use this device with some reluctance as the opposition parties claim that democratic debate has been stifled. A longer session thus gives the government more time.

For the lobbyist this question of time is important. A government that is under great time constraints is more likely to make concessions to get its business through. Secondly the threat of a guillotine must be taken seriously because if carried out the chances of influencing the government are much reduced. If major clauses in a bill cannot be discussed at all they cannot be amended either.

Second Reading

The first reading of a bill is its formal introduction without debate. (The one exception is the 10 minute rule bill procedure which is discussed below.) It is at the second reading that the main parliamentary process starts. There will be at least a week between the first and second readings, which gives lobbyists the chance to prepare their case and publicise their arguments. The second reading is the point at which the House discusses the principle of the bill. This covers both what is in it and what ought to be in it; clearly some of the details in the bill will be crucial. Pressure groups often try to send MPs a briefing for the second reading debate (*see* Figure 5.2). It also gives them the chance of holding briefing meetings at the House for a more detailed discussion with interested MPs.

Should the pressure group try to write to or make contact with all MPs or be more selective? Lobbying takes time and money, so any savings are worthwhile especially as most lobbyists are short of both. The answer depends on how much preliminary work the lobbyist is able to do. A regular study of Hansard, early day motions, speeches, etc. will reveal the MPs in each party who have a particular interest in the subject. Thus it is possible to develop a target list of MPs most worth while approaching. (For more on this see 'How to Approach your MP', Chapter 3.)

It does seem that this process gives pressure groups very little time to get themselves organised to lobby. Sometimes, with rushed or emergency legislation, this is true. More often, however, legislation can be seen coming. The Queen's Speech will probably have given advance warning. Government ministers may have said something about their possible intentions in a white paper or before that in a green paper. It may often be worth while starting lobbying when a green paper or a white paper is published. At an early stage the government may be open-minded about some of its proposals and therefore more susceptible to pressure. So the more effective pressure groups may send out briefing documents when white papers or green papers are published. The various lobbies opposing the Fowler reviews on social security got off the mark at the green paper stage. As regards the public order legislation, this only had a white paper and the NCCL campaigned against many of its provisions from then onwards.

Figure 5.2 NCCL Briefing (Police and Criminal Evidence Bill)

NCCL Briefing

Police and Criminal Evidence Bill 1983

November 1983

National Council for Civil Liberties, 21 Tabard Street, London SE1 4LA

£1.50

For the ordinary constituent a white paper or impending second reading debate gives opportunities for lobbying. Sometimes such approaches are instigated by a pressure group; MPs have received many letters in recent years about such topics as Sunday shopping, *in vitro* fertilisation and abortion, where voting is not necessarily on party lines, as well as about more obviously party political items of legislation such as poll tax, education and trade unions. Sometimes in the case of non-controversial legislation the second reading can, with Commons agreement, be debated in a second reading committee. Obviously lobbying would have to be directed at the committee members whose names can be obtained from the Commons public information office. Subsequent stages are the same as for any other bill.

Committee Stage

After the second reading debate the bill will normally go into committee stage. Unless it is a measure of great urgency or of constitutional significance (joining the EEC or a new representation of the people act) when the committee stage is taken on the floor of the House, it will go into standing committee where there will be the opportunity for a clause by clause, line by line or word by word scrutiny through debate and with detailed amendments (*see* Figure 5.3). Standing committees normally meet in the committee rooms on the first floor. Each standing committee is given an initial letter: A, B, etc. When a committee has completed its work the initial letter will be allocated, if necessary, to the next committee to be established.

At the first meeting of the committee there is a 'sittings motion' which determines when the committee is to meet. Such a motion may be passed on the nod. Sometimes, to the mystification of the public, it can be debated at length. The purpose is probably either to extract some concession about sittings from the government or to show the government that the opposition intends to fight the bill very hard, perhaps eventually to the point of forcing the government to consider a timetable motion. This is the 'guillotine' which means that the government, allegedly to stop wasting time, sets dates by which specific parts of the bill have to be completed. This may mean that some amendments are not discussed at all but merely voted on.

For minor bills the committee stage may last one or two days. Major bills can take several months. For these the committee will usually meet on Tuesday and Thursday mornings at 10.30 am and in the afternoons from 4.30pm. The government then decides how long the committee should sit. This can be late into the night or even through till

Figure 5.3 Amendments (Housing and Planning Bill 1986)

Housing and Planning Bill *continued*

Mr Jeff Rooker
Mr John Fraser
Mr Allen McKay
Mr Allan Roberts

8

Page **18**, line **11** [*Clause 5*], leave out ' or the Housing Corporation '.

Mr Jeff Rooker
Mr John Fraser
Mr Allen McKay
Mr Allan Roberts

9

Page **18**, line **11** [*Clause 5*], after ' Corporation ', insert ' for which Parliamentary approval has been obtained by an affirmative order of the House of Commons '.

Mr Jeff Rooker
Mr John Fraser
Mr Allen McKay
Mr Allan Roberts

10

Page **18**, line **14** [*Clause 5*], at end insert ' and for that purpose reasonably requires
possession and occupation of the dwelling-house '.

Mr Jeff Rooker
Mr John Fraser
Mr Allen McKay
Mr Allan Roberts

11

Page **18**, line **14** [*Clause 5*], at end insert ' provided that possession is not required for
the purposes of refurbishment and subsequent sale or re-letting to another person.'.

Mr Jeff Rooker
Mr John Fraser
Mr Allen McKay
Mr Allan Roberts

12

Page **18**, line **20** [*Clause 5*], after ' dwelling house ' insert ' provided that possession is
not required for the purposes of refurbishment and subsequent sale or re-letting to
another person '.

the morning. I have known a committee dealing with a bill which had been timetabled (see below) to sit three times a week.

If progress in committee is too slow the government may introduce a 'guillotine motion' on the floor of the House. This, in effect, sets a timetable for the rest of the committee stage and for subsequent debates on the floor of the House. MPs may sometimes filibuster; indeed a couple of years ago John Golding MP made a speech lasting 11 hours during the Telecommunications Bill. Government backbenchers hardly ever speak because the minister in charge of the bill wants progress and government supporters merely get in the way! As soon as a guillotine has been imposed this all changes. There is no longer any reason for government backbenchers to sit quietly.

Membership of a standing committee varies in number from a typical 18 to as many as 48 in the case of the Local Government Bill in 1984/85. Party ratios are the same as on the floor of the House of Commons so in the present Parliament a committee of 18 will have 11 Tories, 6 Labour and 1 from the minor parties. The committee membership is determined shortly after the second reading debate. Formally the selection is made by the Committee of Selection but in practice it is the whips of each party who make the decisions. Sometimes MPs are simply assigned without consultation; other bills may be more 'popular' and there is competition at least among opposition MPs. It helps greatly to have spoken in the second reading debate; so does other evidence of interest in the particular subject or possibly a constituency interest. In addition for many bills the whips will try to get a geographical balance and take any other relevant considerations into account.

The membership of a standing committee is important to pressure groups, so much so that they often ask a sympathetic MP to find out as soon as it is published. The Committee of Selection meets every Wednesday when the House is sitting so the names are usually available the following day. Failing a sympathetic MP, phone the public information office at the House of Commons to find out. Once the names are known the pressure groups check whether the MPs have a record of being identified with the subject and what their general approach has been. An early meeting with an interested MP will give the lobby useful information about how the committee will approach the bill, timings, the lines likely to be taken by the various parties etc.

It is usual for the most active pressure groups to prepare detailed amendments to be submitted at committee stage. Indeed some of them may have occasional meetings with the opposition and perhaps separately with government backbenchers on the committee. During the committee stage of the Police and Criminal Evidence Bill the Labour members had weekly planning meetings which were also attended by NCCL and the GLC Police Support Unit. Occasional meetings were also held with the BMA, the Children's Legal Centre, and NAPO; many other organisations sent detailed briefings and were available for consultation. These included the AMA (the Association of Metropolitan Authorities), the Police Federation, the London Association of Community Relations Councils and a number of others.

During the long committee sittings (there were 57 in all, a record!) NCCL and the GLC usually had someone present to provide further help and information. Standing committee meetings are held in the committee rooms off the long first floor corridor. When committee sessions are at their heaviest, usually between January and Easter, the first floor is described as the 'workhouse'. The corridor will be a milling throng of people, MPs, lobbyists and the general public. MPs will be sitting talking about amendments to lobbyists, school parties will be wandering into a particular committee room, there may be a trolley selling coffee and biscuits while at intervals the hubbub will be interrupted by the shout of an attendant: 'Division in 10!' (meaning in 'room 10') and MPs will rush to register their votes in the 30 seconds or so that they have. The committee rooms have space for only 20 people so anyone from a pressure group should be there in good time to be sure of getting a place.

Each committee is chaired by a senior MP appointed by the Speaker. The chairman (sic) is assisted by a clerk with the Hansard reporter next to him and, on the other side, the civil servants who are there to advise the minister. The MPs sit as in the House of Commons, with government MPs to the right of the chair and faced by the opposition. The clerk advises the chair on the selection of amendments. This will indicate which amendments are to be discussed together because they are related, consequential or cover the same topic. Most, but not all amendments will be selected. Some may be out of order, or outside the long title of the bill (*see* Commons Glossary) and so cannot be debated.

Each MP and lobbyist should be armed with the bill, the booklet of amendments and the selection. Ask an MP to get these for you at the start of the sitting as they are put on a table for MPs (and only MPs!). Do not try and help yourself - you are liable to get shouted at by the chair or impeded by the attendant. Also the Hansards for the previous committee sittings are helpful. If you get very bored sitting there do not be tempted to read a newspaper otherwise the attendants will tell you to stop.

Each paragraph of a bill is numbered and is called a 'clause'. (To confuse you still further it is renamed a 'section' when the bill becomes an act.) Amendments are identified under their clause and line number in the bill and may consist of inserts, deletions, or replacements. These may be single words or whole clauses. When the amendments to the whole clauses have been disposed of new clauses can be moved though these may sometimes be debated with earlier amendments. Note that votes are taken in the order in which the amendment is reached in the bill even if it has been debated in conjunction with other amendments to earlier clauses. This can cause confusion as the vote may be taken long after it has been debated.

When a pressure group submits suggested amendments to MPs there are ways of presenting them so that they are easier for MPs to deal with. Remember that on a complicated bill there may be hundreds of amendments put down by the opposition. This is how amendments are worded; they are from the Public Order Bill standing committee on 27 February 1986.

Clause 11, page 7, line 22, leave out subsection (6).

or the following example from the same bill showing how it actually appears in the sheet of amendments. Amendments need only be put down by one MP but in the case of 'official' front bench amendments they will have the names of the frontbenchers on the committee:

Mr Gerald Kaufman
Mr Clive Soley
Mr Ray Powell
Mr Chris Smith
Mr Tony Lloyd
Mr David Clelland

Clause 11, page 7, line 28, at end insert 'but no offence under this subsection is committed unless a person taking part in the procession is charged with committing an offence under sections 1 to 5 of this act during the procession'.

Unless the bill is very simple indeed, with few amendments, I suggest the following points should be borne in mind:

Put each amendment on a separate page even if it is very short. Under the amendment there should be a brief summary of the main argument in support of the amendment. Give the MP who has agreed to put down the amendment a second copy of the wording with room to attach six names as in the example above. This second copy is the one the MP will hand in to the clerk when s/he formally tables it. The following is an example of how NCCL presented amendments to the Criminal Justice Bill in October 1987:

Criminal Justice Bill Amendments
Clause 61 page 39 line 44
After 'other' *insert* 'greater'.

The £10,000 fine threshold is an important safeguard against the use of new confiscation powers in trifling cases. The power to change it should only be in an upward direction.

Amendments may either be changes to clauses such as the above examples, or they can be new clauses. In standing committee new clauses are taken after all the other amendments have been considered. At report stage new clauses are taken first.

It is worth mentioning a variation of the normal standing committee and this is called a special standing committee. Briefly, what happens is this. Before the committee considers detailed amendments it will sit several times taking evidence from witnesses. In practice this is similar to a select committee procedure except that it is directly concerned with a bill. The point of the first stage is to enable the committee to consider arguments for and against the bill's proposals.

My own view is that this is an excellent idea and I would like to see virtually all bills benefit from this procedure. It works much better than the existing process of trying to understand the key issues through debating a series of detailed amendments. My first experience of the procedure was as a member of the special standing committee on the Criminal Attempts Bill. After hearing the evidence from one witness on behalf of the Law Commission the minister in charge of the bill announced that he was going to redraft a part of it. I suppose the ordinary standing committee procedure might have achieved the same result but there is no certainty of this and the process would have been somewhat tortuous. Clearly, for pressure groups the special standing committee procedure offers obvious opportunities. Unfortunately the Government seems not to like the idea and has prevented bills from being debated in this way. Perhaps there will be a change of heart.

Report Stage and Third Reading

After the committee stage the bill returns to the floor of the House of Commons for its report stage and third reading, these two stages being normally taken on the same day. The report stage is in some ways similar to committee stage in that detailed amendments are moved. The Speaker selects those to be debated, but at this stage only a small number tend to be chosen, apart from government amendments which are always debated (*see* Figure 5.4). Amendments that have been fully considered and voted on in committee are less likely to be selected so committee tactics should take this possibility into account.

There may occasionally be major political benefits in debating a

Figure 5.4 Selection of Amendments (Representation of the People Bill)

REPRESENTATION OF THE PEOPLE BILL, AS AMENDED

Consideration of Bill

Mr Speaker's Provisional Selection of Amendments

Govt NC6 + (a) + Govt 16 to Govt 44 + Govt 54 to Govt 59 +
   Govt 61 to Govt 63 + Govt 66 to Govt 71

NC9

Govt 1 + Govt 2 to Govt 8 + Govt 10 to Govt 15

Govt 9 + (a)

Govt 45

Govt 46

Govt 47 + Govt 48 to Govt 51

Govt 52 + Govt 53

60

Govt 64 + Govt 65

Govt 72 + Govt 73

74

Govt 75 + Govt 89

Govt 76 + Govt 77 to Govt 81 + Govt 91

Govt 82 + Govt 84 + 85 + Govt 86 + 87 + Govt 88 + Govt 92

Govt 83

Govt 90

By Order of Mr Speaker

27 February 1985

particular amendment on the floor of the House rather than in committee because of the greater publicity that can be obtained. In that case the best tactic may sometimes be not to table the amendment in committee at all - unless you or an MP are ingenious enough to devise a quite different amendment which will enable the same issue to be raised again. For example during the committee stage of the Police and Criminal Evidence Bill we debated and voted on a number of amendments concerned with 'stop and search'. At report stage the Speaker accepted an amendment that there should be a code of conduct governing stop and search actions by the police. In the event the Government accepted this amendment.

After the third reading the bill goes to the Lords where it passes through the same stages except that the committee stage is on the floor of the House and amendments can be moved at the third reading. If the Lords make any changes these amendments have to come before the Commons again. Then the Commons can only debate these Lords amendments and any further amendments the Commons wants to make to the Lords amendments. It is not an opportunity to raise any other issues. As such changes cannot be predicted in advance the government must allow time for this further stage, all of which adds to the pressure of time on the government referred to earlier.

A disagreement between the two Houses means that the bill may have to be sent from one to the other until agreement on the amendment(s) is reached. If this does not happen the government can either accept the Lords amendments or, in extreme instances, pass the measure again in the following session - and this time the Commons view will automatically prevail. In practice the unelected House of Lords is reluctant to push things so far as this would simply encourage those who believe an unelected second chamber has no place in a democracy to press for its abolition. However, as is made clear in Chapter 10 on the House of Lords, the government has been defeated on a number of occasions in recent years - far more often than in the Commons.

Government legislation thus provides one of the best opportunities for influencing MPs. Apart from lobbying before second reading debates, the start of the committee stage provides even better lobbying opportunities but normally only for more experienced pressure groups. As a tactic, you are more likely to be successsful in amending a government bill than in trying to promote a private members' bill with all the difficulties that this can encounter. After all the government will find time to get its measure through while many private members' bills founder because they run out of time on the floor of the Commons. Indeed when the Alton abortion bill ran out of time, David Alton apparently considered putting down an amendment to the report stage of a government bill: the Criminal Justice Bill. As we go to press the outcome of this tactic is not known.

A report stage may be guillotined; though a decision about this will probably have been made when the timetable motion for the committee was debated. Report stages may last one day though for major bills they can take two or three days. Indeed the time to be allocated on the floor of the House may have been the subject of private negotiations between the parties – the opposition may have agreed to finish the bill by a certain date in committee (without a guillotine) in return for more time at report stage. The benefit is more publicity as debates on the floor of the House command more attention than those upstairs in committee.

Report stage is also a good opportunity for pressure groups and, as in committee stage, they can again recommend specific amendments or new clauses. There is a small public gallery on the floor level of the House - it is called the 'undergallery' and very occasionally MPs can get a ticket for a pressure group member. This enables the lobbyist discreetly to pass notes to the MPs giving further facts to help in the debate and it is only from these few seats that this can be done.

Diagonally opposite is another gallery called the 'box' where civil servants sit. They send notes to the minister via the minister's PPS, who hopes that his/her diligence will be rewarded by eventual promotion to junior ministerial office.

After report stage is the third reading. This will usually follow report stage, often later the same evening. Third reading gives a chance to debate the principles of the bill as a whole but speeches must be confined to what is in the bill and not deal with what has been left out.

Two other committees are involved in the legislative process: the Scottish Grand Committee which can meet in Edinburgh, and the Welsh Grand Committee which can meet in Cardiff. These committees consist of all MPs from Scotland and Wales respectively, although the Welsh Grand Committee also has three English Tory MPs. Their function is to consider non-controversial bills and they can make recommendations on them. They are also able to cover specific subjects and financial estimates. For example the Scottish Grand Committee has debated the NHS, education and the Scottish economy.

Action Check List

1. Study green and white papers when published and lobby on the proposals.
2. Watch the Queen's Speech for statements of specific legislative

intentions; there may be other hints such as answers to PQs.

3. Watch for news about publication of the particular bill and the likely date of second reading. Some newspapers often publish this information. Get a briefing document ready for MPs. This is the right moment for individual constituents to write to their MPs, though they could also have done so soon after the publication of any green or white paper.

4. Decide whether your group's aim is to lobby generally for or against the basic principles or whether you want to get involved in arguing for specific amendments.

5. Decide whether, for second reading, you are going to approach all MPs or be selective.

6. Send copies of your briefings to the House of Commons library (and to the Lords library); perhaps also to civil servants.

7. Following second reading get the list of MPs who will serve on the standing committee (unless to be taken on the floor of the House). This is usually decided by the Committee of Selection which meets on a Thursday. Get names from a helpful MP or phone the House of Commons public information office (01-219 4272).

8. When submitting amendments to MPs, put each one on a separate page with a brief summary of the main argument.

9. Approach sympathetic or all MPs on committee either with general lobbying propositions or with specific amendments. If you have any Labour contacts try to find out how the Labour members will plan their tactics. Sometimes a sympathetic pressure group can get access, attend a meeting or otherwise exert an influence.

10. Decide whether your pressure group has the resources to monitor the progress of the committee, perhaps by attending all or some of the sessions, and whether you intend to provide a regular briefing input.

11. Watch out for report stage dates, assess standing committee amendments and any commitments made by the minister. Discuss report stage tactics with sympathetic MP(s) and establish what amendments or new clauses should be put down. Then prepare briefing notes on them – decide whether the target list should only consist of those who served on the committee or whether there is a case for a wider approach.

12. If you fail in the Commons, get organised to try in the Lords (see Chapter 10).

Private Bills

Private bills are not to be confused with private members' bills. The procedure is quite different and the opportunities for pressure groups are more limited. Nevertheless the serious pressure group should know something about such bills because, from time to time, they contain proposals which are controversial and can be effectively stopped or at least amended.

What are private bills? They are legislation giving powers or benefits to an individual or group of people rather than applying to the whole community. Such bills are usually sponsored by and give powers to local authorities, public corporations and private companies. Strictly speaking private bills could cover a wide range of other issues such as the marriages or divorces of certain people but this is rare nowadays. The following are examples of private bills:

Alexandra Park and Palace
Dartmoor Commons
London Docklands Railway
London Transport
Barclays Bank
Dartford Tunnel
King's College London
Merseyside Development Corporation
Nottinghamshire County Council
British Rail
Felixstowe Dock and Railway
Associated British Ports (Hull Fish Docks)
Hastings Pier
Royal Bank of Scotland
Streatham Park Cemetery
Valerie Mary Hill and Alan Monk (marriage enabling)

Sometimes there may be a public bill which also affects private rights. This is called a 'hybrid bill' and requires a special and more complicated procedure, e.g. the Channel Tunnel legislation. Private bills can start in either House, although if they are politically contentious they are more likely to start in the Commons. Private bills go through the same formal stages as public bills, though the committee procedures are quite different. Private bills also differ from public bills in that they do not have to be passed in one session.

Second readings are usually a formality; the clerk reads out the title of the bill at 2.35pm on a Monday to Thursday. In the absence of objections it then goes straight to committee. It takes only one member to shout 'Object!' and there has to be a second reading debate. Sometimes the motive in objecting is merely to get a general debate on the issue, while at other times there may be a specific aspect of the bill which causes concern.

An example may be of interest. In recent years a number of county councils promoted bills which contained a 'processions clause'. Basically this clause said that the police had to be given a number of days' notice before a demonstration. Some MPs objected strongly to this because they felt that a major change affecting civil liberties ought not to be slipped through in a private bill dealing with, among other things, the licensing of street photographers or ice cream vendors. (In fact the subsequent Public Order Bill had similar provisions and was strongly opposed for this and other reasons.)

The point of objecting to these bills was therefore to persuade the local authorities to drop the processions clauses. The local authorities use parliamentary agents to handle bills for them and they try to find out why MPs object to a bill. Sometimes they can be persuaded to drop the offending clause. If they persist then MPs can effectively cause considerable delay, which is costly for the promoters. Bargaining behind the scenes can therefore prove effective. The NCCL was instrumental in doing a great deal of effective lobbying against these provisions.

To return to the procedures; if there has been objection to a bill the chairman of Ways and Means selects one day between 7pm and 10pm for debate. If an attempt is made to talk the bill out then its supporters will need to have 100 votes to get a closure. (In effect this means that the matter should now be voted on.)

The next stage is that the bill goes to a private bill committee. Here the procedure is quite different from public bills. The private bill will go either to an opposed bill committee or to an unopposed bill committee. The difference lies not in MPs' objections but whether there have been any formal petitions against it – in this context 'petitions' have a special meaning, quite different from normal usage. In either case the committee proceedings are quasi-judicial. MPs serving on an opposed bill committee have to sign a declaration that they have no interest and that their constituents have no local interest in the bill. Arranging a petition against a bill is possible but difficult for a pressure group.

The procedures regarding petitions are complicated and the usual course is to employ professional parliamentary agents, although this is not strictly necessary. One of the petitioners may act as agent for the petition, in which case s/he would have to be registered for this purpose.

Contact the private bill offices at the Commons or at the Lords for more information. This is a very complicated matter indeed, so do not rush into it.

Following the committee stage the bill returns to the floor of the house for report and third reading. Amendments can be put down for debate and again it is possible to 'talk the bill out'; this means that MPs will filibuster till there is no time for further debate that day, as the time set aside is again usually from 7pm to 10pm. Such delays are costly for the promoters and they may decide to cut their losses, compromise on the controversial clause and get the rest of the bill through.

Action Check List

1. Tackling private bills is for experienced lobbyists only.
2. Watch for the announcements of private bills and scrutinise them to see if they contain objectionable provisions.
3. Lobby sympathetic MPs to 'object' so there is a second reading debate; and later to ensure there are amendments for the report stage.
4. Prepare the usual briefings both as regards the principles and detailed objections. The promoters of the bill normally send background documents to all MPs.

Private Members' Bills

Most bills are introduced by the government. However, ordinary MPs, referred to as 'private members', can also introduce legislation. The government controls most of the debating time in the House of Commons. The major problem facing a private member in trying to legislate is that time usually runs out. Even with a big majority in favour, a measure can be made ineffective by blocking tactics and a great deal of lobbying is therefore geared to preventing this from happening. This may seem undemocratic but it is fairly easy to organise.

First, however, it is useful to understand something of how the system works. In fact there are three ways in which private members' bills can be put forward. Do not confuse them with private bills which have been discussed in the previous section.

The three methods of putting forward private members' bills are: ballot bills; 10 minute rule bills; and presentation bills.

In addition a private member's bill can start in the House of Lords and then has to be sponsored by an MP.

Private members' bills have to go through all the same stages, in both Houses, as bills introduced by the government: second reading, committee stage, report stage and third reading. On all Fridays set aside for private members' bills there are invariably a number of such bills awaiting their second reading. Most will not have been reached by 2.30pm; these are called out at that time and any member can, anonymously, shout 'Object'; usually this is done by one of the government whips. In the absence of any such objection the bill is automatically given its second reading and can proceed to its committee stage.

While a private member's bill need only be sponsored by one MP, there is provision for a number of MPs to act as sponsors. This provides an opportunity, where relevant, of demonstrating all-party support. Without this it is difficult for a private member's bill to pass. So you need to consider which MPs might be invited to have their names on the bill. Obviously these will be MPs known to your organisation or who have in some way previously been associated with the issue. Discuss this with the MP who has agred to promote your bill.

Ballot Bills

Let us consider ballot bills first. At the beginning of every parliamentary session is a ballot which all MPs can enter, and in practice over 400 do so. Those that do not are government ministers and PPSs, the shadow cabinet and other senior opposition frontbenchers, and backbenchers who have no stomach for the work involved. But for the 400 plus the ballot result can be a major event; a minor and hardly known MP can become famous or infamous. Some years ago a Scottish Tory MP called John Corrie tried to restrict the right of women to obtain abortions. In the event he failed but the measure was widely known as the 'Corrie bill'. A more recent attempt to limit abortion rights is called the 'Alton bill' after its sponsor. Similarly some years earlier Alf Morris, the Labour MP, had the Chronically Sick and Disabled Persons Act put on the statute book and is well remembered for it, as is Tom Clarke MP who, more recently, succeeded with his bill about disabled people.

The first 20 names that come out of the ballot are listed for debate. In fact only the first six have a reasonable chance of getting a full day's debate. The other 14 take their turn after the days selected by the top six in the hope that they will not need the whole day. Fridays are set aside for this purpose. On this day the House starts at 9.30am and the main debate continues till 2.30pm. Any bill not reached or not completed has to 'queue up' on another Friday.

Despite the difficulties, the top six do have a chance of becoming law provided they are not too hotly opposed. It is not just time for second reading debate that is the problem, as there may also be a lack of time for later stages, especially report. If a government measure makes very slow progress the ruling party can simply make more time available. Theoretically the government can also make extra time available for a private member's bill but in practice this has not happened for many years.

To return to the members who have entered the ballot. Sometimes pressure groups may approach likely MPs well in advance of the day when the ballot takes place to try to get a commitment to introduce a bill. Of course some members will want to work independently without the involvement of a pressure group. But for the majority it is sensible to have the help and support of a pressure group. The ballot occurs every session, usually in November, a few weeks after the Queen's Speech. It is held in a committee room in the House of Commons at noon on the designated day. The proceedings are open to the public and so the press and pressure groups are in attendance. Some MPs may be present so any who are successful may be pounced upon immediately by any of the pressure groups to persuade them to take on their draft bill. Those MPs not there for the ballot will find themselves pursued by phone or other means. The results of the ballot are published in the order paper the following day.

On what basis can MPs be persuaded to take on a particular bill? Obviously a high place in a ballot gives an MP the best possible opportunity of legislating in the area of special interest or commitment. Even so, the average MP may make a different choice if his/her position in the ballot is in the first six compared with lower down. The stark choice is between something that has a chance of getting through or of going down fighting for a cause. The lower the place in the ballot the more likely it is that the MP will be willing to sponsor a bill which is unlikely to succeed. This may be because it is too controversial or perhaps too complicated to get through.

Odds against being in the top six of 400 are pretty long. Yet the former MP, John Corrie (Cunninghame North) came first twice in three years. The first time he introduced his anti-abortion bill which eventually ran out of parliamentary time. Two years later he introduced the Diseases of Fish (Scotland) Bill and this became law. It was generally understood that after the hassles of the abortion controversy he settled for a less demanding option the second time.

Apart from pressure groups, government departments also have bills available 'off the shelf'. These are measures that government departments want to become law but for which no time is currently available. The government whips make these known to backbenchers who come up in the ballot and are able to offer departmental and ministerial help. For the MP the attraction is a bill which the government will encourage and which therefore has a fair chance of getting through with all the kudos which this gains. Of course the MP can take one of these and add to it or make changes before getting it printed. This may present the government with a dilemma as it may be hard for them to decide whether to withdraw support from their own (albeit amended) proposals. David Clark, Labour MP for South Shields, took the government's own bill on wildlife and the countryside and got it through with an important amendment which the government did not really want.

Only one private members' bill at a time can be considered in standing committee whereas several public bills can be in committee simultaneously. This means that the first private member's bill into committee has to be disposed of before the next bill can be considered. It is thus possible for there to be a queue of bills waiting. It is not unknown for MPs deliberately to keep a bill in committee to hamper the chances of a bill later in the queue. On the other hand the government has the power to create another standing committee for private members' bills.

Bills out of standing committee take precedence on the floor of the House over those still waiting for their second readings. Again there may be a queue of bills waiting for their report stages. It is when the bill finally gets back to the floor of the House that there are the best opportunities for its opponents to block it. Provided the Speaker selects several amendments for debate, each presents an opportunity for the bill's opponents to 'talk it out'. Indeed this is what happened to David Alton's abortion bill. Of course the bill's supporters can move the closure, or that the question be now put. This requires a majority vote but also a minimum of 100 in the 'aye lobby'. On the face of it this does not sound like an impossible requirement: only 100 MPs out of 650! Even if debate on a clause comes to an end without a closure, 40 MPs must still take part in a division; this means the Speaker or deputy Speaker, plus four tellers, plus 35 MPs voting. So even a vote of, say, 34 to nil is insufficient. This means that a bill can make no further progress on that Friday.

You may feel that MPs ought to be in the House on Fridays. But remember that Fridays are the days when MPs head for their constituencies, to hold their surgeries, go to meetings, etc. Constituents do not like long-standing commitments broken, schools have to be visited and so on. So it is a real dilemma for an MP. Does s/he meet the local shop stewards about a factory closure or let them down because of the need for 100 MPs to support a bill on, say, the needs of the mentally handicapped? Let's face it, whatever s/he does might be seen to be wrong!

Apart from the bills already mentioned, the following are examples of bills, most of which failed, that have been put forward under this procedure:

Abuse of toxic substances	House buyers
Betting, gaming and lotteries	Immigration offences (amendment)
Caravan and tent sites	Juries (disqualification)
Chronically sick and disabled persons (amendment)	Partnership in Youth Service
Cycle tracks	Sex equality
	Video recordings

10 Minute Rule Bills

Suppose your 'tame' MP doesn't come up in the ballot, what then ? There are other opportunities to introduce a bill. The most obvious is the 10 minute rule bill procedure. During most of the session there is a limited opportunity to introduce a bill on a Tuesday or Wednesday afternoon after question time. In effect this gives the MP the opportunity of talking for about 10 minutes to make the case for the bill. Technically this is a 'first reading' and permission is being sought to get the bill printed for a second reading debate. One MP who wishes to oppose the bill may speak at similar length after which there is a vote; usually these bills tend to go through unopposed at this stage. However it has been known for them to be opposed for tactical reasons. An MP who really supports a bill calls a vote to flush out the MPs who are against it so that there can be campaigns against them in their constituencies. Once a 10 minute bill is passed it joins the Friday queue of those seeking time for a second reading debate. Ahead of it will be the 20 bills that have come top in the ballot and any earlier 10 minute rule bills.

How does an MP get a 10 minute rule bill slot? The answer is an example of parliamentary procedure at its most archaic. The successful MP is the one who appears first in the public bill office on the third floor of the House of Commons at 10am on a Tuesday or Wednesday for debate three weeks later. The earlier in the session the greater the competition tends to be. So getting the slot means arriving early in the morning or, to be on the safe side, bringing in a camp bed and sleeping the night. I have arrived at 7am to find somebody already there and yet on another occasion I walked in at 9am and was first. I once went to the office at about midnight to find a Tory MP firmly established. Why, you may ask, can't there be a better system? When I have asked this question the answer was something like this: if the procedure were made simpler (such as by ballot) too many MPs would go in for it. So it is a form of rationing which limits the demand to those who are willing to bring in their camp beds or arrive for a dawn swoop.

In practice it is one of the most effective means of getting publicity for a cause; a reasonably newsworthy 10 minute rule bill can attract numerous radio and TV interviews, leading articles in *The Times*, *Independent*, *Guardian* etc. Yet the chances of such a bill becoming law are virtually nil. There is simply not the time. Nevertheless many interesting subjects have been the subject of such bills in recent years: abolition of jury vetting; abolition of standing charges for gas and electricity; abolition of the City of London; an independent police complaints system; the rights of tenants in private accommodation; complaints against solicitors; and racial harassment. Note that such bills can only be printed if they pass this first stage. Then the MP can have 120 copies which most pressure groups find useful in their campaigning. If you only want a bill printed then the presentation bill procedure, described below, may be of interest.

The following are examples of recent 10 minute rule bills:

Access to personal files
Access to the countryside
Control of dog nuisance
Control of religious sects and cults
Co-ownership of flats
Emphysema (compensation of coal miners)
Greater access to the countryside
Lead in paint
Marking of gravity (beer and lager)
Motor vehicles rear seat safety provisions
Multi-occupied properties (regulation)
People's right to fuel
Polygraph registration and control
Prevention of delays of trials
Private tenants' rights
Registration and accountability of charities
Right of reply
Standing charges (abolition)
Theft from shops
Working conditions of government trainees

Presentation Bills
Any MP has the right to get a bill printed and presented though there

will almost never be time to debate it. It can however attract a certain amount of publicity, though the only attention it attracts on the floor of the House is when the title is called out by one of the clerks. In recent years this procedure has been used effectively, by Tony Benn for example, with a bill about the Common Market and about withdrawal from Northern Ireland. Other recent examples:

Freedom of information
Generic substitution (National Health Service)
Green belt (preservation from development)
Hereditary peerages
Prohibition of female circumcision
Trade union (amendment)

Private Members' Bills Starting in the House of Lords
Peers may introduce private members' bills which, if they pass through the Lords, then have to be sponsored by an MP. In that case they take their turn on a Friday for a second reading debate.

Action Check List
1. Prepare a draft bill in good time.
2. Approach MPs to ask if they would be willing to sponsor your group's bill if they get a place in the ballot – especially a high place.
3. If you do not succeed be ready to approach those MPs who have secured places in the ballot; can you be present at the ballot?
4. Consider whether you wish to approach an MP to introduce a 10 minute rule bill, or a presentation bill.
5. Discuss with the MP how best you can help him/her, i.e. briefing, press releases and lobbying of other MPs.
6. As regards private members' bills generally, be on the alert for any that are published.
7. The basic principles are then the same as in the case of government legislation (see above), except that lobbying can be more effective in the absence of a party whip. On the other hand there may be pressure groups lobbying against your position.

Statutory Instruments

Quite often an Act of Parliament gives the minister powers in the future to make rules, orders or regulations which have the force of law. This procedure is called secondary, delegated or subordinate legislation It is often used to set charges, or fees, to take account of inflation. It may, however, cover many subjects and, for example, the secretary of state has wide powers to make regulations under the Social Security Act. A great deal of legislation covering Northern Ireland is made under delegated powers.

The opportunities for pressure groups are limited because, with very rare exceptions, SIs, sometimes called 'orders in council', cannot be amended and can only be approved or opposed. In fact not all of them can even be debated; indeed the question of delegated powers is itself often a matter of controversy during the passage of bills in standing committee.

There are three types of delegated legislation:

1. SIs which become law automatically without any parliamentary procedure. These are usually the ones arousing little controversy.
2. SIs which become law unless they are 'prayed' against within a set period, usually 40 days; this means the House passing a motion to annul them. In practice the opposition parties scrutinise the SIs and decide whether they want a debate and a possible vote. This is called the 'negative procedure'.
3. The most important SIs require a motion approving them to be passed within a set period, usually 40 days. This is called the 'affirmative procedure'.

The decision as to which of these three types of delegated powers is to be given to a minister is made during the passage of the main legislation. Standing committees, or rather ministers, can sometimes get this wrong with the result that something which turns out to be of major importance is not subject to the affirmative procedure but must be prayed against to be debated.

If an SI is debated on the floor of the House there is normally a one and a half hour debate. Affirmative orders get the full time, and longer if the government wishes. Negative orders have until 11.30pm starting at 10pm; the start may be later if there are divisions at 10pm, all of which takes time out of the 90 minutes available.

There is no guarantee that an SI that is prayed against will be debated on the floor of the House. In practice there is informal discussion, and argument between the parties as to whether the SI is debated in a standing committee on statutory instruments or on the floor of the House, though the full weight of the opposition will normally secure the latter. Both Houses have the same powers regarding SIs.

Just occasionally the government will allow an SI to be considered and debated in two stages. This is to allow the House to suggest amendments which the government considers, and possibly incorporates, when the SI is brought back a second time for its formal approval. This has sometimes happened in the case of changes in the immigration rules and nationality proposals for Hong Kong. In such instances the first occasion is likely to be longer than the bare one and a half hours. For pressure groups this procedure has the advantage that MPs can be lobbied not only regarding the basic principles involved but also about points of detail which the government can be asked to amend. The other main advantage for lobbyists is that an SI may provide the opportunity for a debate on a topic which seldom otherwise comes before Parliament.

The following is an example of a briefing from the British Medical Association sent to MPs in January 1986:

The motor vehicles (wearing of seat belts) regulations, 1982
The regulations, which were implemented only for a three year trial period, are due to be debated in the House on Monday.
Compulsory front seat belt wearing has resulted in an excess of 200 lives saved and 7,000 serious injuries avoided each year, and the BMA believes that the regulations should be retained indefinitely.
Extensive monitoring during the three year trial period has clearly shown the benefits of seat belt wearing, and I attach examples of some of the medical findings.
I do urge you to vote in favour of the indefinite retention of the regulations.

Attached was a brief statement giving the medical evidence covering reductions in hospital attendances by drivers and front seat passengers, and reductions in types of specific injuries.

A difficulty for lobbyists is knowing when an SI is to be published and indeed whether is is debatable. Sometimes ministers may give hints in answer to PQs or in white or green papers or in their speeches. Even so the publication of an SI can occasionally take everyone by surprise. In the case of SIs which have to be prayed against, Labour has occasionally had competition from the Alliance to be the first to put down the 'prayer'. The advantage is that this gives an entitlement to be called to open the debate. On one occasion, after consulting with PLP colleagues, I arrived at the Commons at 6am only to find a Liberal MP sitting outside the table office looking very smug. After that unfortunate experience we made sure that a Labour MP spent the night on the not very comfortable couch outside the table office.

This is how a prayer against an SI appears on the blue part of the order paper. You will notice it looks similar to EDMs, is printed alongside them and can attract other MPs' signatures. This procedure is explained in Chapter 4. However it can be distinguished from EDMs by the 'SI' in the title:

220 *SOCIAL SECURITY (S.I., 1987, No. 1692)*

Mr Neil Kinnock
Mr Roy Hattersley
Mr Robin Cook
Mr Andrew F. Bennett
Mr Derek Fatchett
Mrs Ann Clwyd

* 11

Mr Jeremy Corbyn

That an humble address be presented to Her Majesty, praying that the Social Security (Widows' Benefit) Transitional Regulations 1987 (*S.I., No.1692*), dated 25 September 1987, a copy of which was laid before this House on 1 October, be annulled.

Action Check List
1. Watch out for publication of SIs.
2. Urge sympathetic MPs to try to get debates on those subject to negative procedure. Try and persuade MPs to press for a debate on the floor of the House.
3. Prepare briefing notes for target (or all) MPs.

6
How an MP Can Help in Other Ways

Letters to the Minister

The most obvious course of action open to an MP is to write to the minister. Indeed MPs probably spend more time writing to the appropriate minister than doing anything else. Of course many of the letters an MP sends to a minister will be about individual constituent's problems. However, the MP will also write quite frequently about policy issues. This is valuable at any time but particularly useful during recesses, especially the Summer, when the MP has fewer other opportunities to raise issues. So the first advice to the lobbyist is that if you want to raise an issue with a minister, do so through your own MP. Clearly if you are a pressure group or trade union, then you will almost certainly have contacts with one or more MPs who can do this for you.

What does an MP do on receiving a letter from a constituent or pressure group about, say, nurses' pay? If the letter asks the MP for his/her own views then the MP simply writes back. But quite often the letter asks the MP to raise the matter with the minister or do something about it (see Figure 6.1). In such instances the member normally photocopies the letter and sends it to the appropriate minister with a covering letter. The MP may be non-committal and merely ask for the minister's comments. Alternatively the member may send a strong supporting letter saying s/he fully agrees with the constituent/trade union, etc. and ask the minister to consider it favourably. Then the MP will pass a copy of the minister's reply to the constituent or pressure group.

How do you decide which minister to approach? There are several ministers in every department and MPs are given a list of their detailed responsibilities. For example, as we saw in Chapter 2, there are five ministers at the Home Office. The convention is that privy councillors write to privy councillors while other MPs write to (or at any rate get replies from) the minister with the specific responsibility. It doesn't matter if the MP writes to the wrong minister – the appropriate one will reply. The importance of this for the lobbyist is merely that when the MP sends you the minister's reply you will seldom have the satisfaction of seeing the secretary of state's signature.

Figure 6.1 Example of a Letter from a Pressure Group (Amnesty)

AMNESTY INTERNATIONAL

Amnesty International British Section, 5 Roberts Place
off Bowling Green Lane, London EC1R 0EJ
Tel: 01-251 8371   Telex: 917621 AIBS   Fax: 01 251 1558
Nobel Peace Prize 1977   UN Human Rights Prize 1978

14 March 1988

The Rt Hon Gerald Kaufman MP
House of Commons
London SW1A 0AA

Dear Mr Kaufman

Sharpeville 6 - Death Sentences confirmed

You will recall my letter of 25th February concerning the death
sentences imposed on the Sharpeville Six in South Africa.   As
you will probably know, the South African authorities have today
refused clemency for the six individuals. They are scheduled to
be executed on Friday 18th March.

It would seem that the only prospect of averting these death
sentences at this politically sensitive time would be a personal
appeal from Mrs Thatcher. I wonder if you would consider
approaching the Prime Minister and urging her to send an urgent
appeal for clemency to President Botha.

The circumstances surrounding the conviction of the Sharpeville
six are well known. Amnesty International opposes the death
penalty in all cases. In this case we are particularly concerned
that the six prisoners were convicted simply because they were
present at the event, and not because of any involvement in the
murder. The Supreme Court acknowledged that:

"..... it has not been proved in the case of any of the six
accused convicted of murder that their conduct had contributed
causally to the death of the deceased.....In the present case I
am dealing with the position of the six accused who have been
convicted of murder solely on the basis of common purpose....."

The appeal court upheld the death sentence.

My thanks in advance for your help on this matter.

Yours sincerely

Jane Cooper
Parliamentary Liaison Officer

Letters about the poll tax, for example, will be answered by the minister for local government at the DoE, who was, in early 1988, Michael Howard MP. On the other hand if a privy councillor writes to a minister at that department the reply will come from the secretary of state, who in early 1988 was Rt Hon Nicholas Ridley MP. Incidentally 'Rt Hon' denotes a privy councillor; these are usually present or former cabinet ministers. In many departments one of the ministers will be a peer; s/he will have specific responsibilities and will answer MPs' letters, etc. However on the floor of the Commons another minister will have to answer PQs and deal with debates on the Lords minister's specific subjects.

Why should you not write directly to the minister? For some major pressure groups who are seen as reasonably 'respectable' by the government this may be satisfactory, because you will get replies signed by the minister. Almost everyone else will merely get an official reply signed by a civil servant. Apart from the fact that ministers' letters are on more attractive notepaper, there are a number of important reasons why issues of importance should go through an MP:

- The reply will be a more considered one and more authoritative, although in the end the draft may differ little from the civil servant's own version. After all the official is probably the same in both cases, except that drafts for the minister's reply go through more layers of the bureaucracy.
- The reply will almost certainly be quicker. If not, the MP can put a PQ to the minister asking when a reply will be ready. This normally works like a charm.
- The minister's reply can be used publicly in press releases, etc. as representing government policy. (Where the issue concerns an individual it might be inappropriate to publicise the letter in case doing so would prejudice a person's right to privacy, unless, of course, that person agrees.)
- You have the satisfaction of knowing that your letter was seen by the minister, so you are exerting more political pressure than you might if it did not get beyond a civil servant's desk.
- It is an advantage that your MP is also involved. If the minister's answer is unsatisfactory you can always ask the MP to try again - but give detailed reasons why the minister's first reply was unsatisfactory. Indeed the MP may, if s/he agrees with you, find other ways of raising the issue.

When you write to your MP, brevity is an advantage. State the case clearly and ask the MP to take the matter to the minister. You may also want to ask the MP for his/her own views so make sure your letter is clear on this point. Remember the civil servants may have to investigate the matter so give enough information to enable this to be done.

In practice the MP has to decide whether an issue is best raised with a minister or locally. For example, a query about the National Health Service may be a matter for decision by the local health authority in which case the minister may either seek the health authority's views or simply ask the health authority to write directly to the MP. So make sure you find a way of pinning responsibility on the minister, for example, by emphasising cash shortages due to central government parsimony. Otherwise accept the fact the MP may contact the health authority and send you its reply. There is more about lobbying these other bodies in Chapter 7.

Incidentally, pressure groups sometimes ask an MP to obtain very detailed information through parliamentary questions. Sometimes it can be quite difficult to phrase the questions so that the full information can be obtained. In such instances why not suggest to the MP that s/he write to the minister asking for the information and explaining that it is probably easier doing this than asking a series of PQs. The only snag is that the information is then not generally available unless you or the MP succeed in making the minister's letter widely known.

Meetings with the Minister

MPs have the right to ask for a meeting with a minister. I have known this to be refused, but refusal is exceptional. The MP may not, unless s/he is a privy councillor, necessarily get to the secretary of state but will have the chance of discussing the issue with the appropriate middle ranking or junior minister together with the civil servants. Such occasions can also be used to discuss an individual constituent's problems, for example about his/her immigration status. Here, however, we are more concerned about policy issues although, from time to time, there have been effective campaigns, with much lobbying, about one person's or one family's immigration problems.

As a lobbyist you may wish, from time to time, to suggest to MPs that they raise an issue personally with the minister. When might this be appropriate? The meeting will be in private, though there may be advantages in publicising the fact that the MP is going to meet the minister to raise the particular issue. Afterwards the minister may not wish to be quoted – sometimes what the minister says will be more revealing if it is 'off the record', though there would be nothing to prevent the MP telling the press what s/he has said to the minister. Very little is normally gained by meeting the minister on a subject where his/her position is firmly entrenched. Sometimes, however, when there is an active campaign MPs are requested as a last resort to see the minister, say about a controversial hospital closure. A meeting with a minister is more likely to be useful when there is a little flexibility in the government's position.

While individual MPs can seek such a meeting, it is more common for a group of MPs to make a joint approach, for example MPs whose constituencies might be affected by a hospital closure. MPs may have interests in common, which may cut across party lines: I once went with a Tory MP to see a minister who was being very critical of Citizens Advice Bureaux. Sometimes MPs go as members of groups; the all-party Friends of Cyprus have lobbied the minister of state at the Home Office about the immigration problem affecting a family of Greek Cypriot origin. On another occasion the Parliamentary Labour Party civil liberties group lobbied a Home Office minister about tightening the laws covering the possession and ownership of guns. This took place several years before the Hungerford shooting tragedy and the minister then was not sympathetic to our arguments.

A key question is whether the MP(s) can be accompanied by a representative from a pressure group. A few pressure groups are seen as 'respectable' enough by the government for them to have direct access to ministers anyway and so do not normally need an MP's help in this.

As regards most pressure groups, the MP can check their 'acceptability' with the minister's private secretary but it will not always be agreed. The virtual right for MPs to meet a minister would be weakened if it were to be used primarily as a means of getting other people to meet the minister. Equally such a presence may make the MP's deputation more effective – after all ministers have their civil servants; why shouldn't MPs have some help as well? In my experience Home Office ministers have, for example, agreed that someone from the National Council for Civil Liberties could be with a Labour MPs' delegation. So if you want to go along with your MP, ask if it is possible. In any case it is essential that MPs going to see a minister are well briefed beforehand and you should suggest a preliminary meeting with your group. It is worth adding that ministers may be more willing to have representatives of a local group come along with the MP where it concerns purely a constituency matter. Where there are local MPs from more than one party perhaps you should suggest a mixed party deputation plus representatives from your group.

Action Check List

1. Contact your own MP and ask him/her to seek the minister's views, etc.
2. If you have local branches, get them to approach their MPs.
3. If you are contacting other MPs, make clear to them why you are doing this, e.g. as part of a national campaign, or because s/he is an opposition frontbencher, otherwise your letter might be passed to the constituency member for your address.
4. Decide whether you also want your own MP to state his/her views on the subject.
5. If you know an MP reasonably well and letters have not got any concession from the minister, would a meeting help? Ask your contact MP; if s/he agrees make sure you can provide a good briefing on the issue.
6. A delegation of MPs could be more effective – in gaining publicity in their constituencies, more weight, etc.
7. Tell the media what is happening, or make sure the MP does so; press release the minister's letter, ensure the press are kept informed about the result of meetings with the minister.

Mass Lobbies

Mass lobbies are when several hundred or perhaps several thousand people turn up at Parliament to lobby their MPs on a specific issue. They can only take place at times when the House is sitting and certain arrangements must be made (see below) both by the organisers and by the MP(s) who have been asked to help. The main aim must be to achieve publicity and a sense of solidarity among the lobbyists who may have arrived from all parts of the country. Organising a mass lobby is a lot of work and my advice is to be sure you cannot achieve the same ends by other means. If the only aim is to get people to see their MPs this can be done more easily by arranging meetings in the constituencies, though this will give the participants less of a sense of achievement. On the other hand, with planning and good organisation you can arrange for a fair proportion of the lobby to get to meet an MP.

One of the most successful lobbies I helped to arrange was in 1980 when Wandsworth parents, teachers, students and children came up the river, early one evening, in two boatloads before coming into the Palace of Westminster. As the boats – with music, placards and balloons – came past the terrace of the Commons the effect was dramatic!

Because of the numbers involved it often happens that quite a few of the lobbyists do not manage to see their MPs. Indeed they may not even get into the Palace of Westminster because space is limited, so it can be a frustrating experience. It is thus doubly important that the organisers plan the event in detail to allow for these problems.

Mass lobbies are arranged on a wide variety of issues and they average about one a week. They are seldom held on a Friday though that might be appropriate to coincide with contentious private members' legislation. Because lobbies can take place only when the House is sitting, they cannot start before 2.30pm on Mondays to Thursdays and 9.30am on Fridays. The following are examples of lobbies in recent years:

Campaign for Nuclear
  Disarmament
Cyprus
National Council for Carers
Dreadnought Seamen's
  Hospital
Open University students
Closure of DHSS resettlement
  units
Austin Rover workers
Sunday trading
Pensioners
National Union of Students
Nurses

Animal rights
World Development Movement
Scottish steel workers
Workers from Westland
  Helicopters
Medical students
National Union of Teachers
Multiple sclerosis
Association of University
  Teachers
Prevention of Terrorism Act
Abortion
Disabled people
London Transport workers

Having established that you want to organise a mass lobby you should decide what you want to happen at Westminster. Remember you are not allowed to march or demonstrate outside or near the Houses of Parliament when they are sitting, so your mass lobby should arrive as individuals. Only about 100 people can actually get into the central lobby at any one time and this will include people who are already going there for other reasons. So if your lobby will be of any size you have to make additional arrangements to involve the lobbyists or they will simply spend the afternoon queueing to get into St Stephen's entrance. There are five possibilities:
1. Get an MP to book the Grand Committee Room off Westminster Hall so that the lobbyists can be addressed by and ask questions of MPs. You will have to decide how long the lobby is likely to last and make the booking accordingly. You can arrange for lobbyists to go into the Grand Committee Room on an hourly shift system.
2. Small groups of lobbyists can meet their MPs in the interview rooms (sometimes called the 'W' rooms) off Westminster Hall. There are six of

these rooms of varying sizes and they hold from 10 to about 40 people. Arrange for MPs to book these rooms. Again a 'shift' system, say half-hourly, is possible (*see* Figure 6.2). In addition, MPs have on occasion talked to small groups of lobbyists in Westminster Hall itself.

3. If you are going to have an even larger lobby then you should also book Central Hall, Westminster and arrange for MPs to speak there.

4. The Commons authorities estimate that in the course of an afternoon and early evening about 1,200 lobbyists can attend meetings with MPs in the Grand Committee Room and in the interview rooms.

5. After the meetings in Central Hall, the Grand Committee Room and in the interview rooms the lobbyists can, if they wish, make their way into the central lobby where they can fill in green cards to see their MPs. Note: in order to ease the flow of people, lobbyists will normally have to leave Westminster Hall through New Palace Yard and into Parliament Square even if they wish to see their MPs. So it means they will have to go back to St Stephen's entrance.

Action Check List

1. Contact 'A' division, Metropolitan Police, Cannon Row Police Station, London SW1; this is essential for all the necessary arrangements.

2. Get an MP to book the Grand Committee Room, and interview rooms and inform the Sergeant at Arms office. In the case of a large lobby you may also find it useful to deal directly with the Sergeant at Arms office.

3. Book Central Hall, Westminster; you could start earlier than 2.30pm at this venue.

4. Arrange speakers and don't forget one or more people to chair the meeting(s). Any one MP may not be free the whole time so you may need several chairs, especially in the Grand Committee Room. The normal pattern is a flow of MPs who each speak for three to five minutes, perhaps interspersed with people from your organisation.

5. Make sure your MP puts a notice into the all-party whip – if the lobby is supported by MPs of two parties; otherwise a notice in the party whip is necessary; usually this will include an estimate of numbers expected.

6. When choosing the date you may wish, ideally, to coincide with a debate on the subject in the Commons. In practice this is hard to arrange because MPs get so little notice (up to eight days) of most forthcoming business. (The exception is that there may be several weeks' notice before private members' bills on Fridays.) The alternative is to arrange the lobby at short notice when the

Figure 6.2 Mass Lobby Arrangements (World Development Movement)

Join Us in a Mass Lobby to PREVENT FUTURE FAMINE
Tues Oct 22 – House of Commons 2-10pm

FIGHT WORLD POVERTY

FIGHT WORLD POVERTY LOBBY
c/o WDM, Bedford Chambers, Covent Garden, London WC2E 8HA 01-836 3672

Following discussions at the Sergeant at Arms office it has been agreed that on the afternoon and evening of Tuesday 22nd October the 'W' interview rooms and, for most of the period, the Grand Committee Room will be used for meetings between MPs and their constituents attending the Fight World Poverty Mass Lobby, arranged by the major development agencies and the churches.

The office of the Sergeant at Arms has asked us to adminster bookings from MPs at half-hourly intervals for meetings with their constituents.

If you would like to book a room for a meeting with your constituents, could you please fill in the form below and return it to Johanna Weeks, Fight World Poverty Lobby, c/o WDM, Bedford Chambers, Covent Garden, London WC2E 8HA.

To: Johanna Weeks, Fight World Poverty Lobby, c/o WDM, Bedford Chambers, Covent Garden, London WC2E 8HA.

Please arrange a room for a meeting with my constituents on Tuesday 22nd October at the Fight World Poverty Lobby.

Name of MP_____

Name of constituency_____

Preferred time of meeting_____ on Tuesday 22nd October.

Contact telephone no. _____

For FWPL office use

Constituency code_____ Time of meeting_____

Room number_____

Details confirmed with MP_____

Constituency coordinator(s) notified _____

This lobby is organised by the development agencies and the Churches.

business is known. If so, remember that the MPs most committed to the subject wish to speak in the debate and will therefore find it harder to leave the chamber. Equally on a Tuesday and Thursday at 3.15pm many MPs will not want to leave during prime minister's questions. If you are unlucky there may be a major statement after 3.30pm which will make it harder for some MPs to leave the chamber.

7. The time of the lobby will also be influenced by how many lobbyists are coming from outside London. You could start soon after 2.30pm but the lobby will probably get into top gear towards 3pm. If you are dealing only with Londoners you could start a little later in the afternoon.

8. If you expect large numbers, you may need stewards outside St Stephen's entrance. They should be easily identifiable, perhaps with armbands.

9. As it is hard to estimate when people may get into the central lobby to see their MPs it is not sensible to try to make precise appointments. However it is essential for the lobbyists to let their MPs know they are coming and that they will be putting in a green card during the afternoon. Then if the MP cannot be there the lobbyists do not have to spend a long time waiting in vain. The only possible exception is if, in planning the event, you have arranged the meetings with MPs in the 'W' rooms.

10. If there are going to be disabled people on the lobby you must make special arrangements and plan them well in advance with your MP and the Sergeant at Arms office. In the past, lobbies of disabled people have met their MPs in Westminster Hall itself because this is easier for wheelchairs; arrangements can also be made for communicating in sign language to deaf people. You will also need to arrange access for minibuses to bring disabled people into New Palace Yard and for parking facilities. The Sergeant at Arms office is always very helpful in these matters but do give plenty of notice.

11. There are no refreshment facilities at Westminster for lobbyists except that an MP can take not more than three people to the members' cafeteria where facilities are limited.

12. Arrange press coverage and photographers.

13. Get an MP to find some way of raising in the chamber the fact that the lobby is taking place. Perhaps there could also be an EDM on the issue or, after the event, congratulating the lobbyists and urging the government to take whatever action the lobbyists have demanded.

Select Committees

The Commons has a large number of select committees, some of which will seldom be of interest to the lobbyist because they are concerned with domestic parliamentary matters. For example there are select committees dealing with privileges, the Ombudsman, members' interests, selection, sound broadcasting and House of Commons services. On the other hand these committees may deal with subjects which affect the methods of lobbying or the information available to lobbyists – an obvious example being the Select Committee on Members' Interests. Lobbying members of these particular select committees is a sophisticated activity for organised pressure groups and probably beyond the scope of an individual.

I am however mainly concerned with those select committees which correspond to and deal with the responsibilities of specific government departments. In addition there is the important Public Accounts Select Committee. This is concerned not with policy but whether public money has been used for the purposes intended and with the economy, efficiency and effectiveness required of public spending. There are also select committees in the House of Lords: these are discussed in Chapter 10.

The departmental select committees are:

Agriculture	Home Affairs
Defence	Industry and Trade
Education and Science	Scottish Affairs
Employment	Social Services
Energy	Transport
Environment	Treasury and Civil Service
Foreign Affairs	Welsh Affairs

Three of these (Treasury, Home and Foreign Affairs) can have sub-committees. For example the Foreign Affairs Committee has at times had a sub-committee on overseas aid, and the Home Affairs had one on race relations and immigration. The Treasury Select Committee has a Treasury and Civil Service Sub-committee. Sub-committees operate, in effect, as separate committees except that their reports go through a final stage of being approved by the main committee.

Each committee is appointed for the life of a Parliament though there are quite often some changes due to resignations. On average the membership is 11 MPs and 5 on the sub-committees. Formally the Committee of Selection proposes appointments and the House approves them, but in practice the party whips have the real influence. The composition of every select committee reflects the government majority in the Commons, though on some of them a Labour MP has the chair. The House of Commons public information office will give you the names of MPs on any particular committee, as will any friendly MP.

Select committees usually meet in public most commonly at 10.30am or at around 4.30pm, but it is important to check the dates and times in advance. Sessions are open to the public except when the committee is discussing its future work or draft reports or is considering matters of security or commercial confidence. The powers of these committees are investigative. They themselves decide on topics or issues which they wish to look into. The outcome is a report to the Commons with recommendations to which the government will subsequently respond. The government may accept or reject the proposals. There are invariably requests for a debate on such a report but only seldom are they granted. It is important to realise that though there is a government 'majority' on each committee the reports do not necessarily endorse ministerial thinking and some reports have been quite embarrassing to ministers.

In the process of carrying out an investigation, select committees interview witnesses who may be ministers, civil servants, outside experts, representatives of other organisations and of pressure groups. However the Public Accounts Committee gives fewer opportunities for outside bodies to give evidence as most of the witnesses tend to be officials. A great deal of evidence is also submitted in writing and select committees may visit various parts of the country as well as travelling abroad.

The following are examples of investigations by select committees:

Agriculture:	Effects of pesticides on human health
	Storm damage of 16 October 1987
Defence:	Protection of British merchant shipping in the Persian Gulf
	Royal Navy's surface fleet: aircraft carriers
Education, Science and Arts:	Special education needs: implementation of the Education Act 1981
	The secondary school curriculum and examinations
Employment:	Urban Development Corporations
	Skills shortages
	Trade union legislation – unions in GCHQ

Energy:	Radioactive waste
	Electricity and gas prices
Environment:	Pollution of rivers and estuaries
	Green Belt, land for housing
Foreign Affairs:	Food and famine relief (sub-Saharan Africa): UK policy
	Falklands islands
	Cyprus
	South East Asia and Indo-China
Home Affairs:	Immigration from the Indian sub-continent
	Refugees
	Police complaints procedures
	Miscarriages of justice
	Compensation and support for victims of crime
Scottish Affairs:	Dampness in housing
	Hospital provision
Social Services:	Resourcing the NHS
	Children in care
	Perinatal and neonatal mortality
	Problems associated with Aids
Trade and Industry:	Future financing of the community
	Post Office
Transport:	Transport in London
	Road safety
Treasury and Civil Service:	The government's economic policy: autumn statement
	International monetary arrangements
	Acceptance of outside appointments by Crown servants
Welsh Affairs:	Impact of regional industrial policy on Wales
	Tourism
Public Accounts Committee:	Regulation of heavy lorries
	Monitoring and control of charities in England and Wales

Examining a few of these reports shows the wide range of organisations and pressure groups that have submitted oral or written evidence. These include:

Cumbrians Opposed to a
  Radioactive Environment
British Nuclear Fuels PLC
Greenpeace
Friends of the Earth
Trades Union Congress
The National Union
  of Seamen
Association of Metropolitan
  Councils
Association of County Councils
Central Electricity Generating
  Board
Town and Country Planning
  Asssociation
Transport 2000
London Amenity and Transport
  Association
London Chamber of Commerce
  and Industry
National Union of Railwaymen
Transport and General Workers'
  Union
National Union of Teachers

Equal Opportunities Commission
Commission for Racial Equality
Joint Council for the Welfare of
  Immigrants
United Kingdom Immigrants
  Advisory Service
Friends of Cyprus
The Government of the Republic
  of Cyprus
Friends of Turkish Cyprus
Amnesty International
Howard League for Penal
  Reform
The British Council
United Nations High
  Commissioner for Refugees
Countryside Commission
Medical Research Council
Terence Higgins Trust
London Lighthouse
Lothian and Borders Police
Scottish Trades Union Congress
Greater Glasgow Health Board

These procedures can clearly be of major interest to a pressure group. But first you must be aware that there is an investigation into a subject area in which you are concerned. Sometimes the press will carry an item but your best source of information is an MP. The Commons public information office will give you information about investigations underway by a particular committee. If your organisation wishes to submit evidence then phone the Commons and ask to speak to the clerk of the appropriate select committee. These officials are extremely helpful and will advise you how to submit written evidence. Getting called to give oral evidence is more difficult as pressure of time means every committee has to be very selective, but it is again worth consulting the clerk and any friendly MP on the committee about your chances of being invited. It is usual for oral evidence to be preceded by written evidence.

If you are giving evidence, especially orally, do your homework. Find out who the members are and see if you know anything about their views on the issue being investigated. Go to a select committee meeting and get the feel of the procedure. Have a look at earlier reports of the committee and study the way written evidence has been presented. These reports also contain verbatim accounts of the examination of witnesses. (These are also published separately some days after the sessions take place.) It is understandable that some witnesses feel a trifle apprehensive before being called but there is really nothing to worry about provided you are clear about what points you want to make and have the facts ready. It is better that your group should be represented by more than one person – I have seen up to five – so someone can look up specific facts while you are dealing with another aspect of the question asked.

The most difficult aspect of lobbying in this area is how to persuade a select committee to investigate a particular topic. At intervals, some time before the current investigation is completed, a committee begins to consider its next subject(s) and this is where there is delicate manoeuvring by the members. The best way you can influence it is through an MP on the committee or preferably one in each of the main parties. Have an informal discussion or at any rate write a letter making out your case. If the lobbying is too obvious it may be counterproductive. Remember MPs on a committee will consider not only the importance of the issue but whether it will make a political impact. In addition government backbenchers may well get a nod and a wink from a minister to avoid potentially embarrassing topics.

Generally speaking there is no point in asking MPs to support a particular investigation where (i) there has already recently been a full enquiry by, say, a royal commission, or (ii) where there is no perception that a real problem exists, or (iii) where the issue is at the centre of controversy between the main political parties.

Select Committee on European Legislation

This committee's functions are to scrutinise proposals for European legislation. It makes regular reports to the Commons covering every document which has been before it. It does not deal with their merits but with whether they raise questions of legal or political importance and what matters of public policy might be affected.

Action Check List
1. Get a list of members of the relevant select committee from an MP or the public information office at the Commons.
2. Find out what is being investigated from (1) above.
3. Discuss with the clerk and with a friendly MP on the committee

the possibilities of giving oral or written evidence.

4. Study procedures and ways in which oral and written evidence are submitted; look at earlier reports and attend a select committee while witnesses are being examined.

5. If you have a suitable topic for a select committee discuss this with an MP who is a member of it.

Party Groups

We have already seen that there are frequent meetings of the whole of the parliamentary Labour Party and of Tory backbenchers in the 1922 Committee. In addition both the Labour and Conservative Parties in Parliament also meet in subject and regional groups. The subject groups correspond, roughly, to the main government departments so there are, for example, both Labour and Tory Home Affairs Groups. In the Labour Party these meetings are attended by the relevant frontbenchers. These groups really have two main functions: first, to consider their approach to forthcoming bills and other Commons business and secondly to consider subjects of concern, which may involve inviting representatives of pressure groups, local authorities, or trade unions to come along (*see* Figure 6.3). In addition there are the meetings of Labour MPs who are on the standing committees of major bills; these are dealt with in Chapter 5.

The lobbyist may have an opportunity to meet members of a party regional or subject group. Certainly in the Labour Party, owing to time constraints, there are invariably more groups who want to meet MPs than can be fitted in at meetings especially as invitations to such groups are the exception rather than the rule. But you may still feel it is worth the effort. Obviously it is not worth trying to get an invitation unless your subject is likely to be of particular interest to Labour MPs. The following are examples of organisations which succeeded in putting their views to Labour backbench groups over the last couple of years or so:

Gas Consultative Councils	British Agro-Chemicals
Inverclyde District Council	Association
British Rail and the Channel	Scottish Consumer Council
Tunnel	Scottish Tourist Board
South Wales NUM	National Union of Teachers
Strathclyde Housing Campaign	Association of London Community
Civil Aviation Authority	Relations Councils
Campaign for the Reform of	Royal College of Nursing
Animal Experimentation	National Aerospace Shop Stewards

Figure 6.3 Example of Typical Week's PLP Backbench Group Meetings

PLP DEPARTMENTAL COMMITTEES
& REGIONAL GROUPS

Monday 24 June	5.00 pm	HOME AFFAIRS COMMITTEE Representation of the People Bill - consideration of Lords Amendments	21 Robin Corbett
Tuesday 25 June	1.45 pm	SCOTTISH EXECUTIVE COMMITTEE Business meeting	W6 David Marshall

	4.00 pm	WEST MIDLANDS GROUP
		a) Representatives from the NGA will
		   be present for a discussion about
		   the dispute with the Wolverhampton
		   Express & Star
		b) Business items
			19
			Peter Snape

	4.00 pm	NORTHERN GROUP Representatives from British Rail will be present	7 Harry Cowans
	5.00 pm	SCOTTISH GROUP Campbell Christie, General Secretary- elect of the STUC, will be present	20 David Marshall
	6.00 pm	JOINT MEETING OF THE EMPLOYMENT, TRADE & INDUSTRY AND TREASURY & CIVIL SERVICE COMMITTEES Campbell Christie, Deputy General Secretary of the Society of Civil and Public Servants, will speak on the Report of a Scrutiny of Administrative and Legislative Requirements "Burdens on Business"	20 Ron Leighton George Park Austin Mitchell
	6.30 pm	FOREIGN AFFAIRS COMMITTEE Prof Erdal Inonu, Leader of the. Social Democratic Party of Turkey, will be present	6 Tom Clarke
Wednesday 26 June	5.00 pm	TRADE & INDUSTRY COMMITTEE: AVIATION SUB-COMMITTEE Representatives from AUEW TASS will be present for a discussion on the future of the Aerospace Industry	18 Lewis Carter-Jones
	5.00 pm	YORKSHIRE GROUP Business meeting	20 Max Madden

British Medical Association	British Olympic Asssociation
Association of Directors	Stock Exchange
of Social Services	plus many other trade unions

You can approach the group either through a friendly MP, or by contacting the chair or secretary of the group by writing to them at the House of Commons (get the name by phoning the Labour Party at the House of Commons) or by contacting the secretary of the parliamentary Labour Party. Say that you would like to bring a deputation of two or three from your organisation to meet a particular group and enclose a small supporting statement; if you feel your group may not be all that well known to the MPs enclose a brief description of your aims plus something about the people who will be coming along.

Meetings usually last an hour and are on a Monday to Thursday evening. Find out before the meeting how long you will have; it is important to arrive in good time. Do not be disappointed if there are very few MPs present or if your meeting is interrupted by a division. Remember the aim of such a meeting is to influence Labour Party policy or tactics in Parliament so you are unlikely to get far by suggesting something which is very much at variance with existing party policy. In the parliamentary Labour Party there are also a number of groups which have semi-official status. They include the PLP Civil Liberties Group, Trade Union Group, Miners' Parliamentary Group and the PLP Latin America, Central America and Caribbean Group.

Many Labour MPs are sponsored by a trade union. This means that their constituency party gets some money from the union with extra at election times. In return MPs are expected to raise issues of concern to the union and generally keep themselves informed of union policy. As each union may have several sponsored MPs the usual practice is for these to meet regularly. For example I was sponsored by COHSE (Confederation of Health Service Employees) and all seven COHSE-sponsored MPs met monthly with officials from that union.

Meetings of the Conservative subject and regional groups are similarly arranged though with the obvious difference that to influence Conservative Party policy is close to attempting to influence the government. You could also try to meet interested groups of MPs from the other parties by approaching them through a friendly member or by phoning their party offices at the Commons.

All-Party (Country) Groups

There are many all-party groups operating at Westminster. They are of

There are many all-party groups operating at Westminster. They are of two kinds, country groups and subject groups. There is a British XXX Group linking Westminster with almost every country on earth. They give MPs and peers a chance of inviting visitors from a particular country to come and speak, there may be occasional meetings at embassies or high commissions, the Foreign Office will invite members of a particular group to meet visitors for lunch and other occasions and the groups try to meet British diplomats posted to those countries. Sometimes the countries themselves may invite MPs to visit. However, most of these foreign trips are arranged through either the Commonwealth Parliamentary Association (CPA) or the Inter Parliamentary Union (IPU) with a selection system which, in theory at least, gives all MPs a fair chance of going somewhere every few years.

It is usually difficult to discover that an MP is going abroad but a friendly MP may be able to find out which members are going on a particular CPA or IPU delegation. However such delegations do not criticise conditions in the host country unless it is to make representations on behalf of a local parliamentarian who might be imprisoned or otherwise have his or her freedom curtailed. Nevertheless if you are concerned about human rights it might still be useful to brief a sympathetic MP who is going abroad. In any case the constraint I have mentioned normally does not apply to visits under other auspices. In practice most of these country groups are not very active though some, like the British American Group, arranges quite a lot of events including sending some of its members to the United States.

These groups are of interest to the lobbyist because their active members probably include MPs who are quite knowledgeable about a particular country, have contacts with politicians there as well as at the embassy or high commission in London, and may sometimes go on visits. The Commons public information office will give you the names of the officers of any particular group but a list of the whole membership is normally not available. Membership of a group does not necessarily indicate a favourable or unfavourable attitude to a country.

All-Party (Subject) Groups

There are very many all-party subject groups; some are well organised and meet regularly; others only have occasional meetings. A great deal depends on whether they are serviced by an outside organisation or merely by an MP or peer. If the latter they are unlikely to have much by way of background documents as MPs or peers are too busy. The most effective all-party groups are those which have the benefit of staff pressure group.

The All-party Penal Affairs Group is one of the most powerful at Westminster and it is serviced by a member of the staff of NACRO (National Association for the Care and Resettlement of Offenders). Other all-party groups with outside support include those dealing with pensioners, mental health, disablement, civil liberties, human rights and race relations. The last-mentioned is supported by money from a charitable trust rather than by a pressure group.

Examples of all-party groups are:

Parliamentary Human Rights Group	Overseas Development Group
Penal Affairs Group	Conservation Committee
Disablement Group	Friends of Cyprus
Pensioners Group	Drug Misuse Committee
Civil Liberties Group	All Party Committee on Crofting
Football Group	Committee for the Release of Soviet Jewry
Race Relations Group	Esperanto Group
Population and Development Group	Channel Tunnel Group
Non Profit-making Clubs	Tourism Committee
Minerals Group	Social Science and Policy Committee
Chemicals Group	Arts and Heritage Group
Racing and Bloodstock Industries Group	Food and Health Forum
Defence Study Group	Space Committee
	Children's Committee

Details of all-party group meetings are announced in the information sent weekly, by each whips office, while Parliament is sitting, to all members – normally called the 'all-party whip'. However if your organisation is actively involved in such a group it helps to send a letter to members. This can be sent either to regular attenders or members of the group or to all MPs depending on your resources and the importance of the event. In fact every all-party group meeting is open to all MPs and peers though strictly speaking many groups have an annual membership fee of £1 or £2.

Such groups provide an opportunity for lobbyists to meet and address MPs. However you do not need to use an all-party group. An alternative is simply to get a friendly MP to book a room and you or s/he can inform MPs that the meeting is taking place. You can't get it announced on the all-party whip and may find it harder to give the meeting an 'all-party' label though two MPs of different parties could get together to make the arrangements. My advice is to use an existing group if it is active and likely to be sympathetic; check this with a friendly MP.

Such meetings can be held at any time but most commonly are from 4pm to about 8pm. Almost always meetings at Westminster last exactly one hour. There is a great deal of pressure on rooms, especially at the times I have mentioned, so you will probably have to leave when the hour is up to make way for another meeting. Do not publicise your meeting to MPs till you have a room available.

If you prefer the idea of an informal meeting ask a sympathetic MP to invite a few colleagues. Only MPs can book rooms at Westminster and the member is supposed to be present throughout the meeting. This is to prevent organisations simply using the MP as a means of getting a room in central London. Some organisations with MPs on their committees hold their AGMs or annual dinners (see below) at the Commons – and of course invite an MP as a speaker. It is obviously easier to ask an MP to talk to your group if the meeting is at the Commons and the member is still available to vote. It is not reasonable if you want to hold a meeting at Westminster simply to contact an MP you may know and ask him/her to book a room. The effect is that the MP is tied up for the evening and cannot do anything else – which will not appeal to the member if s/he has only a tenuous link with your organisation.

It is clear that the most effective all-party groups are those serviced by a pressure group. So why not set one up? The benefits are that you will develop a close and continuing relationship with a small core of committed MPs and you will thus have greater influence. You should set against this the fact that there are far too many meetings for MPs already and attendances may be very low – perhaps two or three. Are you sure you will achieve more in this way than by the occasional ad hoc meeting? Do not set up a new group unless you are sure it covers a topic that will attract a number of MPs and which does not overlap with an existing group. If you want to proceed you must try the idea out on a few MPs and get their reaction. If some of them show interest and are willing to do the work and hold office then you could consider it.

A word of warning. There has been criticism of commercial lobbying firms using Westminster facilities for commercial ends; indeed some MPs want to bring such activities under closer control. There is more discussion of this point in Chapter 14.

Receptions, Drinks or Dinners at Westminster

MPs and peers can book any of four private dining rooms (dining rooms

A,B,C and D) at the Commons for meals or drinks receptions and also the marquee on the terrace. So you might wish to use this facility – the MP has to be present – to invite members along for afternoon tea or drinks or a formal meal. The latter could be your AGM or with tea or drinks you could give a presentation about your group or some specific issue. Lunches or dinners can be quite costly but tea or drinks are obviously more reasonable. The Commons banqueting department will give you details of costs and other arrangements (01-219 3676).

You can also have dinners on Friday and Saturday evenings and during recesses. Indeed at such times you can book the larger Members' Dining Room or the Harcourt Room, but this can be costly. (There is also such a facility in the Lords.)

Exhibitions in the Upper Waiting Hall

The Upper Waiting Hall is available for members to arrange for an exhibition to be held there. This can last for a week when the House is sitting and is intended for MPs and peers rather than the general public. MPs may take six guests to such an exhibition between 10am and 6pm. To use the Upper Waiting Hall for this purpose an MP must first obtain the sponsorship of a government department. If this is refused the MP can 'appeal' to the Accommodation and Administration Sub-committee who wil decide whether the exhibition may proceed. Exhibitions must not contain items of advertising or commercial interest nor any material explicitly intended to further the aims of any political party or group.

Having obtained agreement in principle the MP has to sign the exhibition ballot book in the Sergeant at Arms office, thus becoming eligible for the ballot in the forthcoming exhibition booking period. At this time a preference for dates can be expressed but this is not guaranteed. Applications for bookings close at 4pm on the Monday following the announcement of the appropriate recess dates and the ballot takes place at that time.

The three exhibition booking periods are: (i) Spring, from the end of the Christmas recess until the Thursday before Easter; (ii) Summer, from the end of the Easter recess until the date on which the House is expected to rise for the Summer recess; (iii) Autumn, from the end of the Summer recess until the Friday before Christmas.

When the MP has got his exhibition dates the organisers should contact the deputy assistant Sergeant at Arms on 01-219 3050 to arrange the details. The MP must put down a PQ for written answer asking the secretary of state of the relevant department if he has considered an application for the exhibition. The reply will confirm that agreement has been given and also give the dates.

You may wish to have an opening ceremony on Monday morning in the Upper Waiting Hall and for this any outsiders, including the press, will have to have invitation cards. Following the opening you may also want a reception in one of the dining rooms; contact the banqueting office (01-219 3676) to arrange this. Refreshments may not be served in the Upper Waiting Hall. The use of the Upper Waiting Hall is free but, apart from the exhibits, you may want people there during the day to answer questions, hand out leaflets, etc. Exhibitions may not be overtly party political – I understand that the Low Pay Unit has been refused in the past. The only one I have ever booked was on behalf of Amnesty International. Examples of fairly recent exhibitions are:

British Conference and
   Exhibition Centres
Yorkshire Water-Colour Society
Energy Efficiency Office/
   Eurisol UK
Coronary Prevention Group

Natural History Museum
The Nature Conservancy Council
Gas Safety
Mental Health Foundation
UK Atomic Energy Authority

Some MPs protested about the UK Atomic Energy Authority exhibition because it focused on an extremely contentious issue.

Action Check List

1. Decide whether an exhibition is worth the cost and effort.
2. Get an MP to sponsor it, and approach appropriate government department.
3. Decide roughly when you want to hold it.
4. When your MP has come up in the ballot, approach the Sergeant at Arms department (01-219 3050) to make the necessary arrangements.
5. Do you want a launch ceremony? Speaker? Guests?
6. Do you want a reception, refreshments? Contact the banqueting department (01-219 3676).

MPs' Extra-parliamentary Activity

So far we have only considered what an MP can do within Parliament or with a government department on behalf of a lobby or individual. Now we turn to what is sometimes called 'extra-parliamentary activity'. There is a great deal that MPs can do: sometimes they do it on their own initiative; at other times they act in response to invitations or suggestions from pressure groups or sometimes from individuals. As a pressure group you can achieve many benefits from making your MP work for you. And many MPs welcome the resulting publicity. Nothing stings them more than the oft repeated question: 'Where do MPs go between elections?' or when they do appear in the constituency: 'What brings you here? Is there an election on?' In contrast conscientious MPs welcome the chance of involvement in issues. There is also, of course, the added bonus of some publicity.

Your Own MP or Another?

Normally local groups will invite the MP for their constituency; of course if your group covers several constituencies you will have a choice of member and perhaps of political party as well. If your group's address is in a neighbouring constituency make sure you explain to the MP that s/he represents some of your members. Sometimes you will wish to invite another MP, perhaps because s/he is a minister, opposition frontbencher or has in some way made a reputation on a particular subject. A different MP may attract more publicity than the local member. It would be polite to invite your own MP as well if your speaker is in the same party, but explain to him/her what the aims are. It is a convention in the Commons that MPs speaking in other constituencies inform the local MP of this.

When thinking of MPs to invite do not just go for the top names. These people are probably very busy and may find it hard to find the time; also pressure of events may mean they have to cancel. Ministers are especially hard to get along; if your own MP is a government backbencher s/he might be a means of persuading a minister. In any case your own MP can be helpful in getting a member of his/her own party to come along.

If you are in or near London remember that non-London MPs may not be too keen to accept invitations at the weekend when they want to be in their constituencies. On the other hand some non-London MPs have their homes in London so they may represent a better prospect. Equally if you are far from London it may be hard to get an MP along while Parliament is sitting but if you have no choice of dates it is certainly worth trying. In any case there are always the recesses. Remember that nothing makes an MP vow never to return more than an event which runs over time so that s/he misses the last train.

I have already explained that MPs have little advance notice of parliamentary business; the announcement is normally not made until the Thursday of the previous week. So arrange to check with your guest speaker on the Thursday evening or Friday. MPs may get leave of absence even if there are three line whips but frontbenchers are in greater difficulty as they have to open or wind up debates concerned with their areas of responsibility. So if there is a late cancellation be tolerant – you have been warned.

Local Pressure Groups

Inviting MPs to an event is the best way of getting to know them. Every pressure group should, in its own interest, have some contact with local MP(s). Even if there is no immediate problem, the benefits will be felt later when help is needed. These are examples of events to which I, as the local MP, was invited:

AGM
Ordinary meeting
Reception, wine and cheese, etc.
Opening ceremony (e.g. CAB office, housing association development, parole hostel, industrial unit, dogs' home extension, peace pagoda)
Unveiling a plaque
Planting a tree

Opening a fete or other social event
Attending a picket
Leading a march or demo
Speaking in a debate
Religious service or festival
Sponsored swim or walk
Christmas lunch or other festive event
After lunch or dinner speech

There are certainly many others. Some are obviously normal events to which the MP is invited. Others are special and the MP can either make the speech, cut the tape, etc. or you can get someone else to do this and merely have the MP present. Sometimes this will present no problem. At other times the MP may feel slighted and could even be offended – avoid this by letting the MP know clearly in advance what your plans are. A useful tip is to have the chair of the event mention that the MP is present.

Why Invite an MP?

Before inviting the MP to an event it is important to decide on the aim. It is probably not good enough merely to say 'Let's have the MP along.' Far better to decide on specific objectives. These might include:

1. Get to know the MP, especially if s/he is recently elected or your organisation is newly established. This could be achieved at, say, a wine and cheese party possibly preceding or following an AGM; or indeed at any event at which there is an informal social activity. Have one or two members of your organisation briefed in advance that the MP is coming so that somebody says 'Hello' to him or her on arrival. It is counterproductive to press an MP hard to attend an event and then ignore him/her for the first ten minutes. If the MP has given up some other event to be with you s/he may not be too pleased to be ignored while all those present are busy drinking wine, chatting, eating, etc. Introduce the MP to the officers of your organisation and anybody else you think the MP would like to meet or who would like to meet the MP. Most MPs are fairly easy to talk to and are quite happy to talk a bit about themselves. Do, however, avoid letting your resident bore monopolise the MP for the whole time. It is reasonable to lobby the MP about some matter of concern to the organisation but it is certainly not right to use the opportunity to lobby about everything under the sun merely because the MP is a 'captive' audience. It is advisable to ask the MP at the outset how long s/he can stay.

2. To brief the MP on the aims of the organisation. Invite him/her to a special meeting of officers or try to do it at a social or other event. It is best to give the MP some written summary of the main points.

3. To lobby the MP to take specific action. This might involve asking the MP to make representations to a local authority, a government minister or a quango about financial aid or perhaps about some matter of policy. Other examples might include planning permission, the adverse impact of actual or future government legislation, etc. If such lobbying is not arranged to take place at the House of Commons then it is best done at a special meeting with the organisation's officers.

4. To get the MP publicly committed to a cause, or at least learn where s/he stands. The MP can be invited to speak to a meeting and indicate his/her views. For example the local CND group could invite the local MP(s) to speak about defence policy. A local civil liberties group or police monitoring unit could ask the MP to discuss forthcoming legislation and his/her attitude. In recent years there have been a number of obvious examples: the Police and Criminal Evidence Act and the public order legislation. These are clearly topics of concern to other organisations such as trade union branches who have an interest in knowing their MP's views and whether or not s/he is open to persuasion.

5. To help further a cause to which the MP is already known to be committed in order to gain publicity and wider support. This is as frequent an objective as any. In the recent past I have been asked to speak at an anti-apartheid demo outside the local town hall (the Tory-controlled council banked at Barclays while that bank was still operating in South Africa), speak at a public meeting organised by the local Action for Benefits campaign against the government's social security proposals, march at the front of a national CND demo, speak at a trade union meeting opposing a local closure, speak at a ceremony commemorating migration from France by the Huguenots 300 years ago in order to be able to draw parallels with present day paranoia about migrants, open a new Citizens Advice Bureau to give me a chance to talk about the increasing needs of the unemployed and of social security claimants. Sometimes it is worth while thinking up imaginative 'stunts' which can gain more publicity. For example Amnesty International local groups invited MPs to be locked up in cages as part of the campaign against torture.

6. It is sometimes difficult to know what to do when the local MP is unsympathetic to a cause which affects many people in the constituency. One possibility is to invite him/her to take part in a public debate with an MP from another party whose views are more acceptable. Such a debate can embarrass the local MP, especially if an effective opponent is invited. The local MP will be reluctant to refuse an invitation in his/her own constituency even if s/he dislikes the opponent and the particular audience. I have seen this tactic adopted by local community relations councils represented by Tory MPs with hard-line views on immigration or race relations. Incidentally there can be a problem if the local MP refuses invitations and this may be more common if s/he is a cabinet minister or senior minister. Offer a variety of dates – perhaps even ask the MP to select a date. There is no reason why consistent refusals should

not be publicised in the press and mentioned again during the subsequent election campaign.

Marches, Demos, Sit-ins

If your MP is unsympathetic there is little point in inviting him/her to events except to be able to publicise a refusal to take part. But it is always worth inviting an MP whom you believe supports your aims. Getting the MP along is a clear indication of commitment and encourages the other marchers or demonstrators. If you do invite the MP along, be clear about what you want: just to take part, or perhaps speak at the event. If it is a demo make sure the MP is at the front and visible to the media and public. If the MP cannot be there for the whole event, suggest when and where his/her presence would be most useful.

Representations to Public Bodies and Other Organisations

We have already considered in Chapter 6 how an MP can write on your behalf to a government minister. In fact there are many public bodies and organisations to which the MP can make representations on your behalf. You could of course write directly but if your letter is forwarded by the MP it will probably get a quicker reply, from a more senior level. Since the MP is involved there may also be more publicity for your cause. As in the case of letters to a minister, the MP will normally photocopy your letter and send it off with his own letter which may be supportive or neutral. When you receive the reply from the MP you can of course ask him/her to comment and you can release the whole correspondence to the press.

In addition to writing you can also ask the MP to meet various public bodies and organisations. It might be easier for him/her to ask whether he can be accompanied by representatives from a pressure group.

The following are examples of bodies and organisations to which as an MP I made representations concerning issues, in writing or in person:

Local health authority – hospital closures, budget allocations
British Rail – disabled access to stations
Channel Tunnel plans
Churches – school merger plans
Private firms – planning applications, employment, traffic
   and parking implications of new developments

Local authority – planning, housing policy, education policy

In addition an MP can be helpful in making representations to foreign governments. I was quite often asked to write or send telegrams, generally about human rights abuses. If you ask an MP to help it is probably best to suggest contacting the embassy or the head of government by letter. I am not convinced that telegrams are any more effective and they can be costly. Don't expect an MP to be too enthusiastic about sending long telegrams overseas.

You can also ask your MP to arrange a meeting with an embassy; it may be posssible for the MP to take representatives from a pressure group along. Mostly I had meetings at embassies and high commissions to discuss human rights abuses. However on one occasion I went to the United States Embassy to lobby for more pressure on the Turkish government about that country's continued occupation of a part of Cyprus; I also had a meeting with the Turkish ambassador to urge, vainly, that Greek Cypriot archaeologists should be permitted to visit certain historic sites in the occupied part of the island.

From time to time MPs have opportunities to attend certain events and functions which are of interest to pressure groups. For example, every two years there is the British Army Equipment Exhibition at Aldershot. While one day is set aside for the press, MPs are about the only outsiders allowed on the days when the buyers attend. Even then MPs are accompanied by a civil servant 'minder'. The secrecy is not directed at the exhibits but to protect the identity of the buyers who are all invited by the British government. Most of the latter are men in military uniforms, with red on their hats, lots of gold on their shoulders and their names, ranks and countries displayed on their chests between rows of medals; in the course of half a day I was able to spot buyers from quite a number of the world's repressive regimes.

Overseas Visits by MPs

MPs going on overseas visits have already been referred to briefly in Chapter 6. In fact quite a number of MPs make visits other than those arranged through the Commonwealth Parliamentary Association or the Inter Parliamentary Union, and foreign governments themselves sometimes like to invite MPs. There may be select committee visits. The Parliamentary Human Rights Group occasionally sends MPs abroad to investigate human rights abuses. When MPs go abroad they often meet senior ministers and officials of the countries they visit. So if you are concerned about what is happening in these countries it helps to brief the MPs in case they have a chance of discussing the matter.

Indeed some pressure groups go further and sometimes provide a staff member to accompany MPs. For example I have twice gone on Parliamentary Human Rights Group delegations (to the Philippines under Marcos, and to Nicaragua to observe the elections) accompanied by a person from CIIR (Catholic Institute for International Relations) and the visit was much more successful because of this help and support.

Action Check List

1. Make the purpose of the invitation quite clear.
2. Tell the MP what, if anything, is expected of him/her.
3. Is it an invitation to speak or merely be present? MPs like to be asked to say a few words, but do warn them! I was once asked to attend an event by an organisation of which I knew very little; pop in any time between 6 and 8pm they said. At about 6.45 I arrived to be told at the door 'They're waiting for you to speak.' Without a second to pause for breath I was publicly invited onto the platform and had to speak immediately. Embarrassing!
4. Invite the press to attend, preferably by issuing a press release beforehand; it may be useful to ask the MP for a handout of his/her speech. Inform the MP if there is to be a photocall and at what time; also if there is to be radio or TV coverage – quite an incentive. In any case do ensure a press release after the event particularly if no reporter is present. Check whether the MP wants to do it or if s/he would prefer the organisation concerned to put one out; s/he may ask to check it before it is sent out.
5. Give the MP the time of the whole event but indicate when s/he is wanted and when s/he can get away.
6. In your letter of invitation give your day and evening phone numbers.
7. Do not assume that the MP, especially if newly elected, knows all of the constituency; directions including a map may help.
8. Alert somebody to await the MP at the entrance.
9. Check beforehand how the MP plans to arrive: car, train, etc. If by train offer help with the journey from the station, either by meeting the MP there or by indicating the route to the venue. Inform the MP if car parking is available and what the arrangements are. The MP may need help with transport, perhaps from the House of Commons. If this can be arranged it may be best to offer it at the outset.
10. If the event is to take place when Parliament is sitting, make contingency plans in case the MP is not able to get away. Most MPs

are obliged to accept invitations 'subject to parliamentary business'. In practice this does not usually prevent the MP attending. However the MP may have to return to the House of Commons to vote so it is doubly important to make clear when the event is likely to end. Equally the MP may ask for the programme to be rescheduled to enable him/her to get back to the House on time.

11. Involve your MP, if sympathetic, in marches, demos, etc. so s/he can show support, boost the morale of those taking part, keep an eye on police activity, and get publicity.

12. Ask an MP to make representations to a local authority, health authority, private firms, foreign embassy, foreign government.

13. If you can discover your MP is going abroad s/he may be able to make representations to the foreign government.

14. Thank the MP afterwards by letter and send photos or copies of press cuttings which refer to the MP's attendance.

8

How to Use Election Campaigns

Parliamentary election campaigns can provide particularly good opportunities for pressure groups. Indeed some of the principles outlined here also apply to European and local council elections. In the case of parliamentary and European elections there is rather more that can be done locally either by branches of national bodies or by purely local groups and organisations. Parliamentary election campaigns are very short and there are only about four weeks between the announcement and polling day. So you must prepare your plans well before the election is declared.

National Pressure Groups

Pressure groups which have no local bases probably have to confine themselves to sending questionnaires to candidates. Increasingly the political parties are advising their candidates either not to reply or to be very careful what they say. Mostly they come from groups which seek to get a commitment from the candidate. I suspect most of the answers come from candidates who have little prospect of winning. There seems little reason for a candidate to give up time in the middle of a campaign to answer questions which will not be seen by any of his/her constituents and can only be hostages to fortune.

Obtaining lists of all the candidates, or even just those of the main parties in every constituency, can be a major undertaking since they are not published in the papers till half way through the campaign. Finding out the addresses of candidates is also difficult as not all parties have permanent offices from which the information can be provided. In any case the questionnaires tend to arrive so late in the campaign that the candidates' replies could hardly be made known to the voters. So why should they be answered? My practice in the case of national groups was to answer those with whose views and policies I agreed and to throw away the rest. I suspect this practice is fairly widespread.

So my suggestion is: unless you have a local branch or can in some way indicate that local people will get to know the candidates' answers before polling day, save your postage and don't bother.

Local Pressure Groups

In contrast to national organisations, local groups can take good advantage of election campaigns. Your area may include several constituencies and you will have to decide whether you can manage to cover them all. These are some of the possible lines of action:

Questionnaires

Send a questionnaire to all the parliamentary candidates. The purpose is to get a commitment from each candidate about his/her attitude to a particular issue. It is important that the questionnaire reaches the candidates in good time and that you tell them that the results will be made known to your local membership before polling day. You could add that a failure to reply will also be made known to your membership. It has been known for the results of questionnaires by Catholic churches to be distributed after Mass on the Sunday before polling day.

In practical terms you will have to study the local press, etc. to find out, before the election is called, who the candidates of the main parties will be. Find out also their home addresses or those of their local parties. Some political parties have permanent offices, others rent temporary accommodation when an election is called. It is important that you get your questionnaire drafted and printed well before the election is called. In the past I have received questionnaires from churches, environmental groups, community relations councils, Amnesty International, Third World groups, animal rights groups, Life (an anti-abortion group) and the Cypriot community. The last mentioned have been particularly diligent in publishing the results of questionnaires and generally adopting a high profile during elections. Although I had long been committed to the cause of the Greek Cypriots, their efforts during the 1979 election in particular ensured my active involvement in their cause when I got to Westminster.

Some pressure groups, such as the Greek Cypriots, and, I understand, some Asian groups, have made a point of helping sympathetic MPs in their election campaigns by ensuring that the local community knew what the MP had done to further their cause. They arranged for letters to be sent out in Greek to members of their local community. It is essential if you decide to do something of this kind that you discuss it first with the candidate's agent – because it might, by law, have to be included in the statement of election expenses.

Public Meetings of all the Candidates

You may wish to hold a public meeting with the candidates during the election campaign. There is no need to invite all of them and you can confine the occasion to the main two or three only. During past election campaigns I have taken part in meetings organised by the churches, the Community Relations Council, and local environmental groups.

If you want to hold such a meeting you must plan it before the election is called.You should decide the following:

1. Possible dates and times of a meeting in relation to polling day; e.g. last Sunday evening at 7pm
2. Venue
3. Which candidates to invite
4. Letting your members know of the meeting
5. Who will take the chair, etc.
6. Press publicity
7. Keeping a record of what the candidates have said and distributing it
8. Should a vote be taken at the end of the meeting ?

You may want to brief your members beforehand about the points they could put. Usually the format of such a meeting is likely to be, say, 10 minute speeches by each candidate, followed by perhaps an hour or longer for questions.

I advise you to think hard before inviting candidates from the minor parties. Your purpose is to make sure your members are better informed before voting and if there is a long string of minority-interest candidates the main contenders will have little opportunity of answering more than a few questions. Indeed the sitting MP may not feel like being there at all if he has to spend most of a valuable evening during the campaign listening to a string of other candidates. Equally important is the fact that some of the candidates are likely to refuse to share a platform with, for example, an openly racist candidate. The election laws do not oblige you to invite all the candidates.

If your group has members in several constituencies you may end up with far too many candidates from each party at your meeting. It may be easiest, by agreement with the local agents, to invite one candidate from each party to speak or answer questions.

At what stage during the campaign should such a meeting take place? Sunday evenings are a good time as the candidates are less likely to have other commitments then. Otherwise it is best to start fairly late, say at 8.30pm, so that it does not encroach on canvassing time. Even so there is no guarantee that all the main candidates will be free. They might have other commitments such as a public party meeting, or they may be helping a fellow candidate in a more marginal constituency. (Some candidates simply refuse to attend meetings with the candidates of other parties and there is really little you can do about this except publicise the fact – the other candidates will probably be keen to do this anyway!) Discuss this with the candidates' agents as soon as the election is called so that you can try to avoid clashes. Remember also the problem of election expenses and discuss this with the agents.

Some sitting (often Tory) MPs are reluctant to appear in public debate with other candidates. If that is the case in your constituency your only recourse would be for your group to meet the various candidates individually.

Meetings with the Candidates

Your group or organisation may simply want to have a meeting with all the candidates to find out their views on specific issues. This could be a meeting between each candidate and, say, your executive committee. You will probably want to be able to inform your membership of the outcome so tell the candidates of this and hold the meeting early enough during the campaign to make this a realistic possibility. Give the candidate some advance information about how you will handle the meeting and again, make the arrangements through the agent. I remember receiving a very thorough grilling in one election in the home counties from representatives of a synagogue: they asked me very detailed questions about the Middle East and Israel.

Alerting your Membership

If you decide you have not got the time or resources to plan any event during the election you can, at least, advise your members to take an active part. Make sure, for example, they attend any public meetings to ask the candidates for their views on your particular subject. If they are canvassed by a candidate they should make the most of the opportunity but can also put their question(s) to any party canvassers. They can write to the candidates or phone them about the issue but do not leave this too late in the campaign as there will not be time for an answer.

Action Check List

1. Decide what you want to do well in advance of the election being announced.
2. Find out the names and addresses of the candidates (and agents if possible) from the main parties.

3. If you decide on a questionnaire draft it well in advance and make it short!
4. If you decide on a public meeting, make tentative plans before the election.
5. Alert your members to your plans and what you want them to do during the election campaign.
6. Plan how you will let your members know the views of the candidates before polling day.
7. As soon as the election is called you will have to finalise your plans very quickly. One or two of your active members will have to be ready to spring into action.

9

Influencing Political Parties

This chapter is concerned with how pressure groups can attempt to influence the thinking of political parties. It attempts to throw some light on policy formulation at national and local level and also covers the parties' annual conferences. National lobbying normally involves some considerable effort, and possibly some expenditure. Most of the actions outlined in this chapter will therefore only be advisable for a national lobbying group. If you are a purely local group your aim will not be to change the national policies of political parties, but rather to influence individual politicians, probably councillors, or local party policies. In any case local groups will probably find it beyond their capacity to do the work required and achieve the sophisticated level of organisation that is necessary for national lobbying. This chapter is therefore aimed primarily at national pressure groups.

All the political parties differ in how they develop policy. The Labour Party has the most formal structure but this tends to change quite frequently; the Conservatives, especially in government, delegate power to their senior ministers. At the time of writing it is difficult to be precise about the SLD (Social and Liberal Democrats) as they are in the process of merging. Nor, for similar reasons, am I able to be precise about the Social Democrats who are still evolving their identity and procedures. Given these difficulties and the fact that this book is not intended to be a detailed description of how the parties in Britain function, all I can do is give a few pointers. Of these the most important, if your group lacks active members of any of the parties, is to develop contacts with political activists.

In fact the parties are developing their policies all the time. All government decisions are effectively the policies of the ruling party. Of course there can be conflicts between government or opposition party decisions and the policies made by the formal party decision-making process. This was seen clearly, for example, during the 1974–9 Labour Government.

Nevertheless the opposition parties are forced to make policy decisions all the time; they have to respond to government initiatives whether these concern legislation, or such areas as economic policy,

Influencing Political Parties 137

public spending, defence and foreign policy. All the parties in Parliament have to make many and quick decisions as even an amendment in a standing committee will be judged as representing the party's policy.

This chapter is concerned with the more explicit and often longer-term policy formulation of the parties. In this the main parties have the following features in common:

- An annual conference which debates policy.
- A party head office with officials who work on policy.
- An elected or appointed committee at head office which is in charge of, or at least has some influence on, the party between conferences.
- A regional party structure often with both elected and appointed committees and officials.
- A series of sub-committees/study groups, etc. with responsibility for developing policy in specific areas.
- Certain powers for individual constituency parties or associations to pass resolutions and submit them to the annual conference.
- The important influence of the parliamentary leadership.
- The involvement in policy-making of MPs who are not members of the cabinet or shadow cabinet.
- The power of local constituency parties/associations to select parliamentary candidates in the light, among other things, of their individual views on policy.

All the above have some influence on policy and, for the lobbyist, indicate where pressure might, at least in theory, be applied. In practice there are complications. The Conservative Party in government makes many of its decisions on policy in cabinet or in cabinet committees and this is increasingly the case. It also relies more than the Labour Party on outside bodies for the development of ideas. Labour on the other hand has an important input from trade unions both at local and national levels. Trade unions account for most of the votes at Labour Party conferences and they have 12 of the 29 places on the National Executive Committee and, through their votes, have a major influence on another six.

Major pressure groups will have to identify the key individuals in these policy-making processes. At the present time the Labour Party has a number of policy review committees and your Labour MP or possibly the Labour Party headquarters at Walworth Road in South London will supply details of these including their composition. The policy-making committees of a party may accept submissions from certain pressure groups and it would obviously be helpful for you, the lobbying organisation, to have informal discussions with the appropriate staff person at Walworth Road and also with a member of the relevant committee. Even when these policy review committees have finished their work, my guess is that from time to time there will be other policy sub-committees which may be approached in the same way.

Remember that research staff at each party headquarters spend a great deal of time on policy and on advising their more senior parliamentary and other members. If your group has prepared a policy briefing for MPs, or published some research, do not forget to send copies to the various party head offices.

Opposition frontbenchers may sometimes have their own informal group to consult on policy matters and though these obviously have no official status they could give your group a chance to have some influence. The only advice I can offer is to establish contact with the appropriate frontbencher and ask if you can help. It might be better, in the first instance, to approach the 'junior frontbencher' rather than the shadow cabinet member; the 'junior' will have a narrower range of responsibilities and thus be more of a specialist and may also have more time for informal discussions.

An especially useful booklet is the annual *Labour Party Directory* which costs £2.50 and is obtainable from party headquarters at Walworth Road. Unfortunately it is only available for journalists. This is a mine of useful information and gives details of headquarters and regional staff, addresses and phone numbers of NEC members, MPs and peers, officers of backbench committees, details of frontbench responsibilities, names of research assistants to shadow cabinet members, MEPs, TUC General Council members, etc.

Party Conferences

All the political parties have annual conferences in September or October. Labour and the Tories normally alternate between Brighton and Blackpool. The two main parties avoid going to the same resort in the same year. Indeed all the parties avoid their conferences clashing with each other. The reason for the popularity of Brighton and Blackpool is that for years they were the only resorts which had a sufficiently large conference centre and which also provided plenty of inexpensive accommodation. Since then Bournemouth has also been used and the increasingly high costs of Brighton have caused some dissatisfaction.

At each conference there is normally a hotel where the senior politicians stay and which is a sort of 'headquarters'. Some years ago it was possible simply to walk in and mingle with cabinet ministers or shadow cabinet members. Increased concern with security has changed that easygoing atmosphere and you cannot now get very far without the conference pass issued to delegates and observers. In Blackpool conferences are at the Winter Gardens and the conference hotel is the Imperial. In Brighton the conference is held at the Brighton Centre; the headquarters hotel has varied and most recently was the Ramada while in earlier years it was the Grand.

The Labour Party conference generally starts on the Monday morning and ends at midday on Friday. Sessions are from 9.30am to 12.30pm and from 2pm to about 5pm. There is also provision for a session on the Sunday evening especially if there is a contested leadership or deputy leadership election. However, fringe meetings tend to start on Saturday evening. The Tory conference starts on the Tuesday morning and finishes on Friday afternoon. Sessions are from 9.30am to 12.30pm and from 2.30pm to 5.30pm except on the last Friday when there is a 3.30pm finish. These times are important if you are planning fringe events as discussed below.

Party conferences provide specific opportunities for pressure groups. Assembled in one town will be virtually all the people in a party with an influence on policy- and decision-making. They thus represent a 'captive' audience. So many groups are now aware of this potential, especially at Labour conferences, that there is enormous competition to get the attention of conference delegates. One often has to run a gauntlet of people giving out leaflets on the way in to conference sessions, and I sometimes wonder how many of these efforts end up unread.

Party conferences provide the opportunity for making or renewing a wide range of contacts. Even chance encounters at fringe meetings, receptions, social events or in the bars can be very productive and might not happen anywhere else. In addition conferences enable you to arrange specific events: fringe meetings; receptions; breakfasts, lunches, dinners; stalls and exhibitions; advertising in the conference guide.

Fringe Meetings

Fringe meetings are a key feature of British party conferences. They attract anything from a couple of dozen people to several hundred. The Labour conference has traditionally had most fringe meetings but there are also a large number at Tory conferences. Fringe meetings take place after the conference sessions at midday and in the early evenings. At Labour conferences there are also fringe meetings later into the evenings and also on the Saturday and Sunday before the conference begins.

At Labour conferences fringe meetings are organised either by Labour movement organisations or by outside pressure groups. If the latter they will include one or more speakers from the group plus one or more leading Labour politicians and trade unionists. The size of audience you get depends very much on the appeal of your speakers. Pressure groups tend to invite either politicians and trade unionists who have long been associated with their cause or the frontbench MPs who have a responsibility for the subject area. Remember that the big names must be booked early, otherwise some other group will invite them first.

Examples of Labour movement organisations that have in recent years held fringe meetings are:

Fabian Society

Socialist Health Association

Tribune Group of Labour MPs

Labour Common Market
   Safeguards Campaign

Labour Party Race Action Group

Labour Campaign for Criminal
   Justice

Labour Campaign for Electoral
   Reform

Labour Co-ordinating Committee

The following are examples of trade unions and pressure groups and other organisations that have arranged fringe meetings at Labour conferences:

Inner London Education Authority

Trade Union CND

CND

Coalfield Communities
   Campaign

Low Pay Unit

Centre for Local Economic
   Strategies

National Council for Carers and
   their Elderly Dependants

British Medical Association

The Howard League

War on Want/One World

Vegetarian Society

Royal National Institute for the
   Deaf

Confederation of Health Service
   Employees

Royal College of Nursing

National Union of Teachers

Association of London
   Authorities

Nuclear Energy Information Group

Age Concern

The Open University

Friends of the Earth

National Council for Civil
   Liberties

At recent Conservative conferences there have been fringe meetings by Conservative organisations such as:

Conservative Medical Society
Tory Reform Group
Selsdon Group

Bow Group
Conservative Friends of Israel
Conservative Trade Unionists

In addition there have, in recent years, been meetings by pressure groups such as:

Amnesty International
British Medical Association
British Association of Social
  Workers
National Association of
  Citizens Advice Bureaux
War on Want
National Council for Civil
  Liberties
300 Club

Child Poverty Action Group
National Viewers' and Listeners'
  Association
Water Authorities Association
Save the Children Fund
Workers' Educational
  Association
National Council for Voluntary
  Associations
Channel Tunnel Group

Some of these organisations have also had fringe meetings at Alliance conferences. At Tory conferences some of these organisations will not expect a large number of sympathetic delegates.

Each party publishes a diary of fringe meetings, although in the Labour Party at least not every organisation can secure an entry. For a fee (currently £30) you may get your fringe meeting listed provided you are an organisation affiliated to the Labour Party or otherwise approved for inclusion in the diary. This should not be difficult as any worthwhile pressure group should be all right – the need for approval is intended only to exclude anti-Labour organisations. It is very important to get your fringe meeting in the diary; the deadline for entries is July. If you miss the deadline and fail to get an entry there will almost certainly be a smaller attendance as it means finding other, and more costly, ways of publicising the event. Delegates tend to plan their days at conference with the diary in front of them so unlisted meetings may get missed out.

It is also possible to advertise meetings and other events in the conference guides or handbooks, although there are few in the Tory booklet – perhaps because of cost. The Labour version tends to have many such advertisements, and you may wish to reinforce your diary entry with an ad. In addition you could produce a leaflet – you will have to do this if you miss the deadline for diary entries – and get people to hand it out to delegates as they enter or leave the conference. The difficulty with this is that security at conferences is very tight and you will not be allowed to give out leaflets within the conference complex unless you have a pass. At Blackpool there are several exits so you will need many helpers to reach all the delegates. Leaflets are a useful aid to publicity but should only be seen as an extra.

Some organisations charge for admission to fringe meetings or have a collection, especially if they decide to serve tea and biscuits. Increasingly admission is free. Or you could have a cash bar. It is a good idea to offer refreshments if your meeting is at lunchtime or immediately after the afternoon session of conference. If charges are made at the Labour conference the typical amounts have been 50p or £1.

Each political party has conference organisers and it is essential you should contact them in the first place. The conference centre may have rooms available but these may only be bookable through the parties. In addition the conference organisers may be able to suggest other suitable rooms in nearby hotels, etc. The local tourist information offices are also a useful source regarding meeting venues, maps and inexpensive hotels. The venue is important – if your meeting is too far away from the conference hall or the main conference hotel you will get lower attendances. But the main thing is to book your room early to ensure a suitable venue. Some organisations make their bookings within weeks of the previous conference and you should certainly try to get the arrangements sorted out not too long after Christmas.

Three critical decisions are the date, time and venue. Labour conference fringe meetings tend to start on the Saturday at any time from 7pm till 10pm, and from 10.30am on the Sunday till 10pm; on the main conference days fringe meetings take place at 12.45pm or 1.00pm and in the evenings at various times from 5.15pm till 10pm. At Tory conferences fringe meetings start at 12.30pm or 1pm and in the evenings from 5.30pm till 10pm.

Whatever time and day you choose may seem wrong, as your meeting is almost certain to clash with up to a dozen others. Some organisations like their meetings to take place before the conference debates the subject but this is virtually impossible to arrange as conference agendas are not finalised till just before the conference. If this is a consideration then you should plan your event as early in the week as possible.

If your event is timed to follow a conference session it is best to be fairly close to the conference hall. Later in the evening it is probably best to be nearer the conference headquarters or, if in Brighton, the Pavilion area, which is easily accessible. It is hard to persuade delegates to search for an obscure location or go to a venue so far away that a taxi is necessary. So do consult the conference organisers of the parties, and anyone you know who has attended party conferences. It helps to have a street map of the town.

Popular venues that are well located include:

Brighton	Blackpool
Corn Exchange	Winter Gardens – Opera House
Dome Theatre	Foyer, Windsor Bar, Circle Lounge
Pavilion Theatre	Baronial Hall
Royal Albion Hotel	Imperial Hotel
Old Ship Hotel	Carlton Hotel
Norfolk Resort Hotel	Clifton Hotel
Metropole Hotel	Pembroke Hotel
Queens Hotel	Claremont Hotel
Grand Hotel	
Bedford Hotel	
West Beach Hotel	
Zap Club	
Ramada Hotel	

Receptions

Their objectives are similar to fringe meetings, and they are publicised in the same way. A reception will probably include drinks and a little food, perhaps a buffet, so it will probably take place at lunch time or in the early evening. There would normally be a speech or two but the main benefit lies in the informal contacts that can be made by members of your organisation with delegates, especially with leading politicians and trade unionists. The venues are similar to those used for the fringe meetings described above. In addition to an entry in the conference diary it may help to have invitations printed. These can be sent before the conference to a target list of delegates including, of course, MPs and peers, in order to increase the number attending. Members of your organisation can give out tickets during the earlier part of the conference. Receptions can be expensive, as even a relatively humble reception, with wine, can cost in the region of £300.

Breakfast, Lunch, Dinner

If you can afford the expense you could invite a small number of carefully targetted politicians to a meal at conference. There seems to be more wining and dining at Tory than at other conferences. However, the later part of evenings at Tory conferences is already taken up with formal social events so arranging a small dinner may prove difficult. At least one organisation has taken to arranging midnight champagne parties at Tory conferences because of a shortage of suitable slots at other times!

At the Labour conference your potential dinner guests may already have fringe meeting commitments so it is important to invite them in good time. Lunches and breakfasts may be easier but your guest may not be too keen on a meal if s/he has to make a major speech shortly afterwards. However I have been to successful breakfasts at the invitation of a pressure group. At lunch and dinner you may also be competing with buffets and receptions by the media, trade unions and possibly dinners given by embassies.

Incidentally, the reservations I expressed earlier in the book about wining and dining MPs apply less at conferences but there is still no need for a relatively poor pressure group to seem extravagant. Remember, though, that you can invite MPs and peers throughout the year, whereas conferences give the opportunity of contacting a wider range of politically active delegates.

Stalls and Exhibitions

At many conferences there are now facilities for groups and organisations to book stalls in an exhibition area. Although this costs money it gives you an opportunity to publicise your organisation, handing out or selling publications and other items, and to have useful informal chats. The cost may be as high as £4,000 and you may have to pay extra for exhibitors' passes. There will also be the cost of arranging a display and increasingly use is being made of videos. Remember though that party conferences are frenetic events and only some of the delegates will find time to browse among exhibition stalls. The following organisations are among those that have taken stalls at recent Labour conferences:

Greenpeace
Compassion in World Farming
Nirex
National Union of Students
Coalfields Communities Campaign
Voluntary Service Overseas
National Union of Teachers
Electricity Supply Industry
British Airways
British Telecom

Pre-School Playgroups
　Association
Chile Solidarity Campaign
Campaign for Nuclear
　Disarmament
Terence Higgins Trust
The Anti-Apartheid Movement
War on Want
Nicaragua Solidarity Campaign
Eurotunnel
Royal College of Nursing

In recent years the following have, among others, had stalls at Tory conferences:

Johnson Mathey	Halifax Building Society
Royal College of Nursing	Nirex
British Longwall Mining Association	Glass Manufacturers' Federation
Granada TV	CEGB

It can be quite expensive to rent a stall, arrange displays and have enough people present for the best part of a week. However, if you want to pursue this then contact the offices of the political parties to make the necessary arrangements.

Advertising in the Conference Guide/Handbook

The conference guides or handbooks are a useful (though possibly expensive) advertising medium for your fringe meeting or reception. The Labour guide has more advertisements for fringe meetings than the Tory handbook, which tends to have more commercial advertisers such as property companies, estate agents, financial institutions. Ads in the Labour guide are often placed by trade unions, local authorities and the organisations holding fringe events.

Other Conferences

A number of other conferences may be of interest to the lobbyist. The Labour Party usually has a two-day local government conference at the end of January/beginning of February, a women's conference in June and a one- or two-day conference in each region. These occasions provide more limited opportunities than the annual conference but there are some fringe meetings. Indeed the Labour Local Government Conference is a particularly successful event with quite a number of well-attended fringe meetings. All trade unions, and the TUC, have an annual or biennial conference with fringe meetings and many have exhibition stalls as well.

The TUC's *Congress Guide* contains many advertisers and also gives details of exhibitors. Recently the latter have included:

Allied Anglo Financial Services Ltd	Eurotunnel
	GCHQ trade unions
Anti-Apartheid	Guide Dogs for the Blind
British Airways	Inverness District Council

British Nuclear Fuels plc   NACRO
CEGB   The Open University
Charities Aid Foundation   Nirex
Dr Barnardo's   Unity Trust plc

Check with the organisations themselves about the precise arrangements. I have for example taken part in an NCCL fringe meeting at the TUC on the subject of public order legislation and trade union rights. I have also spoken at fringe meetings at SCPS (now NUCAPS) and COHSE conferences.

The Tory Party also has other conferences: a two-day women's conference in June, a one-day local government conference in March and two-day regional conferences in Scotland and Wales

Action Check List
1. Contact the appropriate political party in good time, perhaps in December.
2. Decide on date, time and place of event.
3. Refreshments, tea, wine.
4. Free or collection or admission charge, if so how much?
5. Book speakers.
6. Book a room for the event, well in advance, say in December.
7. Arrange entry in conference guide or place advertisement in it.
8. For small events decide on your target guest list.
9. Can you afford an exhibition stall?
10. Book hotel/bed & breakfast/flat accommodation in good time, before Easter.
11. Check with party headquarters about arrangements for passes.
12. Exhibition layout and staffing; video?
13. Send copies of briefing documents, etc. to party headquarters.

10

The House of Lords

The House of Lords consists of some 1,200 members, of whom many attend rarely and some never. Of the total, about 800 are hereditary while approximately 350 are appointed as life peers; some of the most active life peers are ex-MPs and these number about 70. There are also 26 bishops of the Church of England, and 28 law lords. In addition 15 hereditary peers have given up their titles for their own lifetimes – the best known of them is Tony Benn: his efforts some years ago made this renunciation possible.

Peers do not get a salary, unless they are ministers, but are paid a daily attendance allowance for 'signing in': currently (1988) this is £57 per attendance for overnight accommodation away from the main residence, plus £21 for subsistence, plus £22 for research and secretarial assistance. Unlike the Commons they do not get free postage for their letters so if you write to a peer it is best to enclose a stamped addressed envelope. However like the Commons they are allowed to make telephone calls free of charge from Westminster to anywhere in the United Kingdom.

There are currently 21 government ministers in the Lords, including whips, most of whom also speak for departments. This compares with 84 ministers, including whips, in the Commons, plus 41 PPSs.

The House of Lords sits at 2.30pm on some Mondays and on Tuesdays and Wednesdays. On Thursdays there is a slightly later start at 3pm. Later in the session, especially after Easter, the House also sits on Fridays at 11am. The Lords is altogether a more relaxed place than the Commons. The concept of a filibustering speech is rare and done much more gently than in the Commons; there is no timetable or guillotine. Sittings quite often last till 10pm or later but rarely after midnight and there are virtually no all-night debates.

While some peers regard themselves as active and committed politicians, others have a different attitude. The latter may drop in to the Lords during the afternoon but tend to leave after 7pm or 7.30pm. So it is important to ensure votes take place earlier in the day to achieve a larger turnout.

It is difficult to say how many peers are active in the Lords. Estimates suggest that of the total of 1,200 some 250 to 300 attend at least half the daily sittings. The Lords sits about 145 days a year (compared with around 175 for the Commons). Altogether it is estimated that 700 Lords attend in the course of a session but we do not know how many simply go in to 'sign on' or use the facilities and do not take part in the work. In 1988 there was much controversy about clause 28 of the 1987 Local Government Bill which sought to ban the promotion of homosexuality. The Lords upheld this clause by a vote of 202 to 122; this was regarded as an exceptionally large turnout.

Office space is even more limited than in the Commons. While ministers get their own offices, as do the leaders of the Labour and Liberal parties and the opposition chief whip, opposition frontbenchers merely have desks with their own phones, in a room that looks a bit like a typing pool.

There is a clear Conservative majority in the Lords but this is less marked if one disregards the inactive peers. From time to time attempts are made to assess how many active peers there are. The most recent was the Report of the Group on the Working of the House and covered the 1987/88 session. Active peers were defined as those who had attended the House, though they had not necessarily spoken, on at least one third of possible sitting days. Table 10.1 gives the breakdown.

Table 10.1 Party Allegiances of Active Peers

Party	Total	H	C
Conservative	168	101	67
Labour	88	7	81
Liberal	27	12	15
SDP	24	7	17
Independent/crossbencher	73	36	37
Total	380	163	217

Note: H = hereditary; C = created, although it also includes peers who were themselves made hereditary peers as opposed to inheriting their titles.

The majority of the Conservatives are hereditary peers while most Labour peers are life peers. About 120 peers take the Labour whip, although some of them are too old to attend frequently, if at all. Most peers are appointed in the Birthday or New Year's Honours Lists. The

Labour Party decided some years ago not to put names forward for any honours, so the only way new Labour peers can be created is through the less frequent 'working peers' list. As a result the number of active Labour peers is declining.

It is worth adding that the Lords have not behaved as a tame 'rubber stamp' for the Thatcher Government. Indeed since 1979 the Lords have defeated the government on 111 occasions though some of these defeats involved backbench Tories as well as opposition peers and may have been on relatively minor matters. In theory the government could have reversed the results of these Lords rebellions with its more committed majority in the Commons; in practice, either for lack of parliamentary time or to avoid further political embarrassment, the Tories have sometimes let their Lords defeats stand. Some of the most interesting occasions occurred during the debates on the proposals to abolish the Greater London Council and the Inner London Education Authority, a period which has many lessons for the lobbyist. The government quite often brings forward concessions in the Lords to meet the wishes of important interest groups there.

Some members of the Lords are wealthy while others depend on pensions or even on their attendance allowances. The average age is 66. The majority went to public schools. About 66 are women and indeed because women comprise a larger proportion of active peers they are proportionately better represented in the Lords than in the Commons. Many of these women peers are very influential. It has been suggested that some women prefer the less conflict-ridden atmosphere of the Lords to the more 'macho' Commons.

As in the Commons the Lords has a system of whips. However the discipline is much more relaxed and the whips have to work hard to get good attendances. It is mainly those who have or who aspire to frontbench responsibilities who are most likely to vote on party lines. Neither side can really expect to pull out all the stops more than a few times every session. The Tories have a very sophisticated whip with a rare use of three liners (the last that I could discover was at the time of GLC abolition), but ways of grading the importance of two liners.

In any case a large number of peers do not take any party whip. For those who do, voting against their party line is commoner and attracts less attention than in the Commons, but it is still a relatively rare occurrence. In the last resort there are virtually no sanctions that the parties can adopt against individual peers who fail to vote as requested. After all peers cannot be removed either by their parties or by the electorate and thus have an even more secure tenure than, say, members of the Supreme Soviet.

All in all the politics in the Lords are more relaxed than in the Commons and certainly couched in more polite language. Even the division lobbies have different names: compared to the Commons 'Aye' and 'Noe' lobbies, the Lords vote 'Content' or 'Not Content'.

All legislation has to pass through both Houses; however, the Lords have more limited powers regarding finance. Although the Finance Bill, for example, comes before the Lords, it is passed quickly without amendments. On other bills the Lords do not usually vote against second readings.

In theory, the powers of both Houses are similar except when there is a conflict between them. Then the Commons have the power to override the Lords subject to a year's delay. In practice, the Lords are reluctant to force a conflict to this point: formally the constraints on the power of the Lords are relatively slight. The real limits are set down by conventions which are themselves not that precise. The more astute peers realise their weakness compared to an elected chamber. There is also the Labour Party threat to abolish them.

In practice the doctrine has evolved that the Lords exists mainly as a revising chamber; where the government brings in legislation which was in its election manifesto then the Lords feel they have no right to reject it. Many peers would also be reluctant to oppose the principle of government proposals even where these were not in the election manifesto.

The subjects that interest the Lords are not necessarily the same as those that command the attention of the Commons or the country at large. For example, debates on farming, the countryside and hunting attract Lords who otherwise seldom attend. Critical votes on the poll tax also attracted peers who otherwise seldom bothered to attend the Lords though this may have been the result of particular pressure from the whips.

Similarities to the Commons

Broadly speaking the procedure in the Lords is similar to that of the Commons. There are opportunities to ask oral and written questions, public and private bills follow approximately the same stages and they deal with statutory instruments as in the Commons. Identical government statements are often made in both Houses and there are also opportunities for general debates and the equivalent of Commons adjournment debates. In fact the procedures of the House of Lords are as complicated as those of the Commons and this chapter merely covers them in brief summary, sufficient for the purpose of the serious pressure group or lobbyist.

Lords who take the party whip attend party meetings along with their MP colleagues, they take part in all-party groups and have the same rights as MPs when writing to ministers or seeking meetings with them. Strictly speaking peers are 'members of Parliament' just as much as members of the Commons but it seems more helpful in this book to distinguish between MPs (House of Commons) and Lords or peers (House of Lords).

Differences from the Commons

Nevertheless there are differences between the two Houses and between the rights and powers of the respective members which are important for the lobbyist to know. A backbench peer has more opportunities to raise an issue or initiate a debate than his or her counterpart in the Commons. The House of Lords has more time and fewer active members who for electoral or other reasons want to attract attention.

Another important difference concerns the position and role of the Lord Chancellor in presiding over debates. He, unlike the Commons Speaker, has no power to discipline debate and keep order. In the Commons MPs address the Speaker while in the Lords peers address each other. This influences the conduct of debates but, more importantly, it affects legislative procedure. There is no selection of amendments so, at least in theory, every one that is tabled can be debated. In addition the arrangement of amendments in groups with a similar or related subject is purely voluntary and can be changed by a peer who moves one of them. Indeed the groupings are drawn up by the government whips' office and not by the clerks.

Questions

Questions in the Lords are not addressed to particular ministers but to the government as a whole. This is because there are relatively few ministers in the Lords and therefore, although they have specific responsibilities in their departments, they have to deal with wider areas when on the front bench. There is no equivalent to the Commons order of questions and a mixture of departmental questions can be taken on the same day. Opposition frontbenchers are prominent in asking supplementaries and are likely to welcome briefings from pressure groups.

The Lords equivalent of the oral question is the starred question. There can be four of these a day: each gives the chance of a mini-debate normally lasting between 5 and 10 minutes. Questions and especially answers and supplementaries are longer than in the Commons. Peers apply to the minute room to get a starred question and may have to wait a week or longer, on a first come first served basis, till their turn comes up, so there is a form of rationing. A peer is limited to two starred questions on any one day and three on the order paper at any one time.

Here are some recent examples of starred questions:

To ask Her Majesty's Government what progress has been made in the introduction of the national breast cancer screening programme. (Baroness Sharples).

To ask Her Majesty's Government what is the present total number of London Regional Transport employees and what was the corresponding number on 1 December 1984. (Lord Jay)

To ask Her Majesty's Government whether they have established any link between alcohol consumption and crowd violence at soccer matches; and, if so, what effects they believe the launching of own-brands of lager by soccer clubs is likely to have. (Baroness Masham of Ilton)

The following are examples of topics raised as starred questions:

Haemophiliacs: AIDS infection
County Courts: legal advice
Consumer protection: code of
  practice
Prisoners' wives: travel
  arrangements
Iran/Iraq conflict
Electricity lines: underground
  replacement
Air transport: EC voting system
Children: special health needs
Chlorofluorocarbons
Weapons reduction: summit
  meeting
Higher education funding
Basic science research: funding
Health service: Birmingham
EC food surpluses: distribution
Mental health: nursing staff levels
Health authority consultation:
  closures
East Cheshire Hospice: finance

In addition there is the possibility of a short debate on an unstarred question at the end of business on a Wednesday. This can be a much longer debate than a Commons adjournment with a number of peers contributing. For example an unstarred question on salmon conservation lasted well over two hours and one asking for the establishment of a press standards council lasted nearly two hours. Peers apply to the minute room for such debates but must negotiate the time with government whips so, in practice, most just go straight to the government whips to make the arrangement. The procedure for ordinary written questions is as in the Commons though relatively few are asked, on some days as few as two or three, and their style is similar to that in the Commons.

Legislation

Like the Commons, the Lords have second reading debates on legislation. There is never a division against the basic motion that 'the bill be now read a second time' although there may be a vote on a reasoned amendment. The committee stages are invariably taken on the floor of the House. Following the committee stage a bill in the Lords then has a report stage as in the Commons, followed by the third reading. Unlike the Commons, amendments can also be introduced at the third reading.

Bills can sometimes start their passage through Parliament in the Lords. Normally less controversial legislation starts in the upper house. This means that the Lords often have to return after the long recess earlier in October than the Commons to dispose of bills that reached them late in the session.

Unlike the Commons the timing of votes is critical. Many peers are willing to be present during the late afternoon and early evening, at which point they leave. This seems to affect the opposition more than the government, perhaps because of differences in the social composition. As a result, the opposition achieves its maximum vote between 3pm and about 5.30pm. During committee and report stage debates the Lords break for dinner at about 7 or 7.30pm and votes after will achieve much less. This is the single most important fact about lobbying the Lords on legislation. The result is that a superb speech may be counterproductive if its effect is to delay the vote. Timetabling and drafting amendments so that the key issues are taken early in the day are therefore points of critical importance.

The rules about amendments to bills in the Lords are much less strict than in the Commons. It is however important to avoid the impression that an amendment is a wrecking amendment – one that is intended to destroy the basis of the legislation – because that would give rise to constitutional objections about the supremacy of the Commons.

One opportunity for the lobbyist is by means of an all-party meeting held either before or immediately after second reading. Such a meeting is sponsored by a peer and gives the lobbyist the opportunity to argue for certain possible amendments. An alternative approach is to make use of one of the established all-party groups (whose members are both MPs and peers), like those concerned with disablement or children.

Less time is allocated to report stage than to committee stage; amendments should not be identical to those that were moved in committee. Unlike the Commons the third reading is quite distinct from report, with a different day; again, unlike the Commons, amendments are possible at third reading. Finally there is another stage sometimes called 'passing' or 'the bill do now pass', which gives an opportunity of a brief debate on the bill as a whole – similar to a Commons third reading. In the case of bills that started in the Lords there may also be a stage of considering Commons amendments; while this provides a further though limited opportunity for lobbyists the Lords will, for constitutional reasons, give way to the Commons.

Peers can also introduce private members' bills. It is easier than in the Commons to get them debated as there is less competition to do so. They are a good means of raising an issue but if they are passed in the Lords they have very little chance of becoming law as they have to join the Friday 'queue' for debating time in the Commons – in competition with private members' bills that started in the Lower House.

Other Debates

A number of other opportunities exist for the opposition and for individual peers to initiate debates. In the earlier part of the session Wednesdays are generally given over to debates. In a sense these are the equivalent of opposition days in the Commons, though some are also used to provide opportunities for backbenchers. These debates, which are limited to five hours, may be split into two separate topics. There are also what are called 'short debates' which take place once a month before Whitsun. Each lasts two and a half hours and there is a ballot three to four weeks ahead.

Government Statements

Government statements and private notice questions are repeated by agreement with the whips but in practice not all come before the Lords. It is rare for a peer to ask for a PNQ. Statements (and PNQs) give Lords the same opportunities as the Commons.

Select Committees

Unlike the Commons the Lords make less use of select committees to investigate departmental issues. There are a number of select committees which deal with internal matters such as staff and procedure. (An important select committee which examines European legislation is described below.) From time to time select committees are established specifically to investigate particular issues. For example in recent years Lords select committees have been established to investigate unemployment, overseas trade, and science and technology. In practice the last mentioned now seems to be permanent; it has recently been carrying out two separate investigations, into space policy and medical research.

These committees are similar to the Commons departmental committees: they interview witnesses, receive written evidence, and then produce a report with recommendations. The government then publishes a response. The Lords always find time to debate these reports.

The Select Committee on European Legislation

This committee, known as the European Communities Committee, is very important. Each House has a select committee which scrutinises European legislative proposals. Of the two the Lords committee is probably of greater importance because it has more time and therefore can go into issues more thoroughly and publish detailed reports.

Chapter 11 describes the European Commission and how it influences legislation. Before a draft regulation or directive is agreed by the Council of Ministers it is usually examined by both the Commons and Lords select committees. If the proposed laws are likely to be significant the select committee(s) can recommend they should be debated. In practice the government will not agree to a draft regulation or directive at the Council of Ministers if it is due to be debated in the Lords or the Commons. The Lords select committee has five sub-committees each responsible for specific subjects:

A – Finance, trade and industry, external relations
B – Energy, transport and technology
C – Social and consumer affairs
D – Agriculture and food
E – Law and institutions
F – Environment

The committee and the sub-committees can call witnesses and receive written evidence on any aspect of the legislative proposals.

Getting into Debates

The public gallery in the Lords is smaller than that of the Commons though the demand for it is smaller. To be on the safe side ask a peer in advance. However in practice it is often easier to get into the public gallery of the Lords than the Commons, although for major occasions the place can be packed. There are also a limited number of seats on the floor level, technically 'below the bar', for advisers. These work the same way as the undergallery in the Commons, in that a person sitting there can be consulted by peers during debates, especially in relation to committee and report stage amendments. You can also attend select committee meetings as in the Commons. The Lords committees meet on the same first floor committeee corridor as Commons committees but at the other (Lords) end.

The House of Lords as the Highest Court of Appeal

This does not concern the lobbyist. Five or sometimes seven law lords hear cases only on matters of public importance and where specific points of law rather than facts are at issue.

How to Contact Members

Lords do not represent anyone, are not accountable and do not need to respond to requests from lobbyists. Nevertheless some of them will undoubtedly want to help. Several points should be kept in mind when you approach them:

1. Targetting the right Lords is doubly important. Their interests can be identified from Hansard speeches and questions, press reports, involvements with charities, voluntary groups, etc. Voting lists from the Lords Hansard can be a particularly useful source of information, not just as regards attitudes to specific issues but also as an indicator of interest. Peers who rarely or never vote will probably be a poor bet for the lobbyist. They are best ignored unless you have some personal contacts with them. As in the Commons there are some members who simply carry more weight and influence, though this quality is probably harder for outsiders to define and recognise than in the Lower House.
2. Ask a friendly peer for advice about who to approach.
3. Former MPs are probably worth particular attention as their previous interests will be easier to discover from their Commons days. In addition they are likely to be younger. Some will have

retained links with their previous constituencies and will be more likely to be interested in and willing to raise local issues. Indeed some peers have put their former constituencies in their titles, e.g. Lord Jay of Battersea, Lord Jenkins of Putney, Lord Graham of Edmonton and Lord Ripon of Hexham. Against this it may be the case that some ex-MPs (not the ones mentioned above), may simply carry less weight and influence than other peers.

4. In any case it helps to know where peers live as they can probably be approached more easily and are likely to be easier to persuade to take up issues on behalf of local pressure groups.

5. Opposition frontbenchers are an especially good prospect for national issues. They are likely to have to devote a great deal of time to their responsibilities and will need advice and briefings regarding debates, amendments to bills, etc. Their names are in the newspapers when first appointed, or in *Vacher's Guide*. You can also phone the Lords information office on 01-219 3107.

6. Some peers have a national reputation because of their concern for specific issues, for example Lord Longford on penal reform, Lord Avebury on human rights, Lord Jenkins on nuclear disarmament and the arts, Lord Ennals on health, Lord Taylor and Baroness Blackstone on education, Baroness Ewart Biggs on Northern Ireland.

7. Pay particular attention to the announcement of the appointment of new peers. They will probably be younger and more willing to be active.

8. Peers do not have their own phone numbers in the Lords unless they are frontbenchers. Provided they are active peers you can leave a message on 01-219 5353; otherwise it may be best to contact them at home if you can discover their address, from *Who's Who, Debrett's* or *Dod's Parliamentary Companion*.

9. Note that a few peers are retained as consultants, etc. For example Lord Graham of Edmonton, now an opposition frontbencher and formerly Ted Graham, MP for Edmonton, acts as parliamentary adviser to the Prison Officers' Association and is able to make good use of his previous Commons experience and his contacts among MPs.

10. Write to active peers at the Lords; for example: Lord Graham of Edmonton, House of Lords, London, SW1A 0PW.

11. Do not write to a peer at the Lords unless the House is sitting and you are certain s/he is a frequent attender and has either a desk or a pigeon hole for letters at the Lords. The list of those who can be written to at Westminster is obtainable from Mr Scott's office,

House of Lords, London, SW1A 0PW, tel 01-219 5566. It comprises over 150 peers. There is not the same restriction as in the Commons about being able to hand deliver only two unstamped letters for MPs. The Lords will accept unstamped letters for the peers on Mr Scott's list. Take them to the peers' lobby which is off the central lobby.

12. For peers not on Mr Scott's list or during recesses, write to their home addresses, not to the Lords. The Lords do not have as organised a system for forwarding mail as the Commons, and your letter could take some time to reach its addressee. As regards bulk mail other than to Mr Scott's list when the House is sitting, the assistant superintendent's guidance says:

Post Office regulations require franked mail requiring re-direction to be posted within 24 hours of delivery. It is not possible to do this in the House of Lords for bulk mail deliveries such as your firm has just addressed to the House of Lords.

To ensure delivery, you are requested *not* to send bulk mail addressed to peers at the House of Lords, but instead to post them to peers' private addresses which can readily be obtained from *Who's Who* and *Debretts'*.

Uses for Pressure Groups

Handled properly, the Lords are an important and fruitful area for the lobbyist. There are a number of reasons why the Lords are worthwhile as a target:

1. On the whole, pressure groups have less direct involvement with the Lords than with the Commons. As peers don't have constituents, don't have to face elections or even re-selection some of them may be willing to give more time to being lobbied.
2. As party loyalties are less rigid it may be easier to persuade a peer to break the whip.
3. The peers without party allegiances may be more willing to support 'lost' causes.
4. The Lords procedures, and the less competitive atmosphere, give individual peers better opportunities to raise issues.
5. Above all, you can win there!

Against these advantages there are are number of difficulties. As they don't get a salary some peers are in full-time employment and will go to the chamber only infrequently. Others may simply refuse to be involved and, for the reasons already discussed, are not vulnerable to pressure or influence, are too old, not interested in politics, or just unavailable. Nevertheless it is still well worth while making the attempt.

Action Check List

1. Study the Lords Hansard.
2. Identify ex-MPs, especially new appointments to the Lords.
3. Opposition frontbenchers are an especially good prospect.
4. Peers have similar powers to MPs regarding writing to ministers, going to see them, being active in all-party groups, approaching foreign embassies, etc.
5. For local pressure groups try to discover if any suitable peers live in the area.
6. Do not waste time and money writing to inactive peers.
7. Once you have identified interested peers they can be involved in many of the same ways as MPs and may have more time.
8. In the case of legislation make use of existing all-party groups or get a sympathetic peer to call an all-party meeting at which your group can provide a briefing on a bill.
9. Remember that peers get free phone calls but not free post. So enclose a stamped addressed envelope for reply to your letters, or give your day and evening phone numbers.
10. Some peers are not wealthy, so offer to meet their travel expenses if you invite them to a meeting or event.

11

The European Parliament and Other International Bodies

It is 15 years since the United Kingdom joined the European Community (EC) which now comprises 12 countries: Belgium, Denmark, France, Germany, Greece, Ireland, Italy, Luxembourg, Netherlands, Portugal, Spain and the UK. The EC is now hoping to establish a single internal market wholly free of frontier controls by 1992. Some 80 other countries – mainly in the developing world – are also linked to the EC by trade (and in some cases aid) agreements.

Anyone concerned with lobbying should know something about the workings of the EC and the role of the European Parliament. Let me stress at the outset that lobbying Members of the European Parliament (MEPs) should normally be in addition to action in the UK and not a substitute for it. However, I can think of at least three exceptions to this: first, where there is a campaign being conducted simultaneously in many or all EC countries on human rights for example; secondly when there is a specific EC issue involved; and thirdly, during election campaigns for the European Parliament.

Before I discuss how to lobby MEPs I want to consider certain wider aspects of decision-making in the EC.

Most people in Britain have only a vague understanding of the EC. British news coverage of it tends to be mainly concerned with the cost of agricultural support (which is a massive 70 per cent of the EC budget), or with the consequential butter mountains and wine lakes which are paid for by European taxpayers. Apart from the tax burden the EC may appear to have little bearing on people's lives, work or leisure. Yet at intervals the EC threatens to make decisions which arouse deep feelings: there is at present concern that VAT harmonisation could result, despite the Prime Minister's denials, in VAT on books, newspapers and even food!

On a more positive note, the EC laws have obliged the British authorities to observe stricter environmental controls (including drinking water standards and cleaner beaches) and greater equality in employment for men and women.

The European Community has now become the biggest trading bloc in the world, with 320 million inhabitants. It is involved in regional

160

development, nuclear research, transport within and between nations, economic planning, job training, foreign aid, worldwide human rights, the environment, agriculture, equal rights, and other important aspects of life in Western Europe. The potential for campaigning is clear. True, the EC is cumbersome, slow moving, bureaucratic and difficult to understand. But like it or not, it is there and it is growing.

Big business and the multinationals have realised the importance of the EC and lobby it extensively and expensively. If they find it useful it is all the more obvious that other campaigning groups and trade unions should also make their views felt.

Where the Power Lies

We need to understand the responsibilities and powers of: the Council of Ministers; the commission and the commissioners; the European Parliament.

These institutions should not be confused with the Council of Europe, which is described briefly at the end of this chapter. Remember also the differences between the European Court of Human Rights in Strasbourg, described later, and the European Community Court of Justice in Luxembourg. The EC Court of Justice is the supreme court in all matters relating to EC law which, in relevant fields, takes precedence over national law. Strictly speaking the EC Court of Justice is not of direct concern to lobbyists.

The Council of Ministers

This is the major decision-making body. Each member state holds the presidency of the community for six months in rotation. There are regular meetings of heads of government (usually twice a year) and of departmental ministers. Since 1974 the heads of government (plus the President of France) have met two or three times a year as the European Council, to agree broad lines of common policy.

The foreign ministers are the senior group of departmental ministers, usually meeting at least monthly. In addition there are parallel meetings of ministers of member states covering finance, transport, the environment, agriculture, trade and industry, energy, tourism, cultural affairs, health, etc. These take place frequently: the agriculture ministers, for example, sometimes meet twice a month, often on the perennial topic of farm surpluses and prices. These ministerial meetings are crucial: key decisions are made in them, for in the last resort the council acts as the government of the community. If the lobbyist wishes to have an influence s/he must exert pressure at a national level as the member governments determine the points of view of their ministers.

The European Commission and the Commissioners

The commission is the executive body in charge of the day-to-day running of the community. It is responsible for drafting proposals for consideration by the council and the parliament. Once agreement is reached the commission ensures that the decisions are implemented, if necessary by taking a national government or other body before the EC Court of Justice. It also produces the first draft of the annual budget, which must be approved both by the council and the parliament.

The European Commission is the civil service of the EC; it has rather more power than the British civil service to initiate matters and formulate policy without the direct guidance of politicians. How does the commission make decisions? It has certain powers delegated to it directly under the treaties and by the council and can make decisions without further reference to anybody. It can for example allocate social or regional grants and fine companies it considers to have violated competition rules.

More important are its powers to propose regulations and directives, the basis of community law. These must be referred to the Council of Ministers and the European Parliament. There is also a consultative stage within the British Parliament, comprising a select committee in each House. (See Chapter 6 for Commons Select Committee and Chapter 10 for the Lords Select Committee.)

Proposals by the commission are sent both to the council (and so on to the 12 national governments) and then to the parliament. There it is usually discussed in detail by a committee. A plenary session of the parliament then considers the committee's report and draft resolution. These are sent to the commission and the Council of Ministers. The parliament has the right to suggest amendments and also, in certain circumstances, to reject them. Following a complicated consultation procedure and majority votes in the parliament it could become community policy, either as a regulation (which is directly enforceable throughout the EC) or as a directive (which requires each national parliament to pass implementing legislation).

Individuals and organisations can have an impact on this process only if they are aware of the existence of draft proposals. Generally these come into the public domain when presented to the parliament. British media coverage of the EC is poor and often limited to what can be made to sound dramatic although the *Financial Times* and the *Independent* give EC matters reasonable attention. Otherwise it is necessary to keep in touch with the European Commission offices in London, Edinburgh, Cardiff and Belfast, to check if your interest or campaign has a European angle. You could also contact the European Parliament's London office or your local MEP. (See p. 228 for addresses and phone numbers.)

In practice there is very little coordinated lobbying across the EC, except on overseas aid and on certain environmental (green) issues, or when trade unions work together through the European Trade Union Confederation (ETUC), or through the Union of Industries of the European Community (UNICE).

Many international organisations and companies keep permanent offices in Brussels to monitor the EC. The CBI has a Euro-office, as do the trade unions and farmers' organisations. Environmental groups, consumers' organisations and development groups have appointed representatives to liaise with the EC. In the field of humanitarian affairs there are also a few permanent representatives, such as the Quaker Council for European Affairs, Joint Task Force on Development Issues, and the Ecumenical Commission for Church and Society in the European Community. In 1984 Amnesty International appointed a staff member to liaise between the EC and Amnesty offices in Europe.

The commission itself comprises 17 commissioners who are appointed by the member states, the larger ones nominating two each and the smaller ones one each. Every commissioner has specific responsibilities, such as social affairs, agriculture, transport, the internal market, external relations. Not only are the commissioners responsible for the work of their departments but they are also answerable to the European Parliament; they can also be dismissed by the parliament though this has never happened. For instance, the commissioners attend the parliament's sittings in Strasbourg, answer oral questions there and, on invitation, appear before parliamentary committees to explain or justify draft proposals.

The commissioners are a curious combination of the politician and the official. They are all political appointments by the member states and hold office for a four-year renewable term. They are acknowledged to be party politicians; in 1983 the present Tory Government appointed Stanley Clinton Davis, formerly a Labour MP and minister, to be a commissioner. His responsibilities are: environment, nuclear safety and transport. The other British commissioner is a Conservative, Lord Cockfield, formerly a minister at the Department of Trade and Industry and responsible for the internal market, customs union service, taxation and financial institutions.

There is no reason why pressure groups should not let their views be known directly to the commissioners. It obviously makes most sense to approach the British commissioners but unless you are from a major and significant pressure group taking part in a campaign coordinated across several European countries I do not advise contacting commissioners from other countries. Indeed I would only approach the British commissioners sparingly. It is far better to approach them through an MEP, as explained below.

As all commissioners are political appointments they are likely to have particularly good links with one of the political groups. It therefore makes sense, if possible, to approach a commissioner through an MEP of his own political persuasion: a left-wing Labour MEP, for example, might not be the best person to persuade Lord Cockfield.

The European Parliament and MEPs

The Parliament comprises 518 members. In 1979 it was directly elected for the first time, in 1984 the second elections were held and the next are due in 1989. Britain sends 81 MEPs to the Parliament, 66 from England, 8 from Scotland, 4 from Wales and 3 from Northern Ireland. The Socialist Group is the largest political group, but it does not have an overall majority. The European People's Party is broadly Christian Democratic in outlook. British Conservative MEPs set up their own group called the European Democrats, now with Spanish and Danish members. The following are the various party groups (January 1988) together with their strength:

Socialists	172 (includes 32 Labour and one SDLP)
European People's Party	118
European Democrats	63 (includes 45 Conservatives)
Communists and allies	46
Liberal and Democratic Reformists	42
European Alliance for Renewal and Democracy	34 (includes one SNP)
Rainbow Group (Greens)	20
European Right (includes Fascists)	16 (includes one Official Ulster Unionist)
Independents	7 (includes one Democratic Ulster Unionist)

The European Parliament is obviously less powerful than the Council of Ministers and the commission. Its role has traditionally been largely consultative and advisory although it has some power over the budget. The parliament may debate all matters relating to the work of the community and also many outside (recent examples include human rights in Chile, South Africa and Poland).

However the Single European Act of 1986 (SEA) has increased the parliament's powers. Draft regulations or directives on any matter related to the completion of the internal market now have both first and second readings in the parliament. At the first reading amendments can be suggested which the council and commission may incorporate. At the second reading the parliament can approve, amend or reject; to override an amendment or rejection requires a unanimous decision by the council. This right is potentially important as it gives, for example, the EP the power to threaten to delay legislation unless the council is willing to compromise. It is too early to give a definitive judgement on this procedure. Suffice it to say that the parliament has been given some powers, but that the procedure has become more complicated!

As far as the budget is concerned, the parliament has both positive and negative powers. It can make amendments to the draft budget originally drawn up by the commission and the council. It can also reject the budget entirely, which it has done twice since 1979 – which leaves the whole community budget in disarray for some weeks or months until a compromise is reached. In contrast the EP has only a limited say over what is called 'obligatory expenditure', that is, spending on policies provided for in the founding treaties, which includes the common agricultural policy. So when the farm ministers agree a certain level of prices there is little the parliament (or the commission) can do about it except protest.

It has 18 committees most of which meet monthly for two or three days in Brussels:

1. Political affairs
2. Agriculture
3. Budgets
4. Economic and monetary affairs
5. Energy and research
6. External economic relations
7. Legal affairs
8. Social affairs and employment
9. Regional policy and regional planning
10. Transport
11. Environment, public health and consumer protection

12. Youth, culture, education and sport
13. Development and cooperation
14. Budgetary control
15. Rules of procedure and petitions
16. International affairs
17. Women's rights
18. Verification of credentials

This chapter deals mainly with how to lobby MEPs, as they are the only politicians we elect directly to represent us in Europe. The basic principles are the same as for MPs but it is useful to understand something of how MEPs operate in order to improve your lobbying effectiveness. The European Parliament meets in plenary session in Strasbourg, while its committees usually meet in Brussels. It is difficult for MEPs to work effectively while living out of a suitcase and moving around so much. The facilities, allowances and office space are better than in the House of Commons but the working conditions are far from ideal. MEPs receive the same salaries as MPs of their own country.

A visitor to Strasbourg will notice the parliament building full of tin boxes in which officials transport papers and documents between Brussels, Luxembourg and Strasbourg. It is obviously inefficient operating from different cities; still, it is an improvement on what used to be. At least plenary sessions are no longer held in Luxembourg. However the benefits to Strasbourg in having the EP meet there are obvious, so it is not surprising that there are vested interests in maintaining the location.

The full parliament meets for five days, Monday to Friday, each month except August, but twice in October; these meetings are usually during the second or third weeks of the month. To see the timetable of relevant dates contact the European Parliament offices as indicated above. These plenary meetings are the main occasions when all MEPs from the 12 countries meet together and are easily accessible, both to each other and to the public.

As we shall see later, the European Parliament operates through political groups. These are important as it is mainly through them that an individual MEP can make the most impact. Both the political groups and committees normally meet in Brussels and although MEPs may arrive around noon and leave the following morning, there are opportunities to lobby them.

There are a great many documents associated with the work of the European Parliament. Unfortunately the Hansard of the parliament, often referred to as the supplement to the official journal, comes out rather late, because it has to be translated into all the EC languages. A record of decisions reached, called 'Texts adopted by the European Parliament', comes out sooner. For more information contact the European Parliament office in London; you will find them most helpful.

How to Contact an MEP

Each MEP from Great Britain represents an area consisting of about eight or nine Westminster parliamentary constituencies and half a million people. As they all spend a lot of time travelling between Strasbourg, Brussels and their own areas it is often difficult to contact them at short notice but most maintain an office with an assistant in their constituencies.

Letters

The European Parliament Information Office at 2 Queen Anne's Gate, London, SW1H 9AA (01-222 0411) has a public information bureau which, among other things, publishes a list of all MEPs with their addresses and telephone numbers which will be sent on request. These are either their home or constituency office numbers or both.

At the same address are the offices of the British Labour Group (01-222 1719) and of the Conservative Group (01-222 1720). Strictly speaking these are the London offices of the Socialist Group and the European Democratic Group respectively.

To save time it is best to write to MEPs at their home or constituency office addresses but if necessary write to your MEP at the European Parliament Information Office, at the address given above, and on page 222.

In an emergency an MEP may be contacted during the Strasbourg session by telephone on 0103388374001; ask for the member or leave a message with the relevant political group office to ask your MEP to call you back. In Brussels the number is 010 322 234 2111. But do try the home or constituency number first, or the parliament's London office which may, incidentally, be able to tell you where the MEP is.

Locally

Not all MEPs hold public advice sessions or surgeries. Even if they do, the large size of their constituencies may make access to advice sessions a problem. However many of them probably welcome local publicity and are therefore reasonably likely to agree to meet local people or groups; alternatively they could be invited to attend and speak at a meeting. See Chapter 7 for more suggestions.

Strasbourg

It is only worthwhile sending a delegation to a meeting of the parliament if your group is planning to spend a lot of money and to put a great deal of effort into lobbying MEPs. It is cheaper to do it in Britain but Strasbourg has the advantage that all MEPs are there together. Going to lobby in Strasbourg is especially important if you are planning an international campaign:

1. To persuade MEPs to support a particular declaration, say under rule 65 (see below) by getting them to attach their signatures.
2. To meet a number of MEPs informally, for specific discussions. This may be easier than trying to get them together to meet at home and obviously applies even more if you want to meet MEPs from several countries.
3. To have informal discussions with several MEPs; again this can be specially important if they are from several countries.

Remember that members of the public need passes to enter the Palais de l'Europe where the EP meets. These have to be obtained in Strasbourg, but let your MEP know in advance and discuss your plans with him/her. If you are from a pressure group, you should also let the European Parliament office in London know of your intentions so that Strasbourg can be alerted to your coming; this may facilitate the issue of passes when you arrive at the Palais de l'Europe.

If you are going to Strasbourg it is best to be there early in the week even though not all MEPs will have arrived. In practice some MEPs leave on Thursdays; Tuesdays, Wednesdays and Thursdays are likely to be the best days for making contacts. It is important that a delegation to Strasbourg is concerned with points of principle on major issues. Lobbying at the last minute may be a waste of time since amendments will have been decided at committee stage and voting intentions agreed in party groups. You should go before the matter has been discussed in committee.

The European Parliament Information Office sometimes has stocks of a free booklet with all MEPs' biographies and photographs to help you identify them – although from time to time it is out of print. Get your local MEP to set up introductions in Strasbourg. Indeed s/he might agree to arrange a meeting with some of his/her colleagues to enable you to put your case or with commissioners who are also in Strasbourg for part of the session week. It ought to be possible to get quite a bit of time with MEPs in Strasbourg provided you have made the necessary arrangements beforehand.

Brussels

You can also consider going to Brussels to lobby a party group or committee. Although MEPs are normally there for under 24 hours there should be time for meetings with them – again provided you organise it well in advance with an MEP.

Note: Do make sure that in any approaches to MEPs you tell them what approaches you have made to MPs and councillors, especially if they are members of the same political party. They will be likely to know each other, and it is much more effective if their efforts are coordinated rather than duplicated. They should be told if other politicians have agreed to raise the issue, when and how.

What MEPs Can Do

Although there is no formal restriction on what issues an MEP can raise, a member will obviously be more effective when dealing with matters which are directly a community responsibility. Basically the community treaties are economic, although there are obviously social and political consequences. The social aspects may be based on economic arguments, for example the absence of equal social rights may have implications for fair and free trade between member countries. There has for some time been a proposal that in all EC countries, following maternity leave, there should be a period of three months' parental leave for either parent up to the child's second birthday. This has so far been resisted by the British government.

While an MEP can technically raise any subject, s/he will obviously achieve more in relation to community issues than where the parliament can merely express an opinion without the commission having any need to respond. An MEP can raise almost any issue relevant to your pressure group and this means the parliament is one more avenue for pressure and public debate.

Any topic relating to trade and industry and employment would be of major concern to the parliament. Issues range from inner-city poverty and racism to agriculture and road building; from conservation to consumer protection. Foreign policy questions and trade and human rights are often raised. Various British organisations have taken civil liberties issues to Europe both in the parliament and in the courts. Note that under the Treaty of Rome the EC does not have power to issue directives or regulations to member states on a range of subjects of which the most important are: social welfare policy, planning, housing and education. This does not mean the European Parliament cannot consider such matters but that its influence is bound to be more limited.

The Informal Approach

Once you have approached your MEP for help, s/he may, for example, contact an individual official at the commission. The result may mean the MEP is sent the required information, perhaps a document that is not confidential. Or the MEP may make the approach through one of the officials of his/her political group or of a committee on which the member sits. Similarly an MEP may make an informal approach to a commissioner.

The Formal Approach

A number of options are open to the MEP. S/he may, for example, put down a resolution in a form somewhat similar to a Commons early day motion, in order to attract support from other members. This may draw attention to an abuse or to some matter of general concern inside or outside the community. The MEP may be able to put pressure on his/her political group or relevant committee which will give the case more weight. Sometimes a text can be agreed by more than one political group and may be debated by the whole parliament; if accepted, it will be passed on to the commission or council with a request for action. Your MEP will be able to judge which is the best approach. Finally an individual or a group of citizens can present a petition to the parliament.

In practice the MEP can do several of these things simultaneously. But because of the constant travel, and the need to translate documents into eight languages, parliamentary procedures move slowly.

It is possible for fact-finding delegations to be sent to a country as a result of such initiatives. In 1985 a number of MEPs representing the Socialist Group visited Britain as part of an inquiry into racism and fascism in Europe. This group subsequently produced a report, 'Against racism and fascism in Europe', which received considerable publicity. More recently there have been fewer such delegation visits because of financial restrictions.

Questions

As at Westminster, MEPs can put down written or oral questions, which can be used either to get information or to draw attention to an issue.

Oral Questions

The plenary session holds two periods of question time each month. On the Tuesday there are questions to the council and foreign ministers and on the Wednesday to the commission. Although based on Commons practice, the Strasbourg question time has become slow and ponderous, partly because everything has to be translated and partly because the replies and the supplementaries are rather lengthy. The political bite which is a feature of the Commons is missing.

Questions are directed at (i) the commission and answered by the commissioners, (ii) the council and answered by a minister from the country having the presidency and (iii) the foreign ministers of the member states meeting in political cooperation and usually answered by the same minister who replies on behalf of the council. When Britain held the presidency this meant, for example, that Lynda Chalker, a minister of state at the Foreign Office, came to Strasbourg every month for six months in order to answer questions. The following is an extract from the Official Journal dealing with oral questions on 8 July 1987:

Question No 63 by Mr McMahon:

Subject: South Africa

Have the foreign ministers had any further discussions on the situation in South Africa following the recent South African elections and the decision by the South African government to expel representatives of the UK media from that country, and have they any proposals to put before the June Summit for the stepping up of sanctions and other measures against the racist regime in South Africa?

ELLEMAN-JENSEN, President-in-Office of the Council of Foreign Ministers. – As I indicated earlier, questions on South Africa are under constant review at all levels of EPC. On 25 May the foreign ministers had a discussion on the result of the whites-only elections in South Africa on 6 May. We noted with grave concern in this connection that there is a serious risk of further polarization of attitudes. We agreed that these elections would be a disappointment to all South Africans, white and black, who are working honourably for a peaceful change in the situation in South Africa. We therefore repeated our call to President Botha to take steps in order to facilitate a national dialogue. We confirmed that the aim of the policy of the Twelve on South Africa remained the complete abolition of apartheid and the introduction in its place of a genuinely democratic and non-racist system of government.

Mr McMahon and two other members asked supplementaries covering then ban on coal imports by Denmark, the effect of further sanctions on people in South Africa and where Denmark was now obtaining its coal.

The following topics illustrate the scope of oral questions:

EC/Japan relations
Nuclear power and earthquakes
Cooperation with Central
  American countries
Sheepmeat regulations
Protection of migratory birds
Beer cans and the environment
Passport checks
Aid to milk producers in France
Shipbuilding
Air transport liberalisation

Fur trade
The internal market
The Turkish application for
  membership
Boycott of Shell
Unemployment and training for
  under 25s
Visa requirements
Relations with Malta
Cyprus

Oral questions have similar benefits to those in the Commons, namely an opportunity to raise an issue and ask a supplementary. It is a quick and easy way for lobbyists to ask an MEP to help and the exchange in parliament can be publicised back home.

Written Questions
Written questions take a long time to be answered. For example 70 answers given in July and September 1987 were published in the Official Journal on 15 October. Of these, two related to questions asked in 1985 though one was a further answer to a question which had already had a reply in that year; 61 had been asked in 1986 and 7 in 1987. The issues covered are similar to those for oral questions. Sometimes the answers can be brief, as in reply to a question about a person imprisoned in Turkey, allegedly tortured and now adopted by Amnesty: 'The Twelve continue to monitor the human rights situation in Turkey and member countries raise as appropriate their concerns.' In contrast there have, for example, been long and detailed answers to questions about the common fisheries policy, sugar, agricultural surpluses and nuclear fuel reprocessing plants.

Debates
An MEP can initiate debates in a number of ways. Generally this involves several MEPs acting together either informally or through a committee or a political group. It helps if support comes from more than

one country. Recent examples of such initiatives have been: nuclear incidents in the European Community, salmon and trout markets, frontier controls on drugs, and the extension of UK territorial waters to 12 nautical miles.

There are, however, three specific procedures to which it is worth drawing attention: rule 63 resolutions which call on the commission or council to respond; rule 64 resolutions for urgent matters; and rule 65 resolutions which require signatures in support from as many MEPs as possible.

Rule 63   An issue can be raised as a 'motion for a resolution' under rule 63 which may call on the commission or the council to take action or take note of the views expressed. Such resolutions are referred to the appropriate committee for further consideration and may eventually be presented for a vote in plenary session, possibly as part of a more comprehensive report. Examples include the use of drugs in sport and the need for a direct transport link between the Channel Tunnel and the Merseyside region.

Rule 64   There is a procedure for debates on urgent matters. Political group or committee backing is required for the urgency debate held each month (rule 64) and the leaders of the political groups have an important influence in determining which urgency motions are to be given debating time. Those motions which have appeal in a number of countries are more likely to be supported than issues of interest in one country only. Thus it is probably better, for example, to raise an environmental issue in the context of several countries than by referring to the problem in one country only. To be accepted under this procedure the topic has to be related to an event that has occurred shortly before the debate and there must also be wide political support for it.

An example of a 'motion for a resolution' under this rule is one which was put forward by four Labour MEPs on behalf of the Socialist Group. They called for assistance following the hurricane in London and southern England and were concerned with a problem in one member country only. After describing the damage the resolution went on:

1. Expresses its sympathy with the families of those who died or were injured and with the many others who suffered serious damage to their homes and property;
2. Calls on the commission to provide appropriate aid to the affected areas in order to assist the local recovery efforts;

3. Calls on the commission to consider giving specific grants to assist in the restoration of specialist centres of botanical study, such as Kew Gardens;

4. Instructs its president to forward this resolution to the commission and council as well as to the government of Great Britain.

Other examples of subjects raised as emergency resolutions are: situation in Haiti; Afghanistan; human rights day; human rights in the Gaza strip; Washington summit; famine in Ethiopia.

Rule 65   Finally individual members can put down written declarations for other members to support by signatures. These have to be confined to community issues. In some respects this procedure (rule 65) is similar to early day motions in the Commons. They must not exceed 200 words. The aim is to get publicity. However if the declaration is signed by half the MEPs (i.e. more than 259) within two months it will then be forwarded to the institution(s) named in the declaration. Using this procedure is only effective if MEPs are given as much notice as possible that they should sign it.

In practice it is not possible in the normal course of events to rely on MEPs collecting the necessary signatures as they are too busy. Some pressure groups have been successful by sending a small number of lobbyists to be present in the area outside the chamber (sometimes called the hemicycle) for a part of the week. If you decide to do this, make sure each of your lobbyists is armed with the *Vade Mecum*, the book with the names and photographs of MEPs so you can identify them. At least one of the lobbyists should be able to speak French as well as English and knowledge of other community languages would be an advantage.

The first step is that the motion or declaration should be signed by several members whose views are respected by their colleagues; others will then be more likely to follow even if it is a subject with which they are not too familiar. Get advice from an MEP on who to approach for this. Party considerations are obviously important: British Conservatives may well object to signing a motion which has only been signed by left wingers, and vice versa.

While it may seem desirable to approach as many MEPs as possible, be careful. Members of the Socialist and Communist Groups will not sign a motion which has fascist signatures. If you approach MEPs asking them to sign a motion, it is important to make it clear that all MEPs are being approached *except the fascists*.

It takes a lot of effort to collect signatures in Strasbourg – though you can also lobby for support from MEPs here in Britain by asking them to add their names. However as many MEPs are seldom in London you may have to contact them either by post or in their constituencies. It would help to make formal approaches to the political groups too so that as much publicity is given to the resolution as possible. This involves a lot of work and expense, but if you are successful your motion wil be agreed by the parliament as policy. Recent examples of declarations which achieved the necessary numbers of signatures are: (i) that there should be a memorial and documentation centre at the site of a former concentration camp at Drutte in West Germany; and (ii) the Helsinki accord and exit visas for Jews to leave the Soviet Union.

In general individual MPs in the Commons have more opportunities to get debates than individual MEPs partly because of procedure and partly because the latter have fewer days for debate. Speeches in Strasbourg do not normally generate the publicity that they would in the British Parliament, but it can still be a good tactic to get local media coverage in Britain.

In the EP each political group is allocated a precise speaking time to divide amongst its members, and this is strictly observed. This will tend to be a set speech representing the viewpoint of the group. It is thus important that the individual MEP gets the support of his/her political group or relevant committee. Additionally, each individual member has the right before (or more usually after) the final vote to give a 90 second explanation of how s/he is going to vote, and this is the most genuinely spontaneous and passionate moment in any debate. In contrast to the Commons, more speeches in the European Parliament are read from prepared texts.

Petitions

Every European Community citizen, acting alone or jointly with others, has the right to make a written request or complaint to the European Parliament. This is called a petition. It must show the name, occupation, nationality and permanent address of each signatory. There is no need to follow any specific form of wording. Its effectiveness depends largely on how much publicity can be obtained for it. Formally the petition is referred to the Committee on Rules of Procedure. The petition may be noted or passed to one of the specialised committees for further action. This may range from passing the petition to the commission and/or council to appointing a rapporteur to prepare a report or even hold public hearings before preparing a report to put before the parliament. Normally, however, the petitions are merely noted. Remember that if the petition is to make any progress it must deal with a community issue.

It is strongly advisable to discuss any petition with an MEP at an early stage. You will need his/her support if you are to make any progress and the MEP may prefer it to be submitted through him/her. This is especially important if you can get the support of an MEP on the relevant committee. However, strictly speaking you do not need to go through an MEP to send a petition to the European Parliament. Address it to: The President, European Parliament, Plateau de Kirchberg, L-2929, Luxembourg.

The following is an example of a petition, 372/87 from the Federation of Heathrow Anti-Noise Groups:

Subject: restoration of the legal rights of British citizens to seek remedy against excessive noise and nuisance by aircraft in flight over Britain

1. This petition has the support of all member associations as well as Members of Parliament; members of the European Parliament; county, borough, and district authorities; and other organisations who wish to be associated with this plea.
2. This petition pleads that the European Parliament supports the restoration of the legal rights of British citizens to seek a remedy against excessive noise and nuisance caused by aircraft in flight over Britain. These common law rights were removed by the United Kingdom Air Navigation Act of 1920 and were not reinstated in subsequent Acts. Therefore the people of Great Britain do not have the same rights as those which are enjoyed by the citizens of other countries in the European community.
3. The British Government did not safeguard the interests of its people after removing their rights as described in paragraph 2. Since that time, the departments responsible for promoting civil aviation are those which are also entrusted with the protection of the airport environment.
4. London Heathrow is the busiest international airport in the world and continues to grow at more than 13% per annum. It is twice the size of Rome or Frankfurt and has the largest urban area and the greatest number of people adversely affected by aircraft noise in Western Europe.

The petition goes on to itemise the various environmental safeguards which have been removed or ignored by the government. These include limits on aircraft movements, planning restrictions, proposals for a fifth terminal, standards for assessing aircraft noise, night flight restrictions and noise insulation. The petition continues:

8. We are grateful for those EC directives which have resulted in the phasing out of non-noise certificated aircraft and the introduction of quieter planes. They have provided a welcome improvement in noise levels at our airports, but the rapidly increasing expansion of traffic has diminished this and it will be further eroded if the commercial pressures of the airlines for more runways and terminals succeed. We further support the European Union Against Aircraft Nuisance. The member countries in this Union are Austria, France, Holland, Switzerland, West Germany and Great Britain. The Federation of Heathrow Anti-Noise Groups is the officially acknowledged British representative of the union.

9. Your petitioners pray that the European Parliament will consult with the European Community Commission and Council on the appropriate action:

(i) To ensure that all Community citizens, including those of Britain, have the right to sue and maintain actions for nuisance created by the expansion of our airports and the increase in aircraft movements, which interfere with the quiet enjoyment of life to which they are entitled under the Declaration of Human Rights.

(ii) To extend the scope of existing directives covering the noise levels of aircraft, to include the frequency and time of day of take-offs and landings at Community airports, since the environmental nuisance is a combination of all these factors.

Other examples of petitions are: difficulties in importing motor vehicles, rights of residence, freedom of movement for travellers, a cartel of car-paint manufacturers, property transactions in Spain, roads, a ban on the export of greyhounds to Spain.

The Economic and Social Committee

This is a consultative body with 189 members comprising employers, trade unions and other interested groups such as farmers and consumers; 24 are from the UK. Before a commission proposal can be adopted by the council an opinion must often be sought from the Economic and Social Committee; it can also act on its own initiative. It may be worth lobbying the British members and you can get their names from the EC information offices in the UK. Additionally this committee gets notice of proposals so through it you may be able to know quite early of subjects coming before the parliament.

Grant applications

A number of organisations have applied successfully for grants from various EC funds, of which the European Social Fund is probably the best known to community groups. The EC offices in the UK have a useful booklet on this and NCVO (National Council for Voluntary Organisations) has published a helpful guide: *Grants from Europe*. If your organisation applies for cash from one of these funds it may be useful to enlist the help and support of an MEP.

Action Check List

1. You should consider lobbying the European Parliament especially as part of a Europe-wide campaign or where there is a specifically EC issue at stake. For other issues I would not advise you to lobby MEPs unless you are also lobbying domestic politicians.
2. Contact your MEP in the constituency rather than in Brussels or Strasbourg.
3. Do not be deterred by the complexities of the procedures.
4. Get the advice of an MEP or of EP's London office.
5. There is no real limit to the issues you can raise though you will probably get further with EC subjects.
6. Given the poor press coverage of the European Parliament, assume you will have to generate any publicity about your lobbying yourself.
7. Despite the hours they spend travelling, MEPs probably have a smaller constituency caseload than MPs and so might be more willing to help you, especially if it enables them to make more political impact.
8. Consider a petition but involve your MEP.
9. Locally make use of your MEP as you would your MP (see Chapter 7).
10. Study what your MEP is doing; check if s/he publishes a local newsletter.
11. It is worth considering an approach to the Economic and Social Committee.

Other International Assemblies

Britain is also represented through Commons MPs or peers at a number of international assemblies. These are the Council of Europe, the Western European Union, and the North Atlantic Assembly.

Council of Europe
The Council of Europe covers 21 countries and is therefore larger than the EC. The Council of Europe Parliamentary Assembly is attended by MPs delegated from the national parliaments. The member countries are: Belgium, France, Luxembourg, Netherlands, United Kingdom, Denmark, Ireland, Italy, Norway, Sweden, Greece, Turkey, Iceland, Federal Republic of Germany, Austria, Cyprus, Switzerland, Malta, Portugal, Spain and Liechtenstein. The Council of Europe is concerned with all forms of non-military cooperation. Its parliamentary assembly has 170 members and meets three times a year. There are 18 MPs on the British delegation. For more information contact the Commons public information office.

Although the council is regarded by some as merely a talking shop, there are opportunities to lobby the MPs in the British delegation on matters affecting international cooperation. Given that Turkey is a member the assembly may, for example, be a forum in which you can raise human rights issues as well as the question of the continued Turkish occupation of part of Cyprus.

Remember also the differences between the European Court of Human Rights in Strasbourg and the European Community Court of Justice in Luxembourg. The European Court of Human Rights and the European Commission of Human Rights were both set up under the Council of Europe in accordance with the terms of the European Convention of Human Rights. The European Court of Human Rights is not of interest to lobbyists, but for individual British citizens it has made important decisions on such issues as immigration.

Western European Union
The Western European Union (WEU) consists of seven member countries: Belgium, France, the Federal Republic of Germany, Italy, Luxembourg, the Netherlands and the UK. It is concerned primarily with defence matters. The Assembly of the WEU meets twice a year and the UK is represented there by the same MPs as those appointed to the Parliamentary Assembly of the Council of Europe.

The North Atlantic Assembly
The North Atlantic Assembly was previously called the Assembly of NATO Parliamentarians. Its aims are to strengthen understanding and political, economic, social and cultural cooperation in NATO member states. The assembly meets once a year. It has 16 member states: Belgium, Canada, Denmark, France, Federal Republic of Germany, Greece, Iceland, Italy, Luxembourg, Netherlands, Norway, Portugal,

Spain, Turkey, UK and the USA. The British delegation currently consists of 14 MPs and 4 peers.

Action Check List

1. Apart from certain international issues like human rights, lobbying members of these three bodies must have a relatively low priority.
2. Check whether your constituency MP, or other MPs with whom you are in contact, are members of these bodies. The Commons or Lords information offices will tell you which MPs or peers are on the British delegations.
3. You could always ask MPs what they are discussing on these bodies, and suggest that they raise issues which are relevant.
4. Otherwise, forget about them.

12
Councillors

This is not intended to be a chapter about local government powers and structure. However, the lobbyist or ordinary concerned citizen needs to understand the local government system in their own area. Local government organisation in Britain is complicated and each local authority is unique. Clearly I can only give pointers here and you will have to fill in the local details. Your main point of contact will be with an elected local councillor.

Structure

There are 449 local authorities in England and Wales and a further 65 in Scotland. The structure of local government varies in different parts of the country. Some areas have a two-tier system while others have a single tier of all-purpose authorities. This means that single-tier authorities are responsible for all local government functions in their area; where there are two tiers the responsibilities are usually divided between the two councils operating in any one area. Each local authority has its own rules and procedures so it is difficult to give precise guidance to the lobbyist which will be equally applicable in all areas.

Broadly, three different patterns of local authority structure exist in Great Britain: (i) London, (ii) the six main urban conurbations and (iii) the rest of the country. Northern Ireland has a different structure.

London

London has 32 boroughs and each is an all-purpose authority except that education in inner London (at the time of writing) comes under the Inner London Education Authority (ILEA) which is currently threatened with abolition by the government, its powers to be transferred to the individual boroughs or to groups of boroughs. London boroughs have responsibility for most other local government functions in the capital. The exceptions include policing which comes under the home secretary, transport (under London Regional Transport), fire services (under a joint board), main roads (Department of Transport) and major planning matters (London Planning Advisory Committee). It is also worth mentioning that some local authority functions have been taken away from the boroughs in the area covered by the London Docklands Development Corporation (LDDC).

The Metropolitan Areas
Six areas in England have only single-tier local government: Greater Manchester; Merseyside; South Yorkshire; West Yorkshire; Tyne and Wear; West Midlands. Within these areas are 36 metropolitan districts, e.g. Manchester, Leeds, Liverpool, Sheffield, St Helens and Newcastle. They are responsible for most local government functions but there are, for example, joint boards for transport and fire services.

The English Counties, Scotland and Wales
The third main type of local government structure is in the rest of the country and this is on a two-tier basis. In England there are 39 county councils (e.g. Derbyshire, Nottinghamshire) and 296 non-metropolitan districts or shire districts (e.g. Ashfield, Brighton, Hartlepool). In Wales there are eight county councils (e.g. Gwent, Mid Glamorgan), below which are 37 Welsh districts (e.g. Islwyn, Swansea). In Scotland the upper tier has nine regional authorities (e.g. Strathclyde, Fife), below which are 53 districts like Glasgow, Motherwell and Edinburgh. There are also three local authorities for the Scottish Islands.

Northern Ireland
There are 26 district councils in Northern Ireland acting as the lower tier. Above them are nine area boards which consist partly of district councillors and partly of persons apointed by the minister. Northern Ireland also has a housing executive which again consists partly of district councillors and partly of ministerial appointments.

Parish/Community Councils
In addition there are parish councils in England and community councils in Scotland and Wales, about 11,000 in total. Some go back to antiquity but, in a sense, they are optional and are only set up if local people, usually in small villages, want them. In England they are set up by district councils but in Scotland and Wales by the secretary of state. No equivalent exists in Northern Ireland.

Powers

In the case of two-tier authorities outside London, the county councils are responsible for education, social services and policing. There are joint responsibilities for roads, and planning and the other functions, especially housing, are carried out by the non-metropolitan districts.

The following indicates the range of local authority functions though the complete list would be many times longer.

County:
- Education
- Social services
- Police
- Fire
- Consumer protection
- Libraries, etc.

District:
- Housing
- Cleansing
- Refuse collection
- Planning
- Highways
- Economic development
- Community and leisure services

Much of the power of local authorities is in their committees or the party groups although the main decisions are ratified by the full council. Normally council meetings are at about six to eight weekly intervals and there will be a full round of committee meetings within this time period. These meetings are open to the public except that on some committee agendas there are confidential items which are taken at the end at which point the public is asked to leave.

In order to get the support of the council for your cause it is important that you should seek to influence the majority party or to try to secure all party support.

In Northern Ireland the district councils are responsible for such functions as entertainments, sport, environmental health, refuse, cleansing and consumer protection. Four of the area boards deal with health and personal social services; the other five handle education and libraries. The housing executive, as its name indicates, deals with housing – building and maintenance.

The powers of parish councils or community councils are limited but can be important locally: village halls, footpaths, rights of way, allotments, car parking, lighting, war memorials and lavatories; they may also be consulted on planning matters.

Despite recent government restrictions local authorities still have some powers to campaign and publicise issues in their areas. Many publish and distribute some sort of newspaper. Also local authorities are often consulted, in advance, about government proposals. And when the government changes the law or procedures so that councils are seriously affected, they clearly make their views known. One topical example concerns the extra costs and work that will be imposed on many councils by the proposals to introduce the poll tax.

Finding Your Councillors

The best way is to phone your local town or county hall and ask the public relations/information department. You may have more than one councillor representing your ward or area. In some local authorities, such as the London boroughs, there are elections for the whole council every fourth year. In other areas one third of the district council seats are up for election annually with county council elections every fourth year.

It is likely that there will be notices outside the town hall or in public libraries about your local councillors' advice sessions or their addresses and phone numbers. The public libraries normally also keep agenda papers for meetings of the full council or of its committees; in any case these papers must, by law, be available for the public at the town hall.

Another possibility is to phone one of the local political parties and ask them. You should also study the local newspapers for information about what councillors are doing, though these news items do not usually give the ward or area they represent. Unlike Parliament you are not obliged to deal only with one of the councillors representing your area. You may prefer to deal with someone from a particular party or who is the chair or member of a particular committee; but if the problem is local it may make sense to approach a councillor who knows the district. Again the town hall will give you details of which committee would be responsible for any particular subject and which councillors are on it. They should also advise you, where relevant, that your subject concerns the other tier of local government in your area.

You can write to your councillor either at his/her home address, which the town hall will probably give you, or at the town hall itself. It is usually fairly easy to arrange a meeting with your councillors and you could phone them at their homes to discuss this. Note that you should not try to contact councillors by phone at the town hall because they also have jobs and are at the town hall only for meetings. The exceptions to this are authority leaders, some of whom are full time and easier to reach at the town hall than at their homes.

Many councillors also have advice sessions, rather like MPs. Some local authorities arrange the venues and publicity for these;

alternatively the councillors may arrange the sessions themselves. Phone the town hall to find out, or look for notices in libraries, community centres, etc. or try the local office (if there is one) of the political party to which the councillor belongs.

How Councillors Raise Issues at Town Halls

Councillors have a number of ways in which they can raise issues:

1. They can write to the appropriate chief officer.
2. They can write to the relevant chair of committee or to the leader of the council.
3. Many local authorities have a period at council meetings when councillors may ask oral questions of committee chairs; there are often also opportunities for written questions.
4. Councillors can ask for items to be put on committee agendas; in some authorities they can get their own papers put on the appropriate agenda.
5. Committees can ask that certain items be referred to meetings of the full council.
6. Some council committees receive deputations of local people who are concerned about a particular issue.
7. Some local authorities have a procedure for dealing with petitions. This may be at committee or at council meetings.
8. Some councils arrange for their elected members to hold 'report-back' meetings, with officials recording the points made.

Subjects Councillors Can Raise

As regards action within the town hall, councillors are obviously limited to issues which are within the local authority's responsibilities. These give plenty of scope, the more so as local authorities are often affected by government legislation and can comment on green and white papers. Certainly councils can themselves make representations to the government. In addition councillors can have an influence, say on policing, even if they lack the formal powers. However most of the effort will inevitably go into persuading the council to take action on local issues.

A frequent topic of local lobbying concerns grants by the local authority to local voluntary organisations and community groups. The council may have a sub-committee which considers grant applications in detail, possibly interviewing representatives of some of the organisations. Even if your local councillor is not on the relevant committee or sub-committee you can still lobby in support of your organisation.

Outside the town hall, councillors are naturally involved in wider issues. In practice, they are able to do many of the same things as MPs. After all they are politicians first and foremost and active members of their local parties. I recall, for example, a successful meeting organised by a local branch of Amnesty International to which they invited local councillors. As a result, the councillors agreed to take part in the international campaign against torture.

Councillors are frequently appointed onto school governing bodies, even if the local authority does not have any educational responsibilities, and thus they are able to show an interest in educational issues. Councils also make many appointments to other bodies such as health authorities. This may enable the council to discuss the policies of these bodies and in addition the councillors serving on them may be a useful target for lobbying.

How Councillors Can Help outside the Town Hall

You can involve councillors in just the same ways as MPs. However, they usually have smaller areas to cover so you may find it easier to make contact with them than with MPs. The drawback is that many councillors also have full-time jobs so it is unreasonable to expect them to be free on weekdays other than in the evenings. Also they will probably attract less publicity than the MP. Here are some suggestions:

1. Invite them to attend your AGM, open meeting, Christmas bazaar, or to serve on your committee. Some organisations have councillors nominated to the committee from the town hall.
2. Ask a councillor to speak at a public meeting; it may be advisable to invite your local councillor regardless of party or to invite one from each of the main parties.
3. Having a march or a demo? Ask the councillors to take part.
4. Get them to write an article in your newsletter.

Issues Affecting Councillors

The following are examples of issues affecting councillors in recent years. It is likely that the local MPs would also have had representations about them:

1. Cuts in council services, e.g. libraries, day nurseries, centres for the mentally ill, home helps, day centres, luncheon clubs.

2. The level of rates and government grant.
3. Privatisation of services.
4. Housing policy, especially attitudes to the homeless, bed and breakfast accommodation, and disposing of empty council properties or of whole estates.
5. The quality of the housing repairs and maintenance service.
6. Road and traffic schemes.
7. Major planning issues, e.g. the future of Battersea Power Station or of Piccadilly Circus, airport developments, disposal of nuclear waste, building on open spaces or in parks.
8. Facilities for the arts and leisure.
9. Childminding and support for the under fives.
10. Cycle routes.
11. The state of the local health service; though this is not a local government service, local authorities are involved because they nominate councillors onto health authorities.

Action Check List

1. Most action indicated for your MP is also appropriate for your councillor(s).
2. Find out the names of your local councillors: are they from the majority party?
3. Decide whether to approach your local councillor(s) or the committee chair, or the leader of the council.
4. Is it a ward issue or does it affect a larger part of the local authority area?
5. Discuss with a councillor whether s/he will ask a question, raise it in committee or in full council or by means of a letter to a chief officer or committee chair.
6. Invite a councillor to meet your group, speak at a meeting, serve on your committee.
7. Assess who are the influential councillors before deciding on your tactics.
8. Decide whether you will be more successful with a low-key informal approach or with a higher profile campaign. This may depend on how 'political' the council is.

13

Publicity: How MPs Can Help

MPs are news; not as often as most of them would wish, but they do get publicity for what they do, for their political statements, their attendance at events, their backing for causes. If an MP is involved you are more likely to attract press interest and have photographs in the local papers. But it is not an infallible formula, particularly if the local MP is overexposed in the newspapers in his/her constituency.

Clearly if your MP asks a question, speaks in a debate, goes on a deputation to see a minister, leads a demo, sponsors a cause you and s/he will want to press release the fact. Indeed most of the suggestions in this book assume that media coverage is one of the main aims.

However there are a number of other ways by which an MP (or other politician) can help you publicise your cause.

The Parliamentary Press Lobby

At Westminster some journalists have access to the press gallery and to the press lobby. A select few have access to the members' lobby where they meet MPs and get comments on non-attributable 'lobby terms'. They are also a useful channel for feeding in information provided it is likely to be of national interest. An opposition MP supporting a policy statement by, say, Shelter or the Child Poverty Action Group (CPAG) is unlikely to be of much interest to journalists at Westminster; a Conservative MP who takes the same line is more likely to attract media coverage.

The quickest way for an MP to issue a press release is to leave copies in the Commons press gallery. It is a good way of drawing attention to, say, a forthcoming 10 minute rule bill or an adjournment debate.

Press Conferences

MPs can hold press conferences at Westminster in one of the committee rooms. The rooms off Westminster Hall (W rooms, Jubilee Room and Grand Committee Room) have the advantage that photography is permitted but the other committee rooms are also used quite frequently.

The MP books the room and leaves copies of a press notice in the press gallery at the Commons announcing the conference. It is best if the pressure group also publicises the event directly to the appropriate reporters. Contacting both the offices of national media and their Westminster correspondents does not, in practice, cause any unnecessary overlap. Such press conferences can be used by pressure groups for example to launch a policy statement, to publicise a new piece of research or to hear from and question a visitor from abroad, perhaps in connection with human rights issues.

Probably the best times for such conferences are Monday to Thursday mornings between 10am and 12 noon. Wednesday mornings have the disadvantage that they clash with meetings of the Parliamentary Labour Party. On Tuesday and Thursday mornings there may be clashes with standing committees especially during the 'peak season' between January and Easter. I personally favour Monday mornings as there is likely to be less competition from other stories.

It would be sensible for the pressure group to consider direct invitations to other MPs to attend the press conference. It is not likely that many will be free, but the presence of even one or two of them will justify your efforts. It would be even better if the press conference were sponsored by a party or all-party parliamentary group, rather than by an individual MP. Usually such a conference is addressed by the MP and a member of your pressure group but it is best not to have too many speakers. Do keep the contributions short. Make sure you have summaries available for distribution to any journalists present. The aim is to interest the press and give them a chance to ask questions. If they get bored they'll go away, fail to ask questions and your efforts will have been wasted.

If your group has something urgent to say you can always ask an MP to inform the Press Association at the Commons. PA has an excellent chief reporter at the Commons. MPs know how to get hold of him at any time, whether or not the House is sitting. If he thinks it is an interesting story he will put it out on the PA tapes and there should be good coverage.

Radio

Both the BBC and IRN have studios at Westminster. The IRN studio is also linked to LBC and other independent local radio stations. While MPs are often invited to be interviewed there is nothing to stop an MP with an interesting story going to the studios, especially to IRN, to see if it is newsworthy.

Although it is harder to get onto the BBC Radio Four *Today* programme an MP can phone the producers with the story. Indeed the same tactic can also work with the early morning TV shows. Obviously your pressure group could make its own approaches but it is sometimes easier for an MP to give a quick interview about, say, the background to a PQ or EDM.

Outside of Westminster your MP will undoubtedly have access to his/her local radio station. S/he may have the sort of relationship with the local station which makes it possible for the MP to suggest an interview. Also there may be programmes other than news items, perhaps phone-ins. When I was an MP, BBC Radio London asked me on several occasions to do my own programme; I chose one or two themes and interviewed local people and groups. The radio station provided a reporter who taped the interviews and then cut and edited the material in accordance with my instructions. A well-briefed MP could mention your pressure group on this sort of programme.

Local Newspapers

Apart from sending out press releases, MPs may also be asked to write occasional articles or do a regular column. Remember your MP may well be searching around for material to fill such a column. If you know your MP at all, why not suggest topics worth covering or even offer something in writing. This could cover a local or national issue or publicise the work of your group. The odds are the MP will be grateful for the material or even for the suggestion. It goes without saying that your ideas ought to be in line with the MP's broad political approach though most MPs will show an interest in virtually any local issue or local group. In fact inviting an MP to a local event you have organised may result not only in media coverage but ensure that your organisation or event is mentioned by the MP in his weekly column.

Photo Opportunities

Many newspapers, especially local ones, like pictures. Alert them to any photo opportunities; indeed you may be able to help create them. They like pictures of MPs doing unusual things. If it is really good the TV companies may be interested. On one occasion London MPs of all parties were asked, on behalf of the Greater London Enterprise Board, to take part in an event to publicise a company which manufactured battery-assisted bicycles. The resulting pictures of MPs cycling and racing round New Palace Yard attracted considerable TV and newspaper coverage.

Action Check List

1. Discuss publicity/press releases with sympathetic MP(s).
2. If your group wants to hold a press conference, approach an MP about holding it at Westminster.
3. Feed material to your local MP for his/her use in press releases or articles.

14
Commercial Lobbying

So far I have concentrated on lobbying by pressure groups, trade unions and concerned individuals. For want of a better term I call this 'social' lobbying, that is, it is done for non-commercial motives which are usually ideological or political. There are, however, other lobbying activities which are commercial rather than social. These fall into two categories. First are the lobbyists employed by commercial interests, such as firms and trade associations, which I would call 'in-house'; and second are lobbying firms which I describe as 'out-of-house' – public affairs consultants.

Both the in-house and out-of-house lobbyists generally seek to further commercial interests, in contrast to social pressure groups that campaign for ideological or political reasons. On the other hand, while public affairs consultants are in business to make money, some of their clients are social or non-commercial organisations (see below).

While commercial lobbyists will probably have greater resources at their disposal, their methods of approach will not, in theory, be very different from those practised by social pressure groups. Commercial lobbyists will therefore develop target lists of MPs, seek to influence the relevant backbench and all-party groups, select and standing committees; they will get PQs and EDMs put down, arrange meetings for MPs, get MPs to arrange meetings with ministers, provide briefings for debates, arrange for MPs to be lobbied in their constituencies, organise petitions, and arrange for MPs to get letters on particular issues.

The lobbyists will pay particular attention to MPs' constituency interests, arrange visits for target MPs to factories, etc., perhaps even abroad. They also have the resources to provide entertainment. Commercial lobbyists place greater weight on contacts with the appropriate civil servants and so do not always think it wise to claim successes publicly. For example, advance warning of possible legislation is specially useful – it is often more effective lobbying against a tentative plan than against a firm proposal to which the minister has already attached his/her name.

Of course, some lobbyists do not readily come into either category. For example the Automobile Association is not a social pressure group, but neither are its lobbying activities directly for commercial ends. The AA and the RAC campaign for more government spending on roads; they claim to represent the motorist. It is therefore appropriate to consider the AA and similar organisations in this chapter.

Criticisms of Commercial Lobbyists

One important criticism of commercial lobbyists is that they have much greater resources than social lobbyists; in other words they are able to 'buy' influence. Some commercial lobbyists behave with absolute integrity but others are less reputable. One organisation advised its local members to invite their MPs to constituency meetings on a particular Friday; this just happened to be the date when a certain private member's bill was before the Commons. The intention was to keep some MPs away from Westminster so that they would not vote for it. The stratagem failed!

On another occasion the Commons was debating a private bill: The Felixstowe Dock and Railway Bill. As there was no whip on this the promoters feared there wouldn't be enough MPs present to ensure its passage. So a lobbying consultancy sought to keep MPs within voting distance of Westminster by throwing a party that evening. The protests were so strong that the event was called off.

Not long ago the Lead Development Association offered to pay for the Commons Environment Committee to go to Sweden, in the context of an investigation into lead and environmental pollution. This offer was rejected after protests.

Another criticism concerns conflicts of interest by some consultants who work for government departments while simultaneously acting for clients as lobbyists. Some consultants earn 'success fees' for a satisfactory outcome: a form of payment which might be considered unethical.

Some public affairs consultants retain an MP on their books. Even MPs' research assistants have been known to be paid for by a lobbying company, and one industry at least has seconded an employee to work full time with an MP. Such examples have helped to give commercial lobbying a doubtful reputation with resulting pressure to bring the whole activity under some sort of control, as in the United States, particularly by establishing a code of conduct for lobbyists. The Commons has since 1986 instituted a compulsory declaration of interests for holders of lobby journalists' and MPs research assistants'/secretaries' passes; these declarations must show other paid occupations. In addition all-party groups must register the names of their officers, the source and extent of financial benefits from outside sources and gainful occupations of any staff. Where a consultancy provides assistance, the ultimate client must be named.

A number of public affairs consultants support these moves and would like to see a proper register of lobbyists established on the lines proposed by MPs like Bob Cryer. One suggestion that has been made is that inclusion in such a register would entitle the holder to have a pass for the Palace of Westminster while unregistered consultants would be denied this right.

In-House Lobbyists

In-house lobbyists with commercial firms operate similarly to those employed by social lobbies. It is their motives that are different. They probably also have greater resources and may on occasion also make use of public affairs consultants. Many firms and organisations employ one or more staff to lobby MPs. I have already mentioned the AA and RAC; they and other organisations represent a particularly vocal 'roads lobby'. A non-commercial organisation like the Royal College of Nursing now employs three people for lobbying.

It is well known that the nuclear industry is active in lobbying MPs. It employs its own staff and sometimes also outside consultants to achieve its ends. This can include counteracting the influence of the anti-nuclear pressure groups.

There has been a battle between the tobacco industry and the medical profession about advertising and sales. After years of pressure and mounting evidence that tobacco is a killer, the government has imposed restrictions on advertising, and would, I believe, have done more but for the success of the tobacco lobby in resisting such pressure.

Public Affairs Consultants

Any organisation may sometimes consider approaching an out-of-house public affairs consultancy either for a specific campaign or on a longer-term basis. These consultancies are used by commercial firms, local authorities and local authority associations, trade unions, trade associations, charities and social pressure groups. Sometimes consultants are engaged to influence a specific piece of legislation, government contract, political decision or maybe just one clause in a bill.

The following example shows how closely some commercial companies monitor the actions of MPs. A number of constituents complained to me about being inundated with direct mail shots personally addressed to them. I asked a question about this in the House of Commons. Shortly afterwards I was telephoned by a public relations company working for

a direct mail firm, and was written to by another direct mail firm. In both cases they wanted to know what had prompted my parliamentary question and what further action I proposed to take.

What do such consultancy firms have to offer?

They provide a political monitoring and information service. At its simplest this means you pay for a daily service which provides cuttings from the Commons and Lords Hansards and the order papers of the two Houses. So you get advance notice of questions about a specific subject, EDMs, select committee investigations, PQ answers and the debates themselves. There are two firms that provide this specific service (see Appendix IV for details). This monitoring service costs roughly £1000 a year.

More typically public affairs consultants provide a lobbying service covering the whole range of activities and this can cost a minimum of £1,000 a month (in addition to the monitoring service described above). Such arrangements are the subject of specific proposals and quotations. Research and printed material, lunches and MPs' visits would all be extras. Some costs can be quite high: a fee of £40,000 has been mentioned for a campaign to modify a major piece of legislation.

You are also paying for experience and judgement. Public affairs consultants should be able to advise on what can, realistically, be achieved by lobbying. There is all the difference between asking for the ideal and failing, and attempting to secure a concession, which, while it falls short of your aims, is better than nothing.

The lobbying companies I spoke to said that they did not waste much time with MEPs. They concentrated on the European Commission, where the real power is. Commercial lobbying of the Commission is an increasingly lucrative occupation for all concerned.

Advantages of Going to a Consultancy

1. They employ people with experience and the appropriate skills. Their staff include former civil servants as well as people who work or have worked at Westminster and understand the procedures well.
2. They can save you money – compare the cost of employing an extra member of staff, including overheads, with the cost of using consultants.
3. They have close contacts in both Houses and, most importantly, with civil servants.
4. They have the facilities for research and targetting – reference books, Hansards and other publications.

5. They have capital equipment, including computers for data bases often used for target lists, thereby saving you the costs of buying expensive equipment and training staff to use it.
6. They have more time than many in-house staff.
7. Some firms are skilled at lobbying the EC and the European Parliament and may have a member of their staff in Brussels.

Some lobbying firms employ ex-MPs on their permanent staff or people who have been active in politics in other ways. For example they may retain sitting members. They therefore have a network of contacts as well as a working knowledge of the systems. Such contacts will include politicians, civil servants and journalists. These social and professional networks are exploited regularly. It is the 'old boy' system, and it works.

Examples
1. The Greater London Council used a consultancy in its campaign to avoid abolition.
2. During the debate over which scheme would be selected for the Channel link to France there were lobbying consultants at work for each interested company.
3. The European Air Bus uses a consultancy to project itself to MPs and peers, arranges for MPs to visit the factory in Toulouse and generally ensures that politicians and civil servants are kept well informed.
4. The Bicycle Association, representing manufacturers, wholesalers and retailers, uses a consultant.
5. Following a government announcement about the disposal of nuclear waste underground at three specific sites a consultancy was retained by the three county councils affected. It lobbied against the plans to use these sites.
6. The campaign to abolish on-course betting duty was run by a consultancy.
7. A consultancy was engaged by bodies representing various sports – swimming, football and athletics – to campaign against the powers under the 1988 Local Government Bill to privatise sports facilities.

Selecting and Briefing Public Affairs Consultants

You have to be quite clear what service you need. Then you should approach two or three firms and tell them what you want. Ask them to produce a proposal and costing, outlining their services and how they can meet your precise needs. Go and see the firm and meet the person(s) who would be your contact. Do you like and respect them? What other people useful to you do they employ or retain? Find out about other clients they are working for and ask them about recent campaigns. Ask to see examples of their work; do they claim any successes? Can you find anyone you know who has used these consultants? It is important your organisation has the skills and experience to evaluate any firms you approach and judge how well they are performing for you.

I have attempted in Appendix IV (pp. 217–23) to include all consultants claiming to provide a public affairs/lobbying service. There may be some omissions as there is no full listing available. Not all firms are members of a professional body. New firms spring up from time to time and existing consultancies merge. A few firms are specialist public affairs consultants while a greater number claim that they include public affairs within a range of public relations services.

Action Check List

1. Can you afford to use consultants? Have you worked out the costs of improving/extending your in-house facilities?
2. Have you the skill and judgement to select and use out-of-house consultants? If not you may make the wrong decisions and not get value for money.
3. How well are they able (a) to target individual parliamentarians likely to respond to constituency pressure and (b) persuade local people to write to him/her? This can be quite a sophisticated operation as consultants do not have obvious networks throughout the country. Check whether the lobbyist can for example mobilise 'professionals' like doctors and lawyers to contact MPs.
4. What experience have they of getting PQs tabled, of arranging EDM and adjournment debates?
5. What priority will they allocate to holding receptions for politicians and wining and dining them?
6. Do they recommend carrying out opinion polls, or advertising? What resources and experience have they for this?
7. Will they make approaches to backbench groups?
8. Monitoring of Hansards, etc.
9. Do they have experience of lobbying the Lords?
10. How good are their contacts with civil servants?
11. What experience do they have of lobbying in Brussels and Strasbourg?
12. Are they ethical?
13. Are you unhappy about any of their other clients e.g. South African connections, tobacco industry, armaments?
14. How impressed are you by their recent work and their claims for any successes they have achieved?
15. Are there any extra charges?

Appendix I: Commons Glossary

Act
: A bill that has passed all its parliamentary stages and received the Royal Assent.

Adjournment debate
: This term refers to a wide range of debates, but for the lobbyist its greatest importance is the last half hour of each Commons day when backbenchers can initiate a debate and obtain a direct response from a minister.

Admission order office
: Situated off the central lobby; issues tickets for the public gallery.

All-party group
: Group of MPs from more than one party and concerned with a specific issue like penal reform, pensioners or human rights; may include peers. Meets at intervals to consider policy and tactics. There is also a large number of all-party country groups concerned with relations between Britain and specific other countries.

Amendment
: Proposal by one or more MPs to alter wording of a motion or of a part of a bill so that it may be voted on.

Annie's Bar
: A bar only for accredited lobby journalists and MPs.

Annunciator/monitor
: TV screens situated throughout Westminster; display subject of debate, member speaking, actual time and time speech started; also shows results of divisions and advance notice of PNQs and statements.

Backbench committee
: Grouping of backbenchers within one party and usually concerned with either specific subject area (e.g. home affairs) or regional interest (e.g. Scotland or the North West); meets regularly, often with frontbenchers, to discuss policy and tactics.

Backbencher	MP without any ministerial or other frontbench responsibilities.
Ballot bills	The 20 bills put forward by private members each session following a ballot. The top six are assured of a second reading debate on a Friday. (See also 10 minute rule bills and presentation bills).
Behind the chair	Informal meeting of frontbenchers from the two main parties, perhaps to resolve disagreements regarding timing on the floor of the chamber, at what time to adjourn, etc. These often take place while a debate is in progress and, by being behind the Speaker's chair are out of sight. Additionally as ministers and opposition frontbenchers have their offices in the area of the House behind the chair their meetings can have more private venues.
Bill	Name given to primary legislation during its passage through Parliament, after which it becomes an act.
Business questions	A period every Thursday pm when the House is sitting, which is devoted to an announcement of the next week's business, normally in response to a private notice question from the leader of the opposition, followed by an almost unrestricted period of questions to the leader of the House. Is sometimes called a 'business statement'.
Campaign Group of MPs	Group of Labour MPs often defined as 'hard left'.
Carriage gates	Entrance to Commons on Parliament Square, for motor vehicles, taxis, parliamentary passholders and others by special arrangement.
Central lobby	Main public access where members of the public go to meet MPs and peers. Gives access to public gallery, and to committee rooms, except those off Westminster Hall.
Committee corridor	Corridor on first floor giving access to committee rooms 1–16.

Committee rooms	Rooms on first and second floors. Used for select and standing committees, backbench and all-party groups, meetings organised by MPs, press conferences, etc. Photography is not permitted.
Committee of Selection	Committee of senior MPs who propose membership of standing and departmentally related select committees. (In practice the whips usually make the decisions except in the case of private members' and private bills.)
Consolidated fund	A bill offering the opportunity for a series of short debates initiated by backbenchers; usually go through the night.
Consolidation Bill	A bill which, as its name suggests, consolidates previous enactments in one new bill; old enactments of no practical use are repealed. There appears to be no opportunity here for a lobbyist.
Delegated legislation	Powers given to minister in main legislation; these are statutory instruments or sometimes called 'orders in council'. Some do not require parliamentary approval. Those that do get up to one and a half hours' debate (usually) without opportunity of amendment.
Despatch box	Large ornate boxes in front of where the prime minister and leader of the opposition sit but used by frontbenchers on both sides to rest their papers when making speeches.
Division	Vote taken in Commons or Lords or in standing committee.
Dod's	Parliamentary reference book.
EDM (early day motion)	A motion printed in order paper, not debated, attracts signatures of supporting MPs and very useful for lobbyists.
Erskine May	Authoritative and detailed description of all aspects of parliamentary procedure and precedents.
Frontbencher	Minister or senior opposition member who speaks from frontbench usually to open or wind up debates.
Grand Committee Room	Large meeting room off Westminster Hall

	often used for meetings on occasion of mass lobbies; photography allowed.
Green card	A card bearing a request from constituent to meet MP; issued in central lobby when House is sitting.
Green paper	Consultative document on future government legislation or other policies in a specific subject area.
Guillotine	Government imposed restriction on debating time for commons committee report, third reading or Lords amendments stages of a bill; also called a timetable; requires a three hour debatable Commons motion.
Hansard	Official verbatim reports of Commons and Lords proceedings plus answers to written questions. There is also a Hansard covering each standing committee.
Harcourt Room	Function room in Commons; may be reserved by MP or peer who was formerly an MP.
House Magazine	Published weekly when Parliament is sitting. Gives detailed information about progress of legislation, previous and current week's business. Very useful. Costs £75 per annum.
Hybrid bill	A public bill which also affects private rights and therefore requires a special and more complicated procedure, e.g. the Channel Tunnel legislation. See also Private bill.
Interview rooms	Small meeting rooms off Westminster Hall, bookable by MPs, also called the 'W' rooms. Photography allowed.
Jubilee Room	Medium-sized meeting room off Westminster Hall, bookable by MPs. Photography allowed.
Letter board	Board in members' lobby from which MPs may collect urgent letters from colleagues or from government departments. Does not function during recess.
Lobby	All purpose parliamentary word having at least four meanings: (i) meeting points within Palace of Westminster, e.g. central lobby, members' lobby, Lords' lobby; (ii) process of

	persuasion, e.g. to lobby one's MP; (iii) those journalists who have access to members' lobby and who discuss with MPs on non-attributable (lobby) terms; and (iv) mass lobby (see below).
Long title (of a bill)	Sets out in general terms the purposes of a bill and should cover everything in it; although the long title can be amended, in practice it defines the scope of possible amendments.
Lord Chancellor	Presides over debates in the House of Lords; is a member of the cabinet, and head of legal system.
Lords Bar	Small humble bar at Lords end of building to which MPs and peers may take guests. It is also the only bar which researchers and other passholders may use without being with a member.
Mass lobby	Organised event whereby large numbers of people seek to lobby their MPs on a particular issue on one afternoon/evening.
Members' cafeteria	Cafeteria on terrace level where MPs may entertain up to three guests.
Members' entrance	Point in New Palace Yard where members often enter and leave Commons. Is also the pick up and dropping point for taxis. MPs take priority over strangers.
Members' lobby	Between central lobby and the chamber. When House is sitting, access only to MPs, certain Commons staff and some journalists. Gives access to whips' offices, members' post office and vote office.
Message board	Board in members' lobby where telephone messages and green cards are left for MPs. Does not function during recess.
Money resolution	Resolution normally taken after second reading of a bill; authorises expenditure resulting from the legislation. Usually taken on the nod, but is debatable for 45 minutes.
New Palace Yard	Area inside carriage gates at Big Ben end of Palace of Westminster.
1922 Committee	Weekly meeting of Conservative MPs;

Norman Shaw (North & South)	frontbenchers may only attend by invitation. Offices for MPs and staff, and some meeting rooms. Situated on Victoria Embankment.
Norman Shaw Conference Room	Meeting room bookable by an MP.
Official opposition	The largest minority party in the House; its leader is leader of the opposition, his senior colleagues are the shadow cabinet and occupy the frontbenches opposite the government ministers.
Official report	See Hansard.
Open question	Oral parliamentary question usually addressed to the prime minister, and so worded that any subject may be raised as a supplementary. Typically: What are her engagements that day?
Opposition day	One of 20 days a session allocated to opposition parties for them to choose what issues are to be debated. Seventeen are for Labour as the official opposition, and three for the second largest opposition party; these debates are often divided into two separate subjects.
Oral question	Question for answer on the floor of the House which gives MPs the chance of asking supplementaries.
Order book	Published daily, shows future business including questions and SIs but excludes EDMs.
Order in council	See Delegated legislation.
Order paper	Daily agenda for Commons (or Lords) business. The full Commons order paper contains additional information on blue paper and is sometimes called the 'vote'.
Other place	House of Lords.
Pair	MP of other party with whom there is agreement about simultaneous absences should there be divisions – usually confined to two line whips (votes) and the whips (MPs responsible in each party) may also have to agree.
Parliamentary clerks	Officials who advise on all aspects of

	parliamentary procedure, from business in the chamber to standing and select committees, public and private bills and the tabling of PQs.
Parliamentary private secretary (PPS)	Government MP with the most junior and unpaid post; currently there are 41. They perform tasks for their minister, and are technically part of the government 'payroll' in that they are constrained in what they can do on the floor of the House or in committee.
Parliamentary question (PQ)	Questions by MPs to ministers must be tabled in advance. May be for oral or written answer.
Payroll or payroll vote	Describes ministers and PPSs who can be relied on to support the government on all voting occasions when there is a government 'line'. This matters specially when there is no official whip. Present total is 125 in the Commons.
Petition	Petition presented to Commons by an MP on behalf of one or more petitioners. There are strict rules regarding wording and presentation.
Planted question	Written or oral question tabled by backbench MP at request of a minister (usually passed on by the minister's PPS). This enables the minister to make information available without the need for a formal statement. Also used in oral questions to raise an 'easy' subject for the minister on a day when s/he expects to have a rough passage.
PLP	Parliamentary Labour Party.
Point of order	A means of interrupting business in the chamber or in committee, often to make a political point which the MP has otherwise been unable to make. Abuse of points of order is frowned upon by the Speaker but much used. Can be done almost anytime but the Speaker often takes points of order after private notice questions and statements.

Policemen's cafeteria (Westminster Hall cafeteria)	Cafeteria off Westminster Hall used by staff and some MPs.
PPS	See Parliamentary private secretary.
Prayer	Two meanings: (i) prayers at beginning of daily Commons sitting; (ii) a motion opposing a government statutory instrument.
Presentation bill	Usually refers to a private member's bill, presented to the House and printed but with virtually no opportunity of time for debate.
Press gallery	In Commons chamber, above Speaker's chair, for use of press, but also refers to other press facilities (catering, etc.) nearby.
Printed paper office	Office in Lords from which peers can obtain official documents.
Prime minister's questions	Two 15-minute periods a week, at 3.15pm on Tuesday and Thursday afternoons when the PM answers oral questions. Used to make political points.
Private bill	Legislation giving powers or benefits to an individual or group of people rather than applying to the whole community. Such bills are usually sponsored by and give powers to local authorities, public corporations, private companies and, rarely, to individuals. See also Hybrid bill.
Private bill office	Office at Westminster dealing with private bills. There are separate offices for the Commons and Lords.
Private member's bill	Bill introduced by individual MP. Three types. See Ballot bill, 10 minute rule bill and presentation bill.
Private notice question (PNQ)	Emergency application to the Speaker, before noon, to allow an oral question to the minister that day on an urgent matter; if granted this gives an opportunity of a short period of supplementary questions.
Privileges, Committee of	Select committee of the House concerned with breaches of privilege both by MPs and, more commonly, by outsiders, often journalists.
Privy councillor	A title bestowed on politicians who hold or have held senior office; called 'Right

	Honourable'; get some priority in being called to speak.
Public Accounts Committee	Influential Commons committee concerned with examining public expenditure incurred by government departments.
Public bill	Bill concerned with matters of public interest as opposed to private bill.
Public bill office	Office at Westminster dealing with public bills; there are separate offices for the Commons and Lords.
Public gallery	Galleries mainly facing Speaker's chair from which the public can listen to debates.
Public information office	Situated in Norman Shaw North Library. Provides parliamentary information for the public including a weekly record of progress of legislation in Parliament.
Pugin Room	Smart bar for MPs and peers and their guests; afternoon tea can also be taken there.
Queen's Speech	Annual speech of government's legislative and other proposals for the coming session, delivered by the Queen in the Lords Chamber at the State Opening of Parliament.
Recess	Period when Commons or Lords are not sitting.
Refreshment departments	Administer all catering facilities at Westminster; each House has a separate department.
Register of Members' Interests	Gives details of MPs' business and other interests. Its weakness is that it is neither compulsory nor comprehensive.
Report stage	Follows committee stage of a bill, taken on floor of House and enables MPs to move those amendments that have been selected by the Speaker.
Royal Assent	A bill becomes an act of Parliament when it has completed all its parliamentary stages and receives the Monarch's assent.
St Stephen's Entrance	Main public entrance to Westminster, opposite rear of Westminster Abbey.
Second reading	The first opportunity of debating a bill; it is a debate to discuss the principle of the legislation. The bill must be approved before it can proceed further.

Second reading committee	A procedure sometimes used for uncontroversial legislation; the second reading debate is held in a committee instead of on the floor of the House.
Select committee	Committee of MPs dealing either with Commons internal matters or with powers to call witnesses and investigate subject areas corresponding to government departments. There is also the Public Accounts Committee, and a number of other select committees.
Selection of amendments	Speaker's decision regarding amendments to be debated in Commons. They are often linked in groups dealing with related matters. A similar procedure is carried out by the chairman (sic) of every standing committee.
Sergeant at Arms	Responsible for aspects of administration of the Commons.
Session	The parliamentary year, usually from the Queen's Speech in November to a week before the next Queen's Speech.
Sittings motion	A motion by a standing committee which determines days and times of its future meetings.
SO 20	Standing Order 20: a procedure under which an individual MP may request a debate, on the same or following day on an urgent matter. The MP can speak for three minutes to make the case.
Solidarity Group	Group of centre-right Labour MPs.
Sound archive	Records proceedings of both Houses. MPs can get the tapes.
Speaker	The MP who is elected to this post by the House and presides over its sittings. A very important post with many other responsibilities; assisted by three deputy speakers.
Special standing committee	A committee dealing with a bill which can call witnesses and receive evidence before moving to consider detailed amendments. A very sensible procedure but seldom used because the government does not like it.

Spring/Summer/ Christmas/Easter Adjournment	Short debate preceding a recess when MPs may speak about any issue.
Standing committee	Committee of MPs which considers detailed clauses of a bill after its second reading stage.
Statement	Statement by a minister usually after 3.30pm followed by a period of questions.
Statutory instrument (SI)	See Delegated legislation.
Strangers	Anyone not an MP or an official of the House.
Strangers' Bar	Bar on terrace level where MPs may entertain guests; sometimes nicknamed 'The Kremlin'.
Strangers' cafeteria	On terrace level for MPs and staff.
Strangers' gallery	Public gallery in the Commons.
Surgery	Another name for MPs' advice sessions where constituents go for help with their problems or to lobby their member. Some require an appointment.
Table office	Where MPs table PQs and EDMs.
Ten minute rule bill	Opportunity for MP to make ten-minute speech supporting a private member's bill. These rarely make further progress but are a good way of drawing attention to an issue.
Terrace	Overlooking the Thames; parts are used for functions. There is a bar and MPs can take you to tea with or without strawberries.
Third Reading	The last opportunity to debate the whole bill; often follows immediately after report stage.
Times Guide	Parliamentary reference book on MPs.
Tribune Group	Soft left group of Labour MPs.
Under gallery	Very small gallery on floor level of the Commons where public may be admitted by special arrangement; useful for pressure groups during a bill's report stage as MPs can go and ask for further information.
Upper committee corridor	On second floor of the Commons giving access to committee rooms 17 to 22.
Upper waiting hall	Small lobby off committee corridor where MPs may sponsor exhibitions.

Upper waiting hall	Small lobby off committee corridor where MPs may sponsor exhibitions.
Usual channels	Term to describe the chief whips and the very helpful and influential civil servant who acts as the liaison official between government and opposition in arranging business.
Vacher's	Parliamentary reference books.
Vesting date	The date on which an act of Parliament becomes effective law. This is stated in the act itself though it may only refer to a part of the measure. Otherwise acts usually take effect on dates to be determined by the minister under powers in the legislation. Some parts of acts can be on statute books for years without becoming operative, sometimes because there has been an intervening election and the new government disagrees with the measure.
Vote	Division
Vote (blues)	Full order paper with EDMs that were tabled, or signed the previous sitting day, and all questions; on Mondays this also lists all EDMs for the session, though not their wording, and all questions for future days and private members' bills (see also Order book).
Vote bundle	Issued daily – includes all of the day's official publications, Hansard, order paper, etc.
Vote office	Where MPs obtain all official Commons and HMSO publications they require for their work; usually available on day of publication. Strictly speaking MPs are restricted to 2 copies of each publication they request but they might have a spare one for a friendly pressure group. Open during recesses.
W rooms	See Interview rooms.
Weekly Information Bulletin	Weekly publication with information about progress of legislation, committees, previous and next week's business, etc. Very Useful.

Westminster Hall	The only medieval part of the Palace, the large hall situated between St Stephen's Entrance and New Palace Yard. Gives access to W rooms, Grand Committee Room and Jubilee Room. Used for state occasions, and gives mass lobbies access to Grand Committee Room; also used for lobbies by disabled people.
Whip	Various meanings: (i) weekly listing of forthcoming business sent out by each party to their MPs, indicating likely votes and their importance; (ii) an indication that parties want MPs to attend by the number of lines: three, two or one or a free vote on matters of conscience or procedure; (iii) the MPs or peers in each party who act as business managers and ensure their members turn up and vote according to party decisions.
White paper	Government proposals for future action or legislation; less open to change than a green paper.
Written question	Question tabled by an MP, published in order paper and the answer in Hansard.

Appendix II: Lords Glossary

Bill do now pass	The motion which gives rise to a short, general winding up debate after the third reading of a bill.
Black Rod	An officer of the House. He summons the Commons to hear the Queen's Speech by banging on the door of the Lower House. Is also responsible for accommodation and other services.
Chairman of committees	An officer of the House, appointed every session; s/he chairs committees of the whole House and has duties in relation to private and hybrid bills and other matters.
Cholmondeley Room	Function room in the House of Lords which may be reserved in the name of a peer.
Clerk of the Parliaments	Chief Clerk (official) to the Lords.
Companion to Standing Orders	Essential reference book produced by the clerks, on Lords procedure. More readable than Erskine May, the Companion is quoted to make procedural points in the Lords.
Content	The division lobby for those voting in favour, like the Aye lobby in the Commons.
Crossbenches	The benches set at right angles to the party benches which give their name to the independent peers who sit there although some crossbenchers actually sit on the opposition benches.
Introduction	The ceremony through which a new peer, other than an hereditary peer succeeding to the title, must go through before taking the oath and becoming a full member of the House of Lords. Introductions usually take place on Wednesdays, two peers at a time.
Leave of absence	Granted to peers who do not attend the House; can be revoked at any time.

Lord Chancellor	Presides over debates in the House of Lords; is a member of the cabinet, and head of legal system.
Minute (of proceedings)	Records what is formally done at a meeting of the House. Printed on the first page of the green order paper which is sometimes incorrectly called the 'minute'.
Mr Scott's office	The mail room in the Lords situated to the left of the peers' lobby; this office advises on which peers can have letters addressed to them at the House.
Money Bill	A bill certified by the Speaker under the Parliament Act 1911 to contain only provisions on national taxation, public money and loans. Such a bill cannot be amended or changed by the Lords and becomes law a month after it is sent to the Lords. The definition is very strict and the majority of finance bills (giving effect to the Budget) are not technically certified.
No day named	Section of the green order paper divided into two parts. Part I consists of motions and unstarred questions waiting to be allocated a day for debate, and Part II consists of motions submitted for the ballots for short debates.
Not content	The division lobby for those voting against, like the Commons Noe lobby.
Order paper (green)	The order paper containing future business as far as it is known with a degree of certainty, written questions, notices of committee sittings and no day named entries.
Order paper (white)	The small slip of paper with the day's business, given to visitors to the galleries.
Printed paper office	Situated near Princes Chamber, is the office from which peers get parliamentary papers, equivalent to the Commons vote office.
Public bill office	The Lords equivalent of the Commons office bearing the same name.
Short debate	A two and a half hour debate, two of which occur every Wednesday before Whitsun. They are allocated by ballot three weeks in advance.

Starred question	Equivalent to Commons oral questions; asked by four peers at the start of business, Monday to Thursday and followed by a mini-debate.
Supply bill	Bill concerning taxation, raising of supply or loans, which, by ancient convention, the Lords may not amend, or in practice reject. Many more bills are supply bills than are certified money bills. Supply bills are identified by a special enacting formula.
Unstarred question	Motion for debate in the form of a question, leading to a debate, not time limited, at the end of business when the House is not sitting late. Similar in function, but much freer and more substantial than a Commons adjournment.
Woolsack	The enormous cushion on which the Lord Chancellor sits when presiding over the House.

Appendix III: European Glossary

Brussels

Headquarters of the EC and Council of Ministers and where committees and political groups normally meet.

CAP

Common Agricultural Policy. The EC's agricultural policy, much criticised for its high costs and for resulting in enormous overproduction leading to butter mountains, wine lakes, etc.

Commission

The European Commission is the civil service of the EC and is headed by 17 commissioners.

Commissioner

One of 17 members of the European Commission appointed for a four-year renewable term and responsible for a policy area. Many commissioners are political appointments by the member states.

Council of Europe

An association of 21 member states with an interest in all forms of non-military cooperation. Its most effective instrument is the European Convention of Human Rights. Members of the British Parliament attend the Council's Parliamentary Assembly several times a year. (Check names with the Commons public information office.) For lobbyists one of the main interests is human rights, especially as Turkey is a member state.

Council of Ministers

The ministers representing the 12 EC member states. In practice the portfolios of the ministers attending will vary depending on the issues being considered. Thus there can be meetings say of agriculture ministers or of transport ministers or of prime ministers.

Directive

EC legal instrument binding on member states

as regards its principles but which leaves national parliaments to decide how it is to be implemented.

European Court of Human Rights — Under the Council of Europe there is the European Commission of Human Rights and the European Court of Human Rights; their purpose is to establish the European Convention of Human Rights. Aggrieved individuals can appeal against the conduct of their governments on human rights matters. Quite a number of British people have won cases.

European Court of Justice — The court of justice of the European Community; is the supreme court of EC law. Not to be confused with the European Court of Human Rights.

Luxembourg — Headquarters of the European Parliament which rarely meets there. Court of Justice and some commission departments are based there.

North Atlantic Assembly — Has 16 member states; its aims are to strengthen understanding and cooperation between NATO member states; its assembly meets once a year.

Official Journal — The EC bulletin which records regulations, directives and other matters; its supplement is the Parliament's 'Hansard' and records questions and all that is said in debates.

Oral questions — Put by MEPs at plenary sessions to the commission, the Council of Ministers or to the Foreign Ministers meeting in Political Cooperation.

Palais de l'Europe — The Strasbourg headquarters of the Council of Europe. Its debating chamber is used for the 12 five-day plenary sessions of the European Parliament.

Plenary session — Meeting of the whole European Parliament; in Strasbourg for a five-day period every month except August and usually twice in October.

Political group — An association of MEPs sharing a political viewpoint, e.g. the Socialist Group, with

	172 members.
Presidency	Every EC country in turn, at six-monthly intervals, takes the chair of the Council of Ministers. This is at meetings at all levels from heads of government downwards.
Rainbow	The immediate record of the European Parliament in plenary sittings, so called because the texts are printed in nine colours corresponding to the community languages. A second meaning is the name for a political grouping, Rainbow Group, comprising some left-wing MEPs including the Greens.
Regional Fund	The EC budget for regional development.
Regulation	EC legal instrument binding on member states.
Single European Act	Gives the Parliament added powers in matters relating to progress towards the EC's internal market by 1992.
Social Fund	The budget to contribute to projects with social objectives, principally training. Approved schemes must normally be half-financed by national governments.
Strasbourg	Headquarters of the Council of Europe, and of European Court of Human Rights. The European Parliament holds its plenary sessions there.
Urgency debate	An opportunity for the Parliament, each month, to debate an issue of current importance; the council or commission may reply.
Western European Union	Consists of seven member countries: Belgium, France, the Federal Republic of Germany, Italy, Luxembourg, the Netherlands and the UK; is concerned primarily with defence matters. The assembly of the WEU meets twice a year.
Written questions	Put by MEPs to the same bodies as in the case of oral questions. Answers come more slowly than at Westminster.

Appendix IV:
Political Lobbying Companies

The following list is in three parts. The first consists of specialist public affairs companies; the second is of firms which are general public relations companies but which claim to provide a public affairs/lobbying service; the third is of firms providing a specialist monitoring service. There is no complete listing of all companies in this area and I have assembled the following from a variety of sources.

Specialist Public Affairs Companies

Advocacy Partnership Ltd:
16 Regency Street
London, SW1P 4DB
Tel: 01-630 1235

Central Lobby Consultants:
9 Old Queen Street
London, SW1H 9JA
Tel: 01-222 1265

Corporate Communications
International Ltd:
PO Box 604
London, SW6 3AG
Tel: 01-736 5976

C.S.M. Parliamentary
Consultants Ltd:
Eagle House
109 Jermyn Street
London, SW1Y 6HB
Tel: 01-839 4887

GJW Government Relations:
64 Clapham Road
London, SW9 0JJ
Tel: 01-582 3119

Good Relations Public Affairs
Limited:
59 Russell Square
London WC1B 4HJ
Tel: 01-631 3434

Ian Greer Associates:
19 Catherine Place
London, SW1E 6OX
Tel: 01-630 5651

The Freeman, Trotman
Partnership:
Orchard House
14 Great Smith Street
London, SW1P 3BU
Tel: 01-222 5161

KPA (formerly Keen Public Affairs Ltd):
66-68 Brewer Street
London, W1R 3PJ
Tel: 01-439 7227

Lloyd-Hughes Associates Ltd:
70 Borough High Street
London, SE1 1XF
Tel: 01-403 5493

Michael Forsyth Ltd:
3-4 St Andrew's Hill
London, EC4 5BY
Tel 01-236 8265

Political Communications Ltd:
29 Tufton Street
London, SW1P 3QL
Tel: 01-222 5024

Political Perceptions:
16-17 Pall Mall
London, SW1Y 5NB
Tel: 01-930 3822

Politics International Ltd:
Gayfere House
22-23 Gayfere Street
London, SW1P 3HP
Tel: 01-222 5161

The Russell Partnership Ltd:
16 Great College Street
London, SW1P 3RX
Tel: 01-222 2096

Sallingbury Casey Limited:
25 Victoria Street
London, SW1H 0EX
Tel: 01-222 0762

Wedgewood Markham Associates Ltd:
17 Saint George Street
London, W1R 9DE
Tel: 01-493 6391

Westminster Strategy Limited:
Number One Dean's Yard
London, SW1P 3NR
Tel: 01-799-9811

Public Relations Companies offering Lobbying Services

McAvoy Wreford Bayley Ltd:
36 Grosvenor Gardens
London, SW1W OEB
Tel: 01-730 4500

Burston-Marsteller Ltd:
24-28 Bloomsbury Way
London, WC1A 2PX
Tel: 01-831 5262

City & Commercial Public
Relations Ltd:
11 Blomfield Street

London, EC2M 7AY
Tel: 01-588 6050

Charles Barker Traverse-Healy Ltd:
30 Farringdon Street
London, EC4A 4EA
Tel: 01-634 1000

Christopher Morgan & Partners:
15 John Adam Street
London, WC2N 6LU
Tel: 01-930 7642

CRP Ltd:
37 Millharbour
London, E14 9TX
Tel: 01-987 0321

Good Relations:
59 Russell Square
London, WC1B 4HJ
Tel: 01-631 1399

The Grayling Group:
1 Queen Victoria Street
London, EC4N 4YL
Tel: 01-489 1853

Hill & Knowlton UK Ltd:
5-11 Theobald's Road
London, WC1X 8SH
Tel: 01-405 8755

The Kingsway Group:
10 Doughty Street
London, WC1N 2PL
Tel: 01-831 6131

Ogilvy & Mather:
Chancery House
Chancery Lane
London, WC2A 1QU
Tel: 01-831 2808

Peter Bloomfield & Co Ltd:
20-21 Suffolk Street
London, SW1Y 4HG
Tel: 01-930 9342

Profile Public Relations Ltd:
Assets House
Elverton Street
London, SW1P 2QG
Tel: 01-828 2905

Rait Orr & Associates:
14 Buckingham Palace Road
London, SW1W 0QP
Tel: 01-828 5961

Reginald Watts Associates Ltd:
1-11 Hay Hill
London W1X 7LF
Tel: 01-491 2121.

Shandwick Consultants:
Dauntsey House
Frederick's Place
Old Jewry
London, EC2R 8AB
Tel: 01-726 4291

Welbeck Public Relations:
43 King Street
London, WC2E 8JS
Tel: 01-836 6677

Westminster Communications:
7 Buckingham Gate
London, SW1E 8JS

Monitoring Services

The following firms provide a monitoring service which may include covering Hansards of both Houses, advance warning of parliamentary questions, select committees and standing committees, EDMs, similar information about the European Parliament and also about the Senate and House of Representatives in Washington.

Parliamentary Monitoring Services:
29 Tufton Street
London, SW1P 3QL
Tel: 01-222 5024

Randall's Parliamentary Service:
7 Buckingham Gate
London, SW1E 8JS
Tel: 01-828 3273

Appendix V: Useful Addresses and Phone Numbers

Westminster, Commons and Lords: if you do not know the extension, call: 01-219 3000

Public Information Office

House of Commons
London SW1A 0AA
Tel: 01 219 4272

Commons

Committee office enquiries 01-219 4300
Private Bill office 01-219 3250
Public Bill office   01-219 3251
Refreshment department 01-219 3677
Messages for MPs 01-219 4343
Sergeant at Arms department 01-219 3070

Lords

Journal and Information Office
House of Lords
London SW1A 0PW
Tel: 01-219 3107 (in recesses: 01-219 3000, ask for House of Lords information)

Messages for peers 01-219 5353
Mr Scott's office 01-219 5566
Refreshment department 01-219 4222
Committee office enquiries 01-219 3231
Private Bill office 01-219 3231
Public Bill office 01-219 3153

European Parliament

European Parliament Information Office
2 Queen Anne's Gate
London SW1H 9AA
Tel: 01-222 0411

Headquarters of Political Parties Represented in the Commons (in alphabetical order)

Conservative Party

(Conservative and Unionist
Central Office)
32 Smith Square
London SW1P 3HH
Tel: 01- 222 9000

Labour Party

150 Walworth Road
London SE17 1JT
Tel: 01-703 0833

Plaid Cymru (Welsh Nationalist
 Party)

51 Cathedral Road
Caerdydd
Cardiff CF19MD
Tel: 0222 31944

Scottish National Party (SNP)

6 North Charlotte Street
Edinburgh EH2 4JH
Tel: 031-226 3661

Sinn Fein

51–55 Falls Road
Belfast BT12 8JG
Tel: 0232 230261

Social Democratic and Labour Party
(SDLP)

38 University Street
Belfest
Tel: 0232-323428

Social Democratic Party (SDP)

25-28 Buckingham Gate
London SW1E 6LD
Tel: 01-821 9661

Social and Liberal Democrats (SLD)

4 Cowley Street
London SW1P 3NB
Tel: 01-222 7999

Ulster Democratic Unionist Party

296 Albert Bridge Road
Belfast BT5 46W
Tel: 0232 458597

Ulster Unionist Party

41-43 Waring Street
Belfast BT1 2EY
Tel: 0232 324601

Bibliography

The Civil Service Year Book (HMSO) £14.75 annually. Detailed listing of government departments and the responsibilities of civil servants. Gives names, phone numbers, plus main parliamentary offices in both Houses with phone numbers.

Debrett's Distinguished People of Today (Debrett's Peerage Ltd, 73/77 Britannia Road, PO Box 357, London, SW6 2JY. Tel: 01-736 6524). £55, includes biographies of all peers.

Debrett's Peerage and Baronetage (same publisher as *Debrett's Distinguished People of Today*, above). £95, details of each peer but probably has more information than is needed for lobbying purposes.

Dod's Parliamentary Companion (Dod's Parliamentary Companion Ltd, Elm Cottage, Chilsham Lane, Herstmonceux, Hailsham, East Sussex BN27 4QQ. Tel 0323 832250). £48, published annually. Biographical information with photographs of MPs, peers, plus procedure, political and social interests, political party organisation, etc.

House of Commons Weekly Information Bulletin (HMSO), £1.95 or £71.30 annually. Very useful source of information about current and future business, progress of legislation, select and standing committees, etc. Includes a little information about the Lords.

The House Magazine (The House Magazine, 12-13 Clerkenwell Green, London EC1R 0DP. Tel: 01-250 1504). Published weekly when Parliament is sitting, costs £75 annually. Very useful source of information on current and future business of both Houses, progress of legislation, select and standing committees and articles by politicians and others.

The London Diplomatic List (HMSO) £3.20 annually. Lists embassies, high commissions, and gives names of diplomatic representatives in London of foreign and Commonwealth countries. Also includes international organisations.

MPs' Chart by Andrew Roth, a shortened one-volume version of *Parliamentary Profiles* (see above); £12.

Parliamentary Profiles by Andrew Roth (Parliamentary Profiles, 2 Queen Anne's Gate Buildings, Dartmouth Street, London, SW1H 9BP, Tel: 01-222 5884) 4 volumes at £33 the set, 'warts and all' biographical details of MPs, gives detailed accounts of specific issues raised in Parliament, and political slant; useful for detailed profiles of particular MPs. Well worth a look as it is the most comprehensive and easy to read reference book, and has some wonderfully biting comments.

Register of Members' Interests (HMSO £7.20). This gives details for each MP of directorships, employments, financial sponsorships, land and property, shareholdings, overseas visits, etc. Worth looking at but is neither comprehensive nor compulsory.

The Times Guide to the House of Commons (Times Books Limited, 16 Golden Square, London, W1R 4BN, Tel: 01-434 3767) price £20, published after each general election, lists all MPs with a photograph of each, gives their majorities and a very brief biography.

Vacher's European Companion and Consultants' Register (same publisher, sales agent as *Parliamentary Companion* above). Published quarterly, £6.25 or £20.50 for an annual subscription. Has information about MEPs from all countries, European institutions including their key staff, plus a list of firms offering European lobbying services.

Vacher's Parliamentary Biographical Guide (same publisher, sales agent as for *Parliamentary Companion* above). Published annually, £20. Biographies, without photographs, of MPs, active peers (475) and British MEPs, plus information about their political and personal interests.

Vacher's Parliamentary Companion (A.S. Kerswill Ltd, 113 High St, Berkhamstead, Herts HP4 2DJ, Tel: 04427 76135. London sales agent: Parliamentary Monitoring Services, 29 Tufton Street, London, SW1P 3QL. Tel: 01-222 5024). Published four times a year; costs £4.75 or £15.25 for an annual subscription. Contains a great deal of information on MPs, peers, procedure, committees, opposition frontbenchers, government departments, etc. Does not include biographical details.

Who's Who (A. & C. Black Ltd, 35 Bedford Row, London, WC1R 4JH. Tel: 01-242 0946); £58, contains short biographies of thousands of people including MPs and peers.

Index

Page numbers followed by '(G)' indicate a reference in the glossary.

adjournment debate, 30, 34, 36, 50, 52–6, 152, 188, 198(G)
affirmative order, 97
all-party group(s), 117, 120, 154, 192, 193, 198(G)
all-party whip, 107
Amnesty International, 3, 70, 101, 113, 122, 126, 132, 163, 172, 186
annunciator, 31, 48, 198(G)

backbench/party group(s), 115–17, 192, 198(G)
ballot, 57, 92, 96
ballot bills, 90, 91, 199(G)
banqueting/refreshment department, 121, 206(G)
blocked subject, 37
British Army Equipment Exhibition, 128
Brussels, 166, 167, 169, 178, 197, 214(G)
business questions/statement, 45, 47, 50, 63, 199(G)

cabinet, 16, 63
Catholic Institute for International Relations (CIIR), 129
Central Hall, Westminster, 107
central lobby, 107, 199(G)
Christmas, Easter, Spring, Summer adjournment, 57, 207(G)
Citizens Advice Bureaux (CAB), 3, 23, 27, 104, 126
Civil Service Year Book, 224
closure, 89
CND, 3, 106, 126
COHSE, 54, 117, 146
Commission (European), 162, 163, 165, 170, 171, 173, 214(G)

Commissioners (European), 162–5, 171, 214(G)
committee corridor, 26, 200(G)
committee of selection, 80, 87, 201(G)
committee stage, 80, 85, 90, 91, 153, 156
Commons Public Information Office, 13, 18, 61, 111, 113, 206(G)
Commons Weekly Information Bulletin, 8, 12, 224
Commonwealth Parliamentary Association, 18, 19, 118, 128
Conservative Party, 137
Conservative Party conference, 138, 140, 143, 146
Consolidated Fund Bill, 1, 52, 56, 200 (G)
Council of Europe, 161, 178, 179, 214(G)
Council of Ministers, 161, 214(G)
Cyprus/Cypriots, 104, 128, 132

Debrett's, 157, 224
Delegated legislation, 97, 200(G)
dining rooms, 120–2
directive (EC), 162, 214(G)
division, 24, 31, 54, 93, 150, 200(G)
Dod's Parliamentary Companion, 6, 157, 200(G), 224
Early Day Motion (EDM), 15, 59, 60, 63–5, 76, 98, 109, 174, 192, 197, 200(G)
Economic and Social Committee, 177, 178
emergency debate, 72
Erskine May, 73, 200(G)
European Community Court of Justice, 161, 162, 179, 215(G)
European Court of Human Rights, 161, 179, 215(G)